P9-CCO-779

Knots

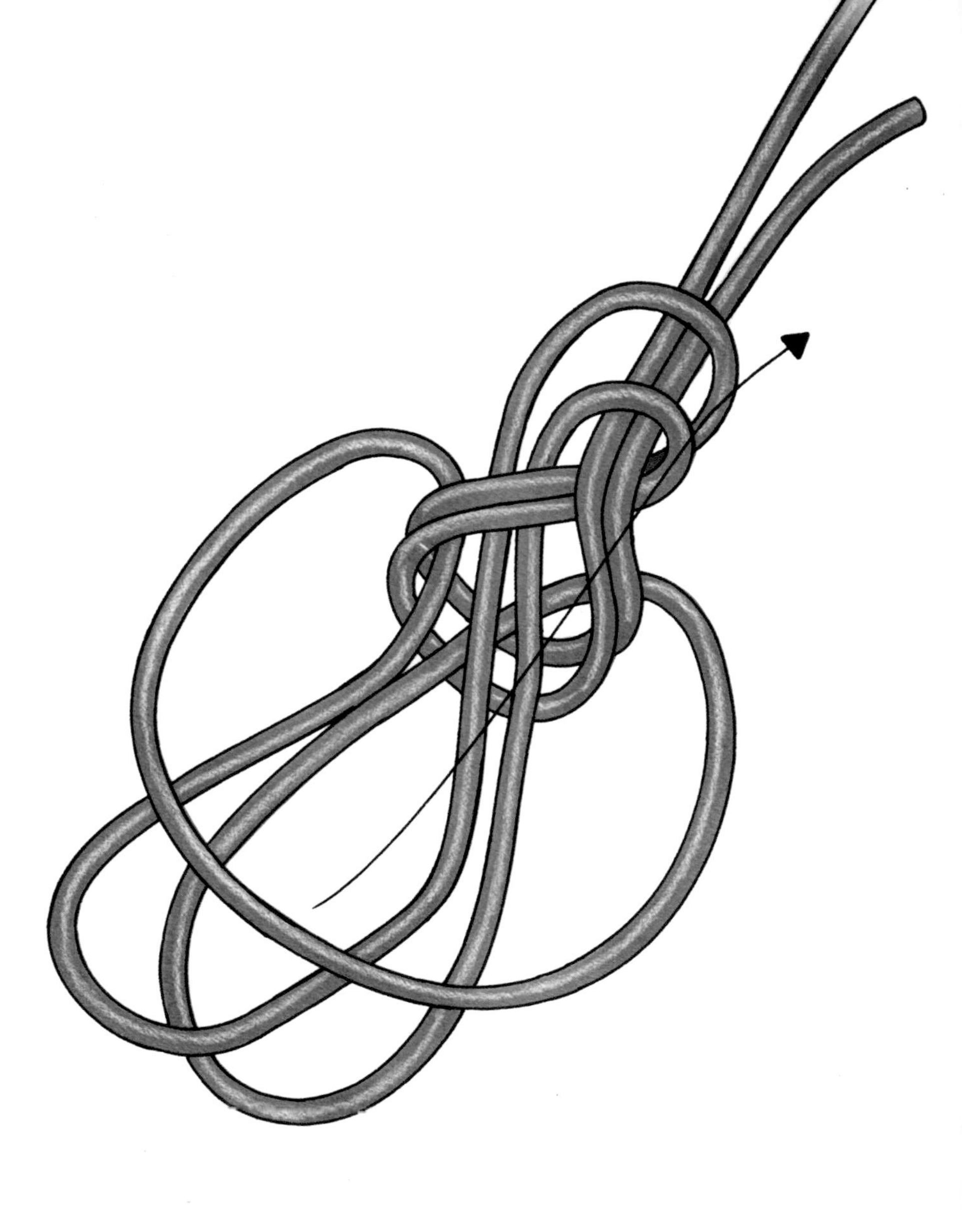

Knots

Richard Hopkins

San Diego, California

This book is dedicated to Brian Field,
a fine knotter and a true gentleman.

ACKNOWLEDGMENTS

The publisher wishes to thank Mark Franklin for creating all the illustrations in this book. The photographs on the front cover, spine, and on pages 26-27, were taken by Simon Clay.

THUNDER BAY
P · R · E · S · S

Thunder Bay Press
An imprint of the Baker & Taylor Publishing Group
10350 Barnes Canyon Road, San Diego, CA 92121
www.thunderbaybooks.com

Produced by PRC Publishing Ltd.,
10 Southcombe Street, London W14 0RA

All notations of errors or omissions should be addressed to Thunder Bay Press, Editorial Department, at the above address. All other correspondence (author inquiries, permissions) concerning the content of this book should be addressed to: Salamander Books, 10 Southcombe Street, London W14 0RA, UK

ISBN-13: 978-1-57145-981-7
ISBN-10: 1-57145-981-2

Library of Congress Cataloging-in-Publication Data

Hopkins, Richard, 1943-
Knots / Richard Hopkins.
p. cm.
Includes bibliographical references and index.
ISBN 1-57145-981-2
1. Knots and splices. I. Title.

VM533.H67 2003
623.88'82--dc21

2003040256

Printed and bound in China

5 6 7 12 11

Contents

Foreword	6
Introduction	7
Equipment	22
Basic Terms & Techniques	28
General Knots	34
Camping Knots	98
Climbing Knots	146
Boating Knots	180
Fishing Knots	214
Glossary	252
Bibliography	254
Index of Knots	255

Foreword

There is no other field of human activity where we happily teach techniques that are thousands of years old and expect them to be accepted without question. Every other human endeavor has changed drastically over the centuries, but still we rely on many of the same techniques in knotting as those used by our distant ancestors. As new materials have been introduced for making rope and cord, some of the old knots do not perform as well as they used to and so new methods of tying have been devised to match the changes, but evolution in knotting has progressed very slowly. Indeed, knowledge of and publicity for new knots has only really occurred in the last twenty years. Developments have come about in some cases because of necessity and in some cases because enthusiasts just wanted to experiment and found (or rediscovered) something that was genuinely useful.

I have tried to keep up with the changes because, at some point in my life, I have had to use nearly all the knots in this book, apart from one or two of the fishing knots, in serious situations, and so I have included a mixture of old and new in the hope that they will cover all your practical knotting requirements as they did mine. Remember that it is no good waiting until you need a knot before learning to tie it. Safety and common sense mean you should learn and then practice, and practice again. There are always chances to hone your skills: while waiting for the bus, on the commuter train, during television commercials, and at many other times during the day. I do not know a single knot tier who does not have a piece of cord in their pocket at all times, close at hand for impromptu practice.

Because knots are so versatile, a knot shown in one section should not be mentally locked to that activity, but may be used in several other applications as your circumstances, ability, and memory dictate.

Read this book, learn some knots, and practice. I'm sure you'll enjoy it as much as I have.

Richard Hopkins

Introduction

Depending on how you define it, cord and knots may have been the very first invention. A heavy stick and sharp stone could be just fortuitous discoveries, but to combine the two effectively into an axe, adze, or spear required cord as a means of joining them together. Imagine early man waking somewhere in Africa. He might be in a simple shelter constructed from branches held together by lashings of flexible twigs or long grass. The point of his spear is held to the shaft by a wrapping of vegetable fibers, the ends of which are intertwined into a simple knot. Simple valuable possessions, such as pretty stones, hand axes, or vegetables not yet eaten are collected in an animal skin and the legs are tied to form a sack. He is ready to face the day. Later the hunter-gatherer discovered archery. Without cord there would have been no bows, just bent sticks. Sinew or plant fiber (perhaps with an early adhesive) held the arrowhead onto the shaft, while a form of knotting or lashing held the string securely to the ends of the bow. The feathers on the arrow were held by a thread wound around the arrow as well as by some resin or bulb juice adhesive. At this point in history the man's axe would have been more sophisticated but still reliant on a lashing to keep its head fixed to the handle.

As humans progressed, many of the other uses of cord with which we are familiar came into use: nets, snares, fishing lines, ship rigging, animal hobbles, tethers, and lashings of all descriptions were developed, while the rope itself became more sophisticated than the simple cords that were used previously. From these simple tools grew agriculture, and ultimately civilization, so there is a strong case for suggesting that our society today might not exist without the foundation provided by cord, rope, and knots!

How do we know that cord has such a long and honorable history? There are no remains of knots from the very early days of human history because natural fibers or sinew did not survive for the archaeologist to excavate. We do know, however, that stone axe heads were fitted to wooden shafts and that spears were pointed with sharpened stone heads. The only practical way to keep the handle and head in effective contact would have been to lash them together. Some types of axe head that have been found are encircled by a groove, which can only have been for the lashings to rest in or to hold a handle that was bent around the stone before being tied securely.

Archaeologists have also found stones with holes in them. These are believed to have been ornamental and as such would have been suspended from cord passing through the hole. Some finds in Czechoslovakia have been identified as jewelry from 35,000 years ago. To reach such a level of sophistication as jewelry suggests that cord was already a common item at this time.

As humans spread across the early continents they would, at some point, have had to cross large expanses of water by means more complicated than swimming and wading, as the waters were too expansive in places. Rafts, coracles, bull boats, even boats made of inflated hide all require knots to be effective, indicating that cord was known a long time ago. However, hard evidence does not exist of knotting before 9,000 years ago. The earliest known knot was found in a net on an island off Finland and dated to this time. It is a sheet bend that is still used in net-making today. The basics of net-making can be seen later in this book.

More recent archaeological finds are relatively frequent, and by the time of the pharaohs we see ropemaking as a specialized craft depicted on wall paintings and on papyrus documents. There are several hieroglyphs depicting cord: they show the measuring cords of surveyors and architects, bundles of flax, spools filled with twine, whips, lasso, tethering rope, fishing nets, sailing ships, and skeins of thread. Other illustrations from this time show how rope was made and used 4,000 years ago. It was already an important component of society.

As we come closer to the present day, evidence of knotting increases, but at the same time it was accepted as an everyday part of life, so we find fewer useful references and have to rely on analysis of artifacts provided by archaeologists and ethnologists. Reference to knots and cords by Shakespeare, Swift, and others emphasizes the common acceptance and importance of knots in ordinary life, but these are relatively recent examples.

Knotting probably reached its peak by the mid to late 1800s when almost every occupation made use of knots in one form or another. Many knots were used for specific purposes by different crafts and the same knot might have several different names depending on the job of the person tying it. This has led, for example, to a number of knots being known as the weaver's knot, and causes confusion when trying to identify exactly what is meant in old texts, although any one of a selection of knots would adequately carry out the task.

Reliable books on knots did not appear until around the early 1800s, although from the early 1600s there had been volumes of advice for sailors and others, which included information on knots. Then in 1944 *The Ashley Book of Knots* was produced and even today this is the standard work for knot tiers, although there are several other very fine books, Graumont and Hensel's *Encyclopædia of Knots and Fancy Ropework* being probably the most comprehensive. It is, of course, important to remember that advances in ropemaking materials mean that some of Ashley's advice requires updating, but it is still an impressive guide to all aspects of the craft. In *The Ashley Book of Knots* the author mentions, in chapter two, eighty-five occupations and specific knots associated with them, and later in the book mentions other jobs that make great use of knots. Of course there are also many common knots, which would be useful to all, and anyone might tie ornamental knots.

There is a tendency today to think that knotting was only carried out by sailors, and that they produced the finest and most complicated knots. It is true that in the days of sail, knowledge of a wide range of knots and proficiency in applied ropework for shifting heavy loads was an essential skill, but this was for work—not decoration. Indeed, the cowboys of the American plains are considered to have made more elaborate and complicated knots to ornament their equipment and costume than any sailors ever did. Practical knots and pretty knots are not always compatible, though a properly tied practical knot usually looks good.

This is not to take any credit from the skill of the crews of the American whaling ships, whose voyages away from home sometimes lasted up to four years and who had a lot of free time while searching for the elusive, oil-rich whales, with only simple materials, such as cord, on which to exercise their ingenuity and relieve the boredom. Some of their knotting is pure art, and even today the ornamental side of knotting appeals to almost all knot tiers, even if they do not feel particularly artistic.

Knotting developed in many different places not only for practical reasons, but as an artistic outlet. The Chinese still produce ornamental knots, which have their own distinct history and significance. Quite complicated compilations of knots, using appropriate colors, are made to provide blessings on the birth of a child or the opening of a new business venture. Added to the spiritual dimension is the fact that they look good and make wonderful ornaments. As an aside it is worth mentioning that the best Chinese knots always contain a small mistake to show the gods that the tier was only a mere mortal, not able to produce the perfection that is the prerogative of the gods. This protects the tier from the jealousy and anger of the gods.

Other cultures found other uses for knots. The Incas made use of knotted cords to maintain their records and accounts. This was done by tying a variety of knots in cords hanging from a central line. Combinations of knots and varying spacings and colors had their special meanings.

Exact details of how this worked are still unclear, as most of the Inca civilization was destroyed by the Spanish in the sixteenth century and a complete explanation was not retained.

South Sea islanders used cords spread over a frame to represent wave patterns and directions, forming useful navigational aids that enabled them to cross great distances with an accuracy that would baffle modern navigators deprived of their charts. Admittedly, a lot of other lore was also passed down orally, but the cords were an excellent memory aid.

Knots occur in other areas in a magical context. They were used to store winds for sailors, and when becalmed a knot was untied to release a wind and allow the journey to continue. This superstition is mentioned as current in Newfoundland by E. Annie Proulx in her novel *The Shipping News*. Even the artistic, zoomorphic "Celtic" knots (which are actually Pictish) probably had a spiritual significance, as they occur on so many ritual objects and burial stones and were later adopted by the monks when illuminating early books such as the *Book of Kells*.

Knots were also used for medical purposes, certain knots being considered to be beneficial for particular injuries. Quite complicated lashings are described to help some injuries; for example, the square knot, or reef knot as it is also known, was historically used for tying the supports to heal fractures. Today, the same knot is always used to secure the ends of a sling in modern first aid.

If you believe knotting to be a subject with no modern application, try learning a few and see how often they come in handy. An ability to tie knots has been of use to me in every job I have had, even though it did not appear in any job specification.

Left: The square, or reef, knot has been used by doctors and healers for centuries, originally for holding splints in place. It is still used for a similar purpose—tying off slings.

Television takes armchair travelers to all parts of the globe, and you may have noticed that whenever the presenter of an anthropological documentary visits primitive cultures, the subject of ropemaking and knotting is frequently used to demonstrate ingenuity and invention. One aspect of these programs is that they demonstrate how cord can be made from a wide variety of natural materials: from the bark of trees, roots, bramble, nettles, coconut husks, grasses, intestines, hide, and leaves. Some materials are better than others and some are specific to certain areas of the world.

It was discovered early on that some fibers produced stronger cord than others, and as agriculture developed, these plants were selectively improved. Because of the specific conditions required to grow some of these plants and the enormous demand for rope, an important international trade developed in the raw materials and, should a war threaten supplies, then the merchants rapidly started to look for new sources. Thus, we now get natural fiber ropes made from Russian and Italian hemp, manila, cotton, coir, and sisal.

Russian and Italian hemp and flax are called "soft" cordage because they come from bast or stem fibers, whereas manila and sisal are "hard" cordage, being made from structural or leaf fibers. Some confusion can arise because manila is often called Manila hemp, a practice that arose many years ago when it was being developed as a rope material.

Rope is still made from these fibers in almost the same way as it has been for centuries, though there have been improvements in equipment and technique. The raw material is cleaned and hackled, or combed, to get all the fibers pointing in the same direction. These fibers are then sprinkled with a lubricant (whale oil was often used) and twisted to form yarn. Several yarns are then twisted in the opposite direction to form strands. These strands are finally twisted to form cord or rope. For some of the larger ropes there may be over 300 yarns in each strand and three or more strands to make a rope. At each stage the direction of twist is reversed and thus the rope stays together because the attempts of each yarn to unwind is countered by the reverse twist applied to the strands.

Controlling the degree of tension and amount of twist applied during the manufacture of the rope was a task requiring skill, and many improvements to the equipment were made over the years. For a long time the twisting of the strands was done by hand and the industry was highly labor-intensive. Imagine how much effort must have been put into making an eighteen-inch-circumference manila rope by hand. Sometimes as many as forty men would be working the cranks to twist and close the strands of a large cable. A coil, 120 fathoms long (about 710 feet), weighed about four tons. Made by modern machinery today, with more precise control over tension and quality, a similar coil still weighs three tons.

The cords would be strung out along the length of the ropewalk and the strands, fixed to hooks on a large wheel, would be twisted by cranking the wheel. When the tension was set, a wooden "top" would be allowed to travel along the ropewalk, feeding the strands into place and closing them into a rope, all under the close control of the master, who monitored the tension and twist. Ropewalks were cool in summer and cold in winter, as they were well ventilated to ensure that the fibers remained dry, preventing rot. With the draft, dust from the fibers, and smell from the tar, they were not the most pleasant places in which to work.

When little tension is applied to the strands during the laying process, a soft-laid rope is produced. This is very flexible, but not as hard-wearing as a rope produced when the strands

Above: Shown in this illustration is an early machine for twisting rope. It was called a "ropejack." A man would have controlled the "top" while another turned the wheel.

are held under strong tension and twist before and during the laying. The hard-laid and soft-laid ropes should not be confused with the hard and soft cordage mentioned earlier.

Over the years, starting in the late 1700s, improvements were introduced to the machinery and other equipment used in producing a consistent product. When explained, some of these improvements now seem obvious, but their introduction was often opposed. Nevertheless, the tide of progress was not to be stopped and new techniques greatly improved the quality and reliability of the ropes. The Industrial Revolution saw steam power replace muscle in turning the machines and crude early models were followed by machines with more sophisticated devices to control the position of the individual strands, adjustments to the length of the strands depending on their position in the rope, and many other ingenious inventions. Modern factories, not limited by the length of the ropewalk, can make lengths of rope almost continuously and at an amazing speed, with a degree of quality that the old ropemakers could only dream about.

Almost as soon as synthetic fibers were invented, they were made into cordage. This was not always a success, but perseverance and new techniques mean that most major rope users today rely on synthetic rope of one sort or another. Indeed, there is now a wider range of synthetic ropes than those made from natural fibers. Unlike traditional ropes, the properties of the modern ropes can be more accurately ascertained and an individual rope can be selected to suit the application required. The synthetic families from which ropes are made are polyethylene, polypropylene, polyester, and polyamide. In these families are many variations, meaning that ropes of almost any specification can be made.

Although synthetic laid rope is available, especially at the cheaper end of the market, the most common form of synthetic is braided rope. This might be just a braided tube, a braid around straight strands, a braid around laid strands, a braid around braided strands, or a braid around braided strands with a core of straight or laid strands. Each type of rope has its own characteristics and requires special techniques to splice. Sometimes new knots have to be learned to ensure that they are secure when tied.

Wire ropes, which have been around for about 150 years, are outside the scope of this book, though they have a fascinating range of applications.

There have been more changes in rope production in the last sixty years than in the previous sixty thousand, and the task of the rope supplier has become more technical in order to cope with these changes and to provide accurate information and advice to customers.

Care & Safety

"United we stand, divided we fall" might have been thought up as the motto for rope care. No matter what type of rope we are using, the strength of the rope depends on every strand doing its duty as designed. This ability is severely reduced by dirt and grit, which can cause unseen damage and, if not guarded against, may lead to possible failure at the least opportune moment. It is one thing for your parcel to come undone if a knot fails, but quite another when you are relying on a rope as your sole route up or down a cliff face. Most of this section will seem like common sense, but, until the reasons for the action have been explained, there will be no incentive to obey the simple rules that will prolong the life of the rope and may save yours.

- Ropes, natural fiber or synthetic, do not like excessive exposure to bright sunlight, although some ropes have ultraviolet inhibitors included in their composition. You can see this in orange-colored "binder twine." The orange is in fact the anti-ultraviolet agent.

- Acid contamination should be avoided, as should contact with other chemicals. Synthetics are vulnerable to solvent attack, which may not always leave visible signs of weakness. Apart from direct contact, chemical damage can be caused by fumes, perhaps from the car when ropes are hung in a garage or if transported in the trunk along with a spare can of fuel. Some chemical attack may show as staining, but it is not always obvious.

- Grease and oils attack in two ways. First as a chemical attack, and also by holding dirt and grit, which then work into the body of the rope and can grind away at the fibers in the strands while hidden away from view.

- Heat is not good for rope, whether it comes from campfire sparks or friction. At the end of a rappel, especially a fast descent, the device used is generally quite warm. During the descent the hot device is moving along the rope, spreading the heat generated over its full length, so this is not a problem, but at the end of the drop, the hot metal sits on one very small area of the rope and it is good practice to remove it from the rope as quickly as possible in order to reduce the time it is in contact. Fusing of the sheath of a rope or glazing of the strands can occur. This is usually easily visible and may require that the rope be withdrawn from service.

• Cold can produce its own subtle effect. If rope freezes, then the freedom of movement of the fibers is severely reduced, so if the frozen rope is then used, there could be internal damage, as the load would be carried unevenly by the yarns, possibly causing some of them to break. Ice crystals can also be sharp enough to cut yarns.

• Capillary action means that rope will take up water and become much heavier to carry. It also becomes weaker, though the exact degree will vary between different designs. This may be overcome to a large degree by choosing ropes that have been impregnated with a water repellent.

• It is good practice to wash ropes regularly in a synthetic detergent, natural soap flakes, or a proprietary rope shampoo. Ensure that they are well rinsed and then allow to dry, spread out in a cool, well-ventilated place. Drying rope over a heater can have a deleterious effect. Caving ropes especially benefit from cleaning, as they tend to be used in messier situations than most other ropes. Some people recommend that new ropes be washed before their first use in order to help the sheath to close onto the core and to reduce shrinkage. Ropes exposed to the sea will benefit from a rinse to remove salt crystals, which can become abrasive.

• Abrasion can occur from almost everything the rope contacts. Sharp rock edges can be covered with padding, special rollers can lift the rope clear of the edge, or simple canvas sleeves can be attached around the rope for protection.

• It is to be emphasized that one must NOT stand on the rope because, apart from the abrasion this causes, if the rope is jerked it may pull a person off balance, the rope could wrap around a leg or neck, and someone might make an involuntarily rapid descent.

• Similarly, no one should stand within a loop or coil, because if the rope comes under load rapidly, there will not be enough time to get to a safe position. Standing under anything being hoisted or lowered must also be avoided, for obious reasons.

• Remember to look where you are going when rope or cordage is involved. It is easy to trip over tent lines and other guylines, or walk into picket lines, to your great embarrassment and the possible inconvenience of others.

• All the care in the world will not prevent the rope from becoming tangled unless it is coiled correctly. A loose rope will appear to twist itself into terrible tangles out of spite, even though very little has been done with it, so it should always be kept tidy.

There are several ways in which a rope may be coiled. The simplest is the way that most people use to coil up an extension cord: it is wrapped from the hand, around the elbow, and up into the hand, forming small coils. This is repeated until the end of the line is reached and then a variety of methods can be used to finish off the coil.

The way in which the coil is to be used may affect the way it is finished off. For an extension cord or clothesline, it is sufficient to wrap the loose end of the cord a few times around the coil and tuck the end under a turn or two of the wrapping. With larger or heavier rope this is not usually enough to keep everything together and larger coils are required, perhaps stretching from the waist to the ground.

Some methods of coiling have been given names such as a “mountaineer's coil” or a “caver's coil” because these activities have certain requirements. A climber wants a rope that will uncoil easily and is easy to carry, whereas a caver wants a rope that will uncoil easily but not catch or snag on the rocks in a cave. Thus, in the illustrations, you can see that the climber puts a whipping on the coil and secures the ends of the rope so that he can immediately undo the tie and use the rope. The caver, on the other hand, uses the two ends of the rope to make a square knot and then wraps a length from each end around the coil before finishing off with another knot. The individual coils are thus kept together and unlikely to snag.

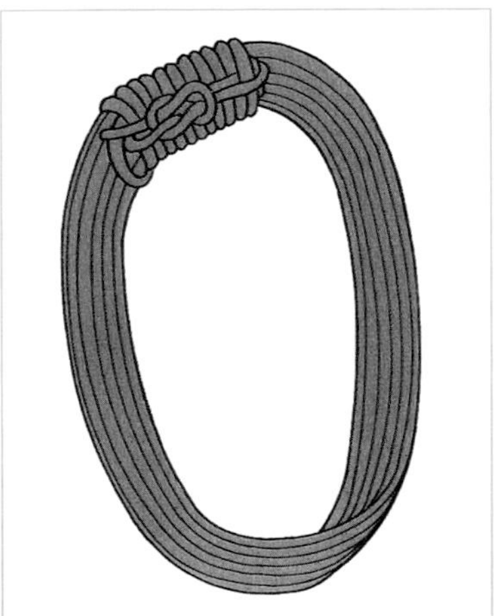

This page: This is a climber's coil, which utilizes a whipping to hold the coil secure. This has the advantage of quick release, should the climber need the rope in a hurry.

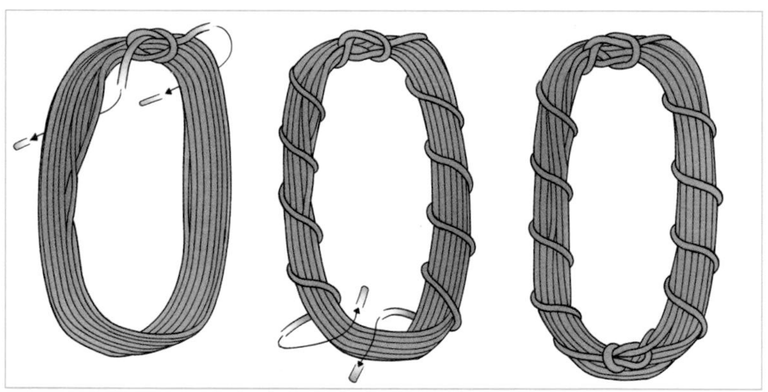

Above: A caver's coil is wrapped around with excess rope to keep it from snagging.

Below: A skein coil is useful for general purposes, such as keeping a clothesline neat.

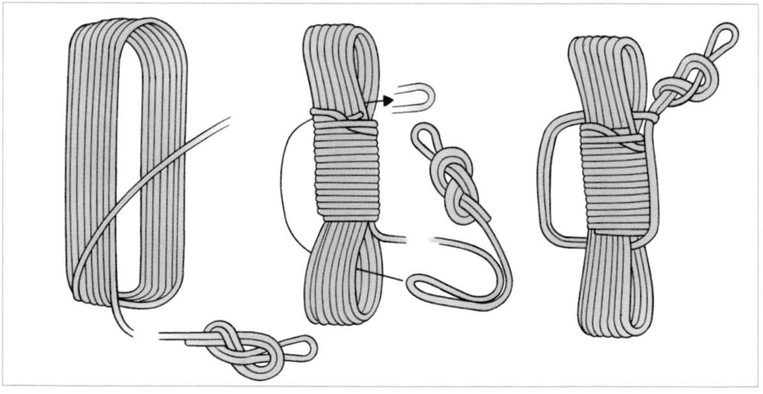

In spite of these names, it does not mean that every climber or caver coils his or her rope in the same fashion. There are many other ways of preparing the rope coils, and in modern practice ropes are also often carried in rope bags or sacks, which, if properly designed, will protect them from mud, grit, and anything that might snag the rope. They are also more manageable, especially underground.

To load a rope into a bag is simpler than might be imagined. First tie a large knot in the end of the rope. (This will keep anyone from falling off the end of the rope.) Put the knot into the bag. Hold the rim of the bag with one hand and let the rope run under the thumb of the bag-holding hand. With the other hand, which is inside the bag, just pull the rope in and let go. Bring the hand back to the holding thumb, take another length of rope, and pull that in. This is repeated in a rhythmic fashion until the end of the rope is reached. Again, it is handy to tie a knot near the end so that it may be found easily when the rope is to be used. It is not necessary to coil the rope as it goes in. In fact, coils are to be avoided as they can cause kinks, which are inconvenient when the rope is in use. Having read how carefully whale-lines were coiled into their tubs, and having seen the care taken when loading rocket lines to avoid kinks, when I first saw braided rappelling rope being shoved into a bag with no apparent care, I was amazed, and this amazement became even greater when later I saw the same rope flow smoothly out of the bag without tangling. It may take a few attempts before you get the rhythm and feel comfortable with a long rope, but it is a useful trick to master. It can often be quicker than coiling, and you do not have to support the weight of the rope, which is a great help to tired arms at the end of a busy day.

Try to ensure that when a rope runs through a block (pulley), the block is the correct size for the rope. If the revolving part (sheave) is the wrong size, the rope may either sit in the bottom of the pulley and slip, or if the rope is too big, it may overflow the sheave and jam. Approximately one third of the circumference of the rope should be in contact with the sheave. The shape of the groove in the sheave is also important, as different rope types work better with certain patterns. For example, Kevlar rope works better with a wider, shallower groove than it does with the rounded groove favored by manila.

The sheave should normally be at least four times the diameter of the rope itself to ensure that the rope does not have too great an included angle or, in simple terms, does not have too tight a bend. However, a compromise often has to be made, especially when there is a lot of gear to be carried (large packs are heavy), but manufacturers of sporting equipment can usually provide a useful lightweight selection from which you can choose.

For storage you will, ideally, have a cool, dark, well-ventilated room or cupboard. In here the rope is hung in coils, either from untreated wooden pegs or from loops of rope hanging from hooks. Do not let the coils hang in disarray from a rusty nail.

As a responsible rope user you will mark each rope with its length, type, and date purchased. There are several methods by which this can be done and you must choose the method with which you are happiest. I write the details on a piece of plastic tape and then secure it under a two-inch length of clear shrink wrap tubing that I attach with a hot air gun (a blow-dryer will do).

It is sensible, if the rope is used for climbing, caving, or any situation where life may be at risk, to maintain a register of use for each rope. This will say how many rappels have been carried out, if any falls occurred on the rope, if it was used to haul unusual loads, how long it was exposed to the elements, etc. Filling in the record is almost as important as putting the rope back in its bag. From this information, and inspection of the rope, you will be able to judge, when you have learned more and gained sufficient experience, whether or not the rope is safe to use again or should be discarded.

Choice of Rope

Your choice of rope or cord depends on what you intend to do with it and how much you can afford to spend. Do not spare pennies when selecting your ropes, but there is no need to bankrupt yourself. Be selective in your choice but try to have an idea of your requirements before you are seduced by the specifications of a wonder rope. If you shop in the right stores, you will find a wide range from which you can select the most suitable.

- For camping purposes it is useful to have a supply of light, braided nylon cord for general camp chores. The sort sold as "paracord" is ideal. You will find it is handy to have a selection of cord from six to eleven millimeters in diameter for more elaborate projects.

• When fishing, you have a vast range of lines from which to choose, and much will depend on the type of fish you are hunting. Tackle shops are the best source of information, as they know what is most effective in their area.

• Boat users will usually require a range of lines, all different, for specific purposes. A canoeist might want a bungee or "shock" cord, a light floating line, a flexible throw line, webbing, and some light lanyards. A sailor could need natural-fiber rope in a variety of sizes if he is a traditionalist or, more practically, would use a similar range of synthetic ropes. One rope may be required to float, another may need to be relatively nonstretch, others will benefit from a degree of give, and if ornamental work is to be done, a cord that ties easily is essential.

• For vertical travel, the range of ropes is also wide. In this field the specialty manufacturers can provide you with a fantastic selection in a vast range of sizes, thicknesses, and colors. Rope seems to have become almost a fashion accessory, but the color coding helps to identify each rope and its function. Ropes are available that will stretch in the event of a fall—by up to ten percent to absorb shock—and there are also ropes that hardly stretch, for precise placement when rappelling or for work access. Also available are thinner cords for Prusik loops and lanyards, ropes for single or double rope technique, tapered ropes, water-repellent treated ropes, fine but very strong Kevlar cords for fire self-rescue equipment, special rescue ropes, and even a silent rope for the military (but this may be hard to find).

All of these activities can put the participant at risk, though fishing and camping tend to be less dangerous than climbing or sailing, but because the best place to practice these sports is away from populated areas, there is an inbuilt hazard level. When life is at risk I cannot emphasize enough how important it is to get proper training and instruction before you use the knots or information in this book. Never think that you have learned it all. There are always new facts to learn and this is what makes knotting (and life) interesting.

Equipment

To tie knots you will need very simple equipment—your fingers. With these alone it is possible to tie all of the knots in this book. There is an old maritime saying, "every finger a marlinespike," which suggests that the old-time sailors were proud of the skill in their fingers. However, there are one or two items that make life much simpler for the knot tier today. This is not cheating; the old sailors used these tools as well, so by acquiring a level of proficiency in their use today, you are helping to carry on an age-old traditional craft. I am sure that if the old-timers had access to modern equipment, they would jump at the chance to use it.

Before equipment is discussed it is worth considering the fingers. Usually the rope does not have to be held in a particular fashion, but the hands must be allowed to do the work and you should be flexible in both your physical and mental approaches so that your hands are able to adapt to the requirements of knot tying.

After fingers, the most useful tool for a knot tier is a knife. This needs to be sharp and a sheath knife is generally more practical than a folding knife, but a pointed blade is not usually needed. A strong blade that will not bend but will hold an edge is ideal. The purpose of the knife is to cut the cord or rope. You may well find that you need more than one knife, as there are many ways and places to cut cord. A cutting board or small section of a board is useful, so that pressure can be applied, ensuring a clean cut that does not put the dining table at risk. A slicing motion with downward pressure gives a clean cut. To cut large rope, a sharp axe and a solid billet of wood give the best results. Place the axe on a firm surface with the edge up and the rope lying across it. While holding the axe handle, firmly smack down hard on the rope with the billet of wood and the rope should be cut through cleanly. It goes without saying that this is best done out of the living areas of the home. This technique may also be carried out with the knife, which is why a strong sheath knife is popular. Place the cutting board on the floor before hitting the knife—if the board is rested on your knee, it will hurt.

The toolboxes of knot tiers contain a wide variety of favorite tools to cut rope, from kitchen knives to Swiss Army knives, through riggers knives to craft knives. Razor blades, craft knife blades, and scalpels are popular, and I have also seen a curved life-raft knife and even an all-steel postmortem knife in a knot tier's kit. As long as the knife will cut cleanly and you find it comfortable and safe to use, then it is acceptable.

Cutting tools do not stop at the knife, however. Any cutting item with a sharp blade can be adapted for your purposes. Depending on what type of work you are doing, and the type of rope, any of the following might be useful: bonsai root clippers, nail clippers, heavy-duty wire cutters, side cutters, scissors of all sizes, and, in extremes, even items like cigar cutters can be utilized. Most of these will need a sharpening device and again a wide selection can be found, from oilstone to tungsten carbide wheel gadgets.

Before cutting any cord you should apply a whipping or a constrictor knot on either side of where you wish to cut, or have wound a length of masking tape around the site of the cut before slicing through the middle of the tape. This leaves both cut ends tidily secure, unable to unravel and easy to work with. The tool that seems most popular to seal the ends of synthetic rope is a disposable gas cigarette lighter, though advanced lighters, which are miniature blowtorches, offer a fine, precise flame. This technique is often called a "butane back splice." Gas or electric hot knives that melt and seal the cord as they cut it can also be purchased.

Sealing a rope is an acquired art. I generally use an old carving knife, heated on a gas stove, with which the cord is first cut.

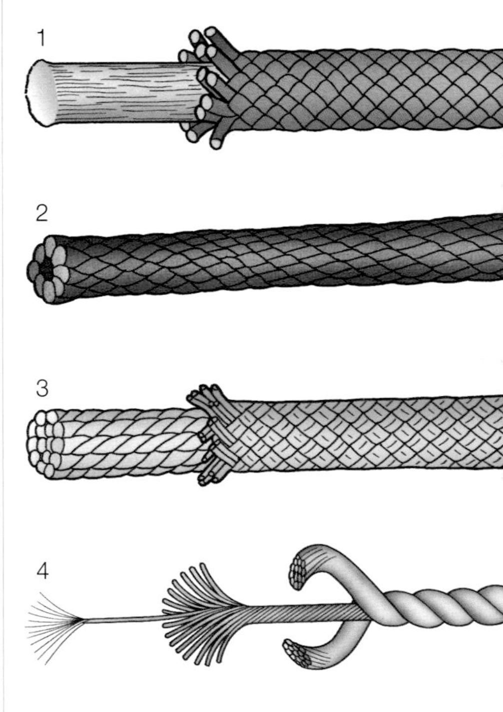

Above: Static kernmantle rope, used for rappelling (1); braided rope (2); dynamic kernmantle, which is used in climbing and has more stretch (3); and laid rope, which is made of fiber yarn (4).

Then, holding the red-hot blade parallel to my cutting block, I rotate the end of the cord between the blade and the board. It requires a small amount of practice, but you will soon be able to cut and seal the rope in one go, and get a slight taper on the end of the cord at the same time. It is worth spending a little time practicing this technique. It will put you in good stead later in your knotting career.

When hot-sealing synthetic cord, it is very important that you remember to do it in a very well-ventilated site, as the fumes given off by burning nylon are not healthy. The ends of the rope also get very hot when this operation is being performed, so do not touch the melted ends until you are sure they have cooled.

Another important tool for knot tiers is the spike, and it comes in a huge variety of forms for general and more specialized use. There are steel spikes, marlinespikes of assorted sizes with round points, diamond shaped points, and (the best shape) something like a cross between a duck's bill and a screwdriver. There are wooden spikes or "fids," fashioned from a variety of hardwoods (lignum vitae is a favorite). Spikes are tapered and come in several sizes, some have a metal collar and flat end so they can be stood upright on the floor, and some are so big as to need two men to manipulate. The most usual size these days is about nine inches long and is very versatile, being used easily on several sizes of rope.

Another improvement on the fid or spike, known as a Swedish fid, consists of a tapered steel channel with a wooden handle. The fid is used to separate the strands of a rope when knotting so that another strand may be passed into the opening. The Swedish fid, because of its angular shape, allows the new working end to be passed easily by laying it in the groove of the channel. When the Swedish fid is withdrawn, it carries the new strand with it. Many other devices have been produced to perform this task, and one of the most successful is the gripfid, which holds the new strand and pulls it through the opened-up strands of the rope.

As with the marlinespikes and the fids, tools to carry out the separation of rope strands come in many sizes and knot tiers have also been most ingenious in converting other everyday objects into tools. If you know what you are doing, then small fids can be made from windshield wiper fittings, umbrella spokes, small plastic tubes, and a very small one for working with tiny cord can even be made from a hypodermic needle.

Sadly, not everyone has fingers that can cope with all the old skills, and thinner cord does not lend itself so well to blunt or less-nimble digits. To replace fingers, the toolbox offers long-nose pliers in many sizes, from jewelers' sizes up to electricians'. Tweezers and forceps, in many sizes and styles (one of the most popular is the artery forceps), are very useful, as they not only lock onto the cord, but also tend to have serrated jaws, which will hold securely when manipulating cord. Because they are available in so many sizes, tweezers and forceps can be found in the toolboxes of lace makers and ship riggers, and most knot tiers in between.

Another device that will get where fingers cannot is a wire loop. There does not seem to be a name for this gadget, yet all knotters know it: a doubled length of wire with the ends contained in a handle. The closed end of the loop may be inserted into a knot or through a rope. A strand can then be placed in the loop, which is withdrawn, pulling the desired strand with it. The wire is usually thin but the thickness depends to some extent on the size of cord with which you are working. It is a very versatile tool and allows for the capture and hiding of short ends when finishing off some knots.

Frequently, making a knot tidy will take longer than the initial tying. A small spike or pricker is invaluable for this and, like the other tools in the box, they are available in many shapes and sizes. Some are similar to ice picks, others look like bradawls, or are improvised devices that defy easy identification, while their use is obvious. The artery forceps and small pliers are also used for the tidying process, so they more than justify their place in the toolbox.

In order to tie knots you can get by with just your fingers, but a knife, Swedish fid, wire loop, and perhaps artery forceps or long-nose pliers will make a perfectly adequate tool kit for most practical knot tying. However, if you have trouble handling very small stuff you may find that proprietary devices or gadgets sold in fishing tackle shops will be of great assistance for some of the knots that appear later in this book.

However, tying knots can become addictive, and if you were to look into the tool kits of real obsessives or professionals, you might also find such items as paper clips, clothespins, netting needles, drinking straws, special splicing needles and tools for braided rope, threaded hollow needles, bag ties, knitting machine needles, football lacing needles, rug-making latch hooks, beeswax, whipping twine, masking tape, glue, hooks, clamps, hairpins, nail clippers, and a host of other implements that have been pressed into service. It can be a real education delving into the depths of other peoples' tool kits and asking, "What do you use this for?" As you become more enthusiastic about knot tying, you will probably find that items are added to your own tool kit that are not covered here. Remember that if there doesn't seem to be a tool that suits the job, your own ingenuity might be able to supply one.

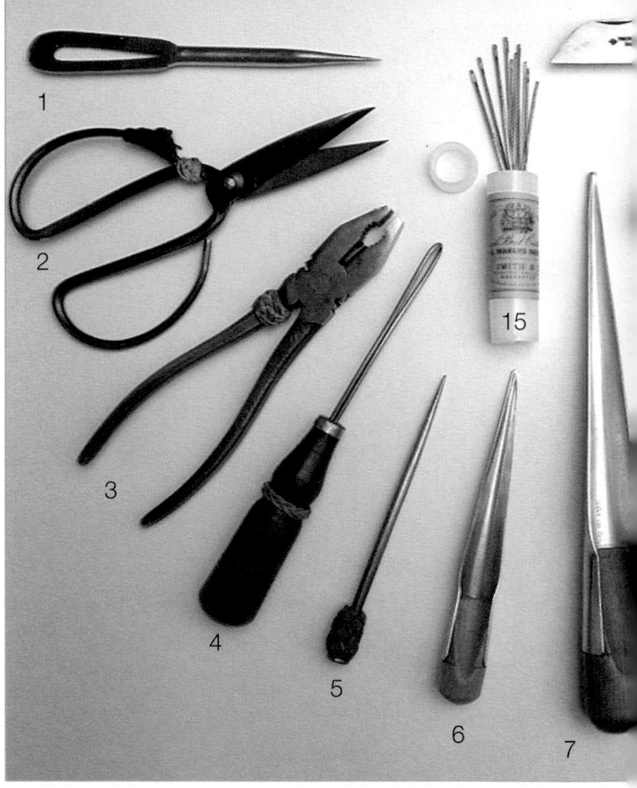

1 Groove spike with a shackle key, used for separating strands; similar to the Swedish fid

2 Scissors

3 Pliers

4 Large wire loop

5 Thin pricker

6 Small Swedish fid

7 Large Swedish fid

8 Small wire loop

9 Disposable cigarette lighter

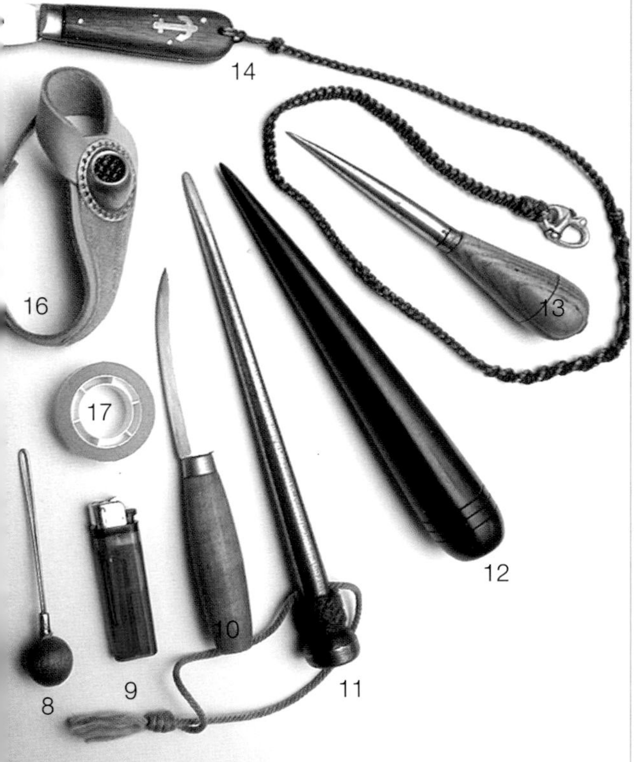

10	Sheath knife
11	Steel marlinespike
12	Wooden fid
13	Pricker
14	Folding knife with lanyard
15	Sailmaker's needles
16	Sailmaker's palm, used like a large thimble and fitted over the palm of the hand to protect the flesh
17	Tape

Basic Terms & Techniques

As with most disciplines, knot tying has its own vocabulary, which will be useful for you to be familiar with. This will not entail learning a whole lot of new words, but you will need to know what we call different parts of the rope and some basic techniques. For ease of reference, there is a short glossary on pages 252 and 253.

Everyone knows the rhetorical question, "How long is a piece of string?" A knot tier will tell you that it is the length between the standing end and the working end. If you are working with a piece of rope, the end you are using is the working end. The other end, which can be thought of as standing around doing nothing, is the standing end. The standing end may, in fact, be involved with another knot, but since only one end at a time is usually being worked, you do not need to worry about this. The part of the rope between the end and the action is known as the working part, and similarly that part near the standing end is called the standing part.

If the rope is doubled so that two strands lie close to one another, a bight has been formed. For some knots, we take a bight and tie around it, or we may pass a bight through a ring before tying off. For many knots it is often easier to pass a bight than to find the working end, feed it through, and then perhaps have to pass it back again.

When we double the rope, we cross one side over the other to form a loop, making a crossing turn. This may be over or under, depending on which way the working end goes. If there is something upright, such as a stick, inside the loop of the crossing turn, and the working part sits on top of the standing part, then a half hitch has been created. It will be fairly obvious that if the working part goes under the standing part it will just fall down and nothing will have been formed. Try it. A half hitch does very little on its own, but when combined with another half hitch or round turns, it forms the basis of some very useful knots.

I will try not to confuse you with over and under, but if you know that a crossing turn could be one or the other, it will make the instructions easier to understand when things go wrong. Believe me, there will be occasions when a knot will not want to cooperate. It once took three days and twelve instruction books before I succeeded in tying one ornamental knot.

Hang the rope over a bar and you have taken a turn around the bar. Wrap the rope around the bar again and you have a round turn. Now try to make a half hitch around the standing part of the rope. You can go on either side of the standing part, but will only get a half hitch if the working end goes around and over the working part, otherwise it just falls away again. Now make another half hitch exactly the same as the first. If everything has gone according to plan you now have your first knot, a round turn and two half hitches (see page 59 for a pictorial guide to this knot). It will all look rather loose at first, but if you hold the working end and pull on the standing part the knot will tighten up and it will give a secure fastening for mooring a boat or securing the end for a myriad of other jobs.

This practice will have shown you many useful things. You have now learned some of the terminology, the difference between over and under when applied to a half hitch, and the difference between a turn and a round turn. You may also have found, while you were tying, that the working end was not quite long enough and that you needed to feed more cord into the knot to complete it. This is a common problem and one that can have serious consequences in practical knotting. If the working end is not long enough on completion of a knot, then, when a load is applied, the knot may fail because, as the slack is taken up, the short tail pulls out from the rest of the knot. When learning to tie a knot this is not a problem, but it is good practice to leave a tail of at least six inches in thin cord or fifteen inches in thicker cords or rope. There is then enough cord to put in a thumb knot or two half hitches as security for the main knot when a life may be at risk.

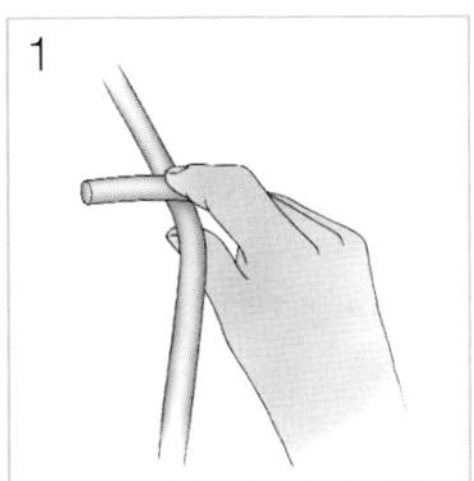

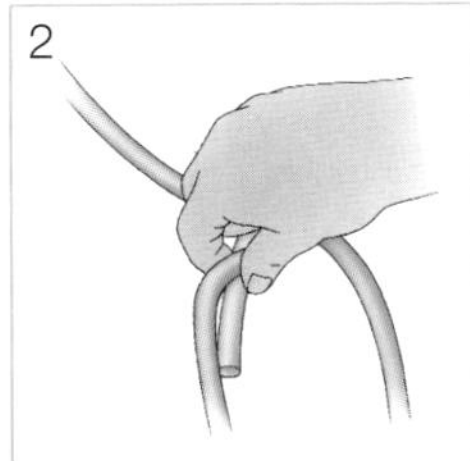

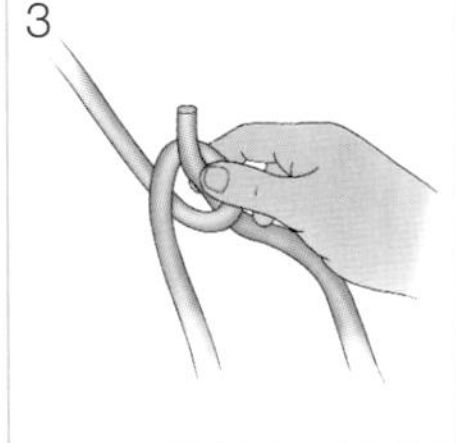

Above: A useful one-handed way to start a bowline. The working end is laid across the standing part (1); the hand twists over to bring the working end into the loop (2); and up to bring the end out through the resulting crossing turn (3).

Not every application will require the security backup. In fact, the action of many knots, especially those requiring easy release, would be neutralized by security hitches.

Spill is another term used in knotting. A knot may be distorted and turned from one knot into another by spilling it. Spilling may occur when load is applied to the wrong end when tensioning a knot. Sometimes this may be intentional, as in one method for tying the bowline, but is usually not intended. Thus if the wrong two cords leaving a square knot (reef knot) are pulled firmly, the knot will distort and form a lark's head. This then could slide off the short end of the other half of the square knot and is why this particular knot should never be used to join two lines in rescue work.

When knots are tied they are usually loose and are drawn tighter as the slack is worked out. In many cases this is done without thinking and is part of the routine of tying the knot. Sometimes, however, the slack has to be worked out systematically to fair up the knot and get everything in the correct position. This is where the pricker and artery forceps are most useful.

With some knots you feed the cord around a second or third time alongside the cord that you first tied. This is called doubling or trebling the knot and is seen most often in Turk's heads or mats and other ornamental work. During doubling (and trebling) it can take a long time to pass the full length of the cord through all the loops and turns of a knot. Some time may be saved by passing a bight from the middle of the working part, instead of a single working end, as then you can pull through twice as much cord each time. When making some mats, for example, it is easier to make the working part into a hank and feed it through in one go, paying out cord as it travels. Care must be taken to work the slack mat into its correct form after the necessary doubling or trebling has taken place.

Whipping

Even if you have heat-sealed the end of the rope, it may help to whip the ends, as this will stiffen the end of the rope, making it easier to pass under strands or through loops. It also looks more tidy and professional.

There are several ways to whip the end of a rope. The method I am about to describe is the simplest, and although it may not be quite as secure as some methods, it is the easiest to learn and generally very effective.

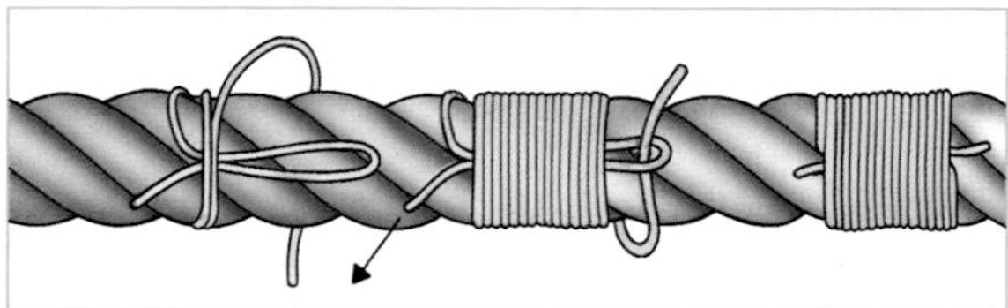

Left: Stages in applying a simple whipping.

Take a length of whipping twine. This is thin, strong, and usually waxed. Make a bight near one end to give a long end and a short end. The short end needs to be at least twice the diameter of the rope to which the whipping will be applied, while the long end can remain on the reel.

Place the bight on the cord with the closed end of the bight facing the end of the rope and about one and a half rope diameters from the end. Hold it in place with your thumb. Starting at the end farthest from the rope end, wind the long end of the twine around the rope and over the bight of whipping twine. Pull tight. Continue to wrap the twine tightly around the rope, moving along toward the end of the rope. Keep the turns as close together as possible. When you have wrapped a length equal to roughly the diameter of the rope, and have pulled each turn taut, the last of the bight of twine, which you have been covering, should be visible as a loop sticking out from the wrapping. Cut the wrapping twine from the reel, leaving a few inches to work with and maintain pressure with your thumb to stop everything from unraveling. Pass the cut end through the loop as though you are threading a needle. The single end of twine projecting from the start of the wrapping is now pulled to drag the loop back and out of sight under the wraps. Pliers or forceps are useful here, as the thin twine can easily cut your fingers when pulled. Before the cut end emerges from the start, you stop pulling and trim the ends of the twine carefully, level with the ends or the wrapping.

In the illustration, the starting strand is rather loose. After threading the cut end through the loop, the loop, or one side of it (trial and error shows which side to pull, as the bight sometimes twists when out of sight), needs to be pulled to take up the slack at the start. The first end is then pulled to reduce the size of the loop and the pull is continued to lock everything in place. A little practice may be required to ensure that you do not pull the top end free from the bottom, in which case the whipping would unravel, but the technique is quickly mastered and you will be able to proudly whip the ends of every cord you use.

Hitching and Lashing

In this section I shall only deal with two simple methods of tying up bundles. Other methods are described later in the book, but for the moment it is useful to concentrate on the differences between these two simple ties.

The easiest hitching is half hitching. We have seen that a half hitch on its own is not very secure, but when a series of half hitches are applied along a bundle, then we get a simple and useful lashing. This can be used to tie a sail to a spar or to tie up a parcel.

One end of the cord is secured around the bundle (in illustration 2 on page 33, a clove hitch is used) and then a series of half hitches is run along the bundle to hold it all together.

Leaving the anchor point, the cord is run along the parcel, passed around the parcel, and then crossed under then over itself, as when forming a half hitch. Your thumb is then put on the crossing to hold it in place, and the process is repeated. At the end of the parcel the cord is tied off, perhaps with a couple of half hitches around itself.

A more secure lashing using the marling hitch can be seen in illustration 1. At first glance there is very little difference between this and the half hitching. However, as you look more closely, you will see that after leaving the anchoring turn (here a timber hitch has been used) the cord is taken along the parcel and around it, but when crossing over, it comes over the first turn and then tucks under before continuing to repeat the procedure. This locks the turns more securely than the other method and is the only way in which a hammock should be lashed for stowing. The lashing should be pulled taut at each crossing as it is tied.

If the parcel could be removed while the two lashings were left in place, the half hitch rope would come undone and could easily be pulled out into a continuous length, but the marling rope would be a series of thumb knots and it would take quite a time to undo them all and get back to a clear rope. This clearly shows the difference between the two systems and why the marling hitch is to be preferred.

Later in the book, methods to lash poles together will be shown and this will allow you, with a little ingenuity, to move weights, build bridges, or even just make a washboard. If you know how to tie poles together, there is no limit to what might be achieved.

If you have attempted the whipping and hitching just described, you will have started to get used to the feel of rope. Practice is the key to successful knot tying, it helps make one feel comfortable with rope, develops muscle memory, and builds confidence.

Another very useful thing to learn is to twist the wrist when holding a cord. We will work with the right wrist for the moment, but the idea can be applied to either side, amending the instructions accordingly.

Hold a piece of cord in the palm of your right hand with the working end between the first finger and thumb while the other fingers hold the cord into the palm. The rest of the cord can hang down below the little finger. Your hand should be a little in front of you, with the back of the hand facing up and about level with your stomach. Turn your wrist down toward the floor, then in toward your stomach and then away from you so that the back of the hand is now facing down and the rope, still between the thumb and finger, and in the palm, is pointing away from you.

This extremely simple move, a mere twist of the wrist, will be helpful when tying some very useful knots, and it is a technique worth learning and practicing.

Right: The first illustration shows the marling hitch. Below, in the second picture, is half hitching.

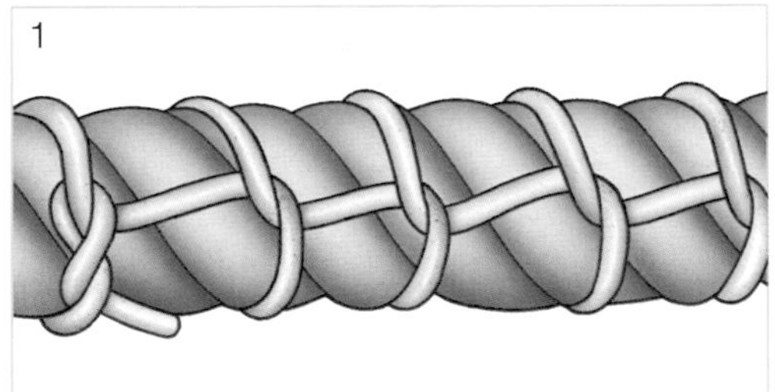

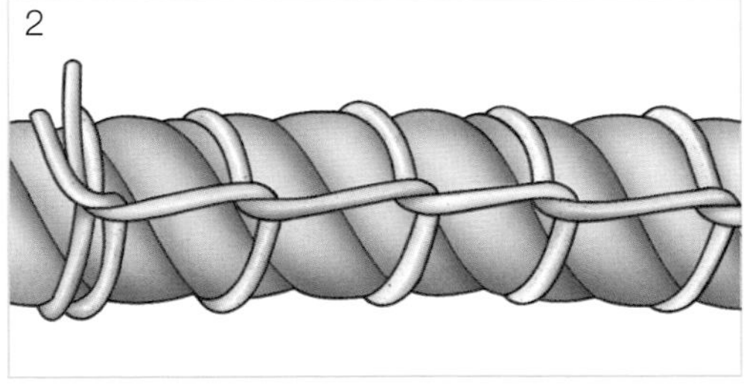

General Knots

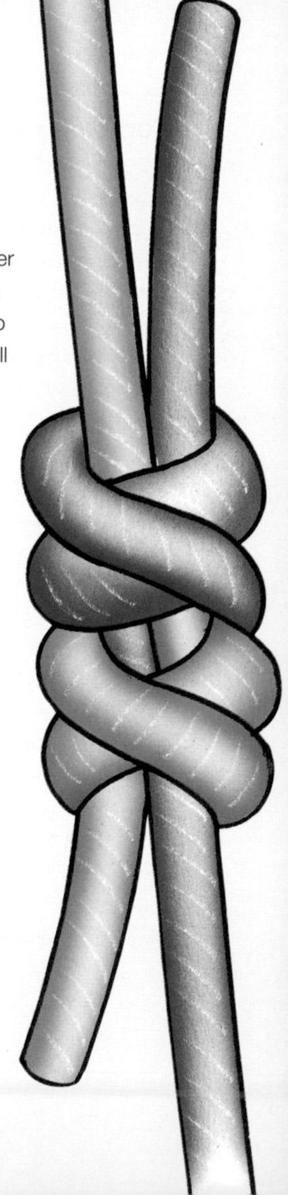

The knots in this section are worth learning by everyone, whether or not they wish to concentrate later on one of the other sections of this book. A mixture of old and new knots has been included and in some cases more than one method is shown to tie a particularly useful knot. This is because some situations will not let you work in the position or direction that you have used when learning a knot, and knowing more than one method builds confidence and helps to encourage mental flexibility.

The knots are not in any particular order, though the first few are among the simplest of knots. None are at all difficult to tie, but at first there may be a few that do not cooperate. Don't give up when this happens. Stop, try to work out where the mistake has occurred, and then correct it.

Contents of General Knots

Thumb or Overhand Knot 36
Double Overhand or Blood Knot 37
Overhand Loop or Thumb Knot in the Bight 38
Overhand Knot with Draw Loop 39
Square Knot (Reef Knot) 40
Reef Bow 42
Hunter's or Rigger's Bend 44
Fisherman's, Englishman's, or True Lover's Knot 46
Double Fisherman's Knot or Grapevine 48
Treble Fisherman's Knot 49
Figure Eight 51
Figure Eight Loop 52
Figure Eight Loop: Threaded 53
Sheet Bend 54
Double Sheet Bend 56
One-Way Sheet Bend 57
Ashley's Stopper Knot 58
Round Turn & Two Half Hitches 59
Bowline (1) 60
Bowline (2) 62
Clove Hitch (1) on a Bar or Ring 64
Clove Hitch (2) over a Pin or Bollard 66
Timber Hitch 67
Killick Hitch 68
Honda or Bowstring Knot 69
Rolling Hitch 70
Tundj 72
Clara 73
Highwayman's Hitch 74
Constrictor Knot 76
Boa 78
Marlinespike Hitch 80
Hangman's Knot 82
Hangman's Knot: A Fishing Application 84
Monkey's Fist 86
Cat's Paw 88
Single Cat's Paw 89
Handcuff Knot 90
Tomfool Knot 91
Fireman's Chair Knot 92
Simple Simon Over 94
Double Simple Simon 95
Simple Simon Under 95
Single Strand Diamond or Lanyard 96

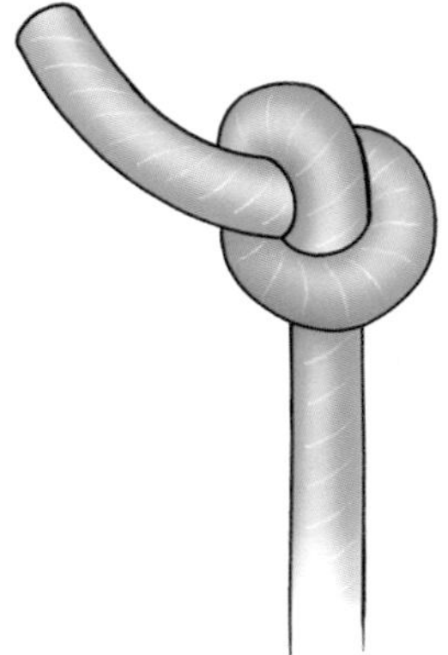

Thumb or Overhand Knot

This is the simplest of all knots and has certainly been known for many thousands of years. It is tied at the end of a light line to keep it from fraying, or to prevent the end from passing through a block and getting lost. As a result it is known as a "stopper" knot.

There are many versions, but this is the one that can be tied by everyone. It can be hard to untie once it has had any pressure put on it.

1 Take the rope and make a loop near the working end. (Remember, this is called a crossing turn.) The loop can be formed by taking a turn around your thumb. Pass the end of the rope across the standing part and then through the loop.

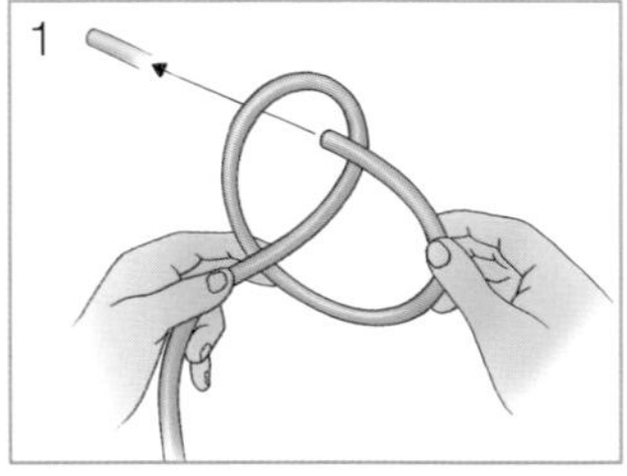

2 Your rope should now look like the illustration. Pulling the ends away from one another takes up the slack to give a thumb knot.

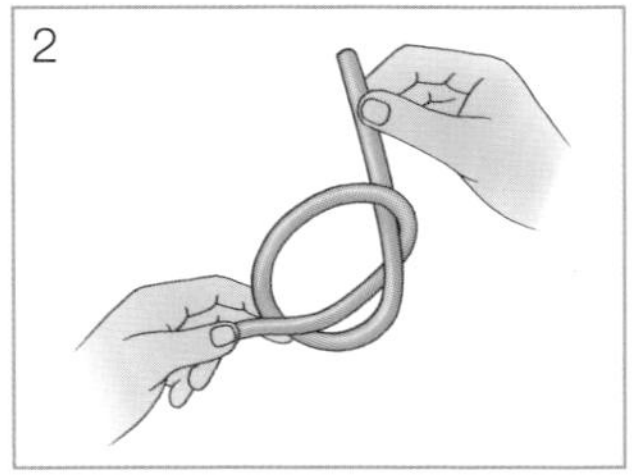

The thumb knot can be tied in two ways; the crossing may be over or under the standing part. While this does not affect the knot it does demonstrate the difference between the over or under forms. With complicated knots, going the wrong way may have disastrous consequences, so always note which way you go.

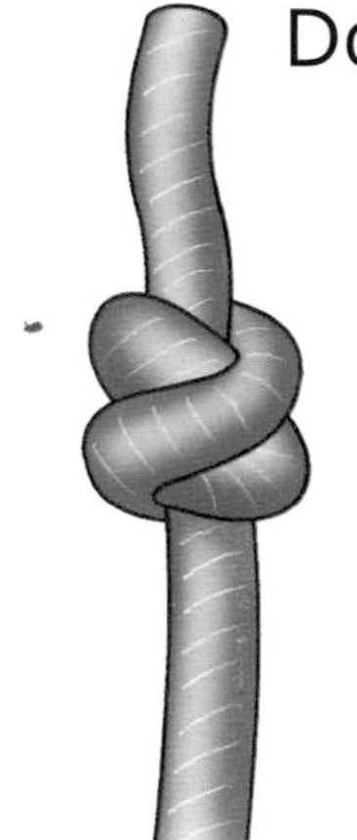

Double Overhand or Blood Knot

This is a simple variation on the previous knot. If the working end is taken a second time around the standing part before the loop is pulled closed, we get a double overhand knot, often known as a blood knot. It is said that this knot was tied in the strands of a cat-o'-nine-tails to cut into the flesh during punishment, and this gave it its name.

1 Again, take the rope and make a loop near the working end. Pass the end of the rope across the standing part and then through the loop as with the previous knot, but this time repeat.

2 Pull the ends to take up the slack.

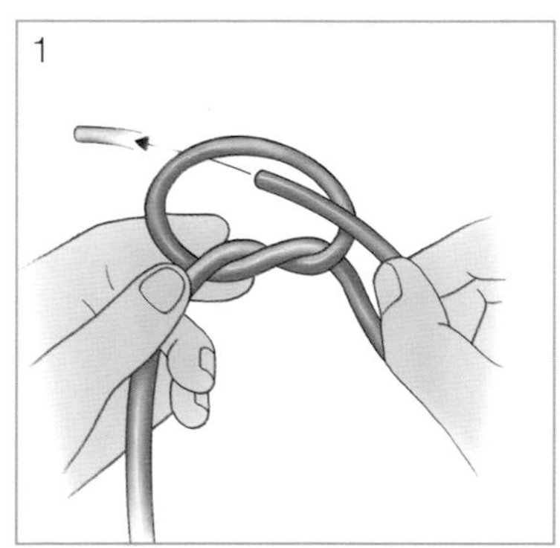

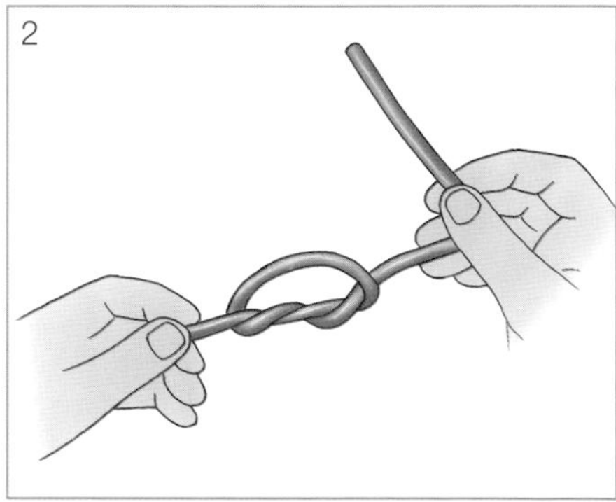

Overhand Loop or Thumb Knot in the Bight

This is the simplest loop to tie in the end of a cord and is most frequently used when in a hurry, as when fastening a parcel. It is quite versatile and can be used for a number of purposes. If you wish to hang something heavy on it, though, it might be wise to make a different choice as it can be hard to undo after loading.

1 Make a bight in the cord, allowing a reasonable length of the line to be doubled.

2 & 3 Tie a thumb knot, as before, with the doubled bight and pull the bight to tighten the knot.

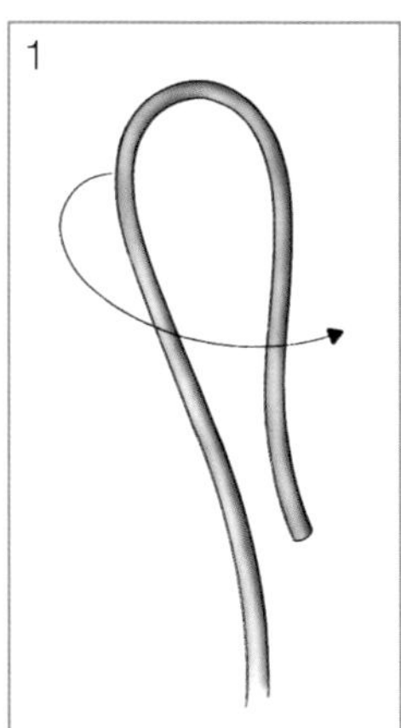

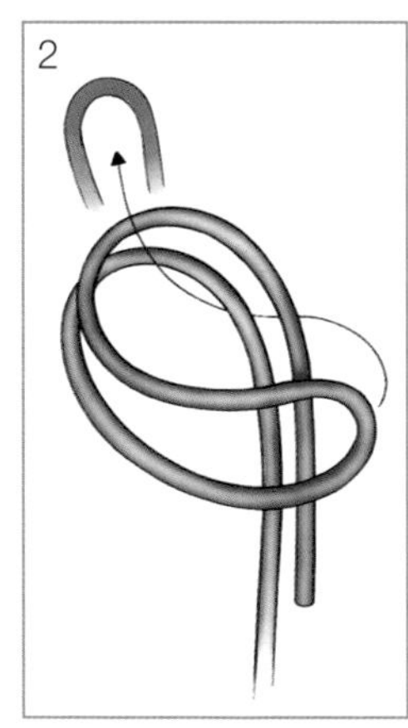

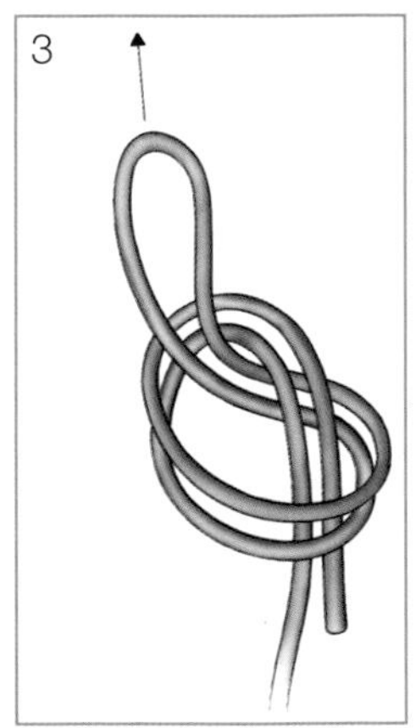

Overhand Knot with Draw Loop

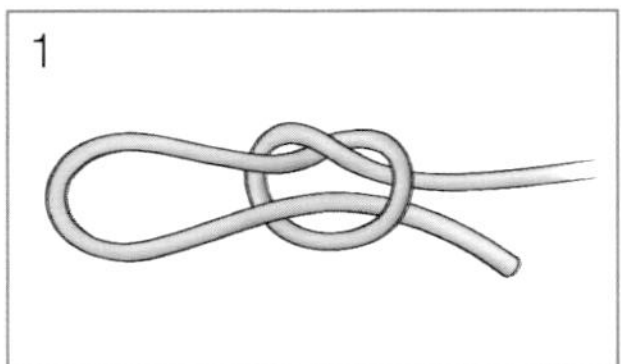

Because the overhand knot can be hard to untie, this variation produces a stopper knot that can easily be removed from the line.

1 Form a thumb knot in the normal manner but before you pull it tight, bring the working end back through the loop.

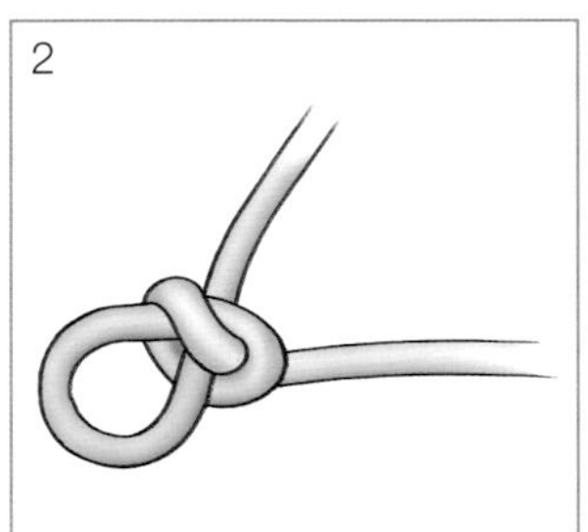

2 Work the loop closed, trapping the working end. Pulling on the end will draw the loop through the thumb knot and untie it.

You must make sure that the working end comes back into the loop alongside itself to form the draw loop and does not come up from the wrong side, which would create a blood knot.

3 If you form the loop around the standing part of the cord, when pulled taut the loop will slide along the standing part to make a simple slip knot or noose. In this form the knot has been used in primitive snares, but there are better knots to use for this.

Square Knot (Reef Knot)

In America, this knot is known as the square knot, but elsewhere it is named after its use for reefing the sails of ships. It was known several thousand years ago and was widely used in jewelry. Some say that it was once called the Herakles knot for a physician who recommended it as the knot to use when bandaging wounds. Others have suggested that Hercules (Herakles) used the knot to tie the legs of the hide of the Cithaeron lion when using it as a cloak.

Today the knot is used to join the ends of a triangular bandage when forming a sling, as the knot will lie flat and not be too uncomfortable.

1 Take one end of the rope in each hand. Cross one end over the other and then take one of the ends down, under the other rope, and bring it up and across the first rope.

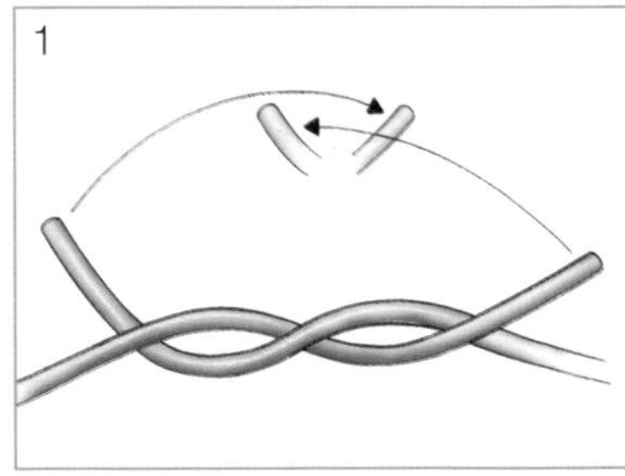

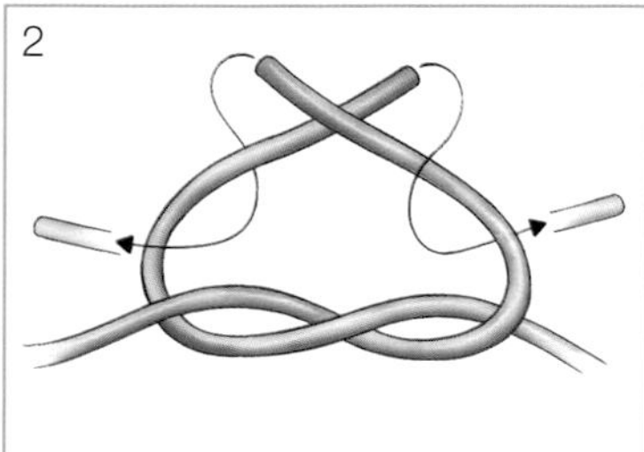

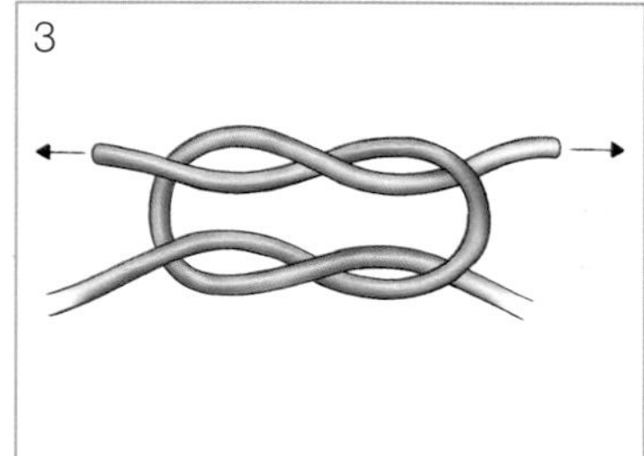

2 The next move takes the end that has come out on top and crosses it over the second cord. To achieve this, the ends must be turned to point back the way they came from. It is brought down and led up through the loop that has been formed. As it leaves the loop it should be running alongside itself and the other cord will be doing the same but traveling in the opposite direction.

3 If you hold each end close to its own standing part and pull both pairs away from each other, the knot will tighten.

If you get the second series of crossings wrong you will be left with a granny knot. It is immediately recognizable: The working ends do not lie alongside their own standing parts. When this happens you will very soon find that everything falls apart and you have to start again. It is more efficient to get it right the first time.

Don't use this knot when there is another person connected to the rope. Take one working end and its standing part and pull them in opposite directions. You will see the knot spill and the resulting lark's head formed by the other cord could easily slide off the first cord, sending a climber to the bottom of the cliff. It only takes a stubborn tuft of grass to spill a reef knot, so do not use it except on string. There are many far better knots you can use to join two ropes.

Reef Bow

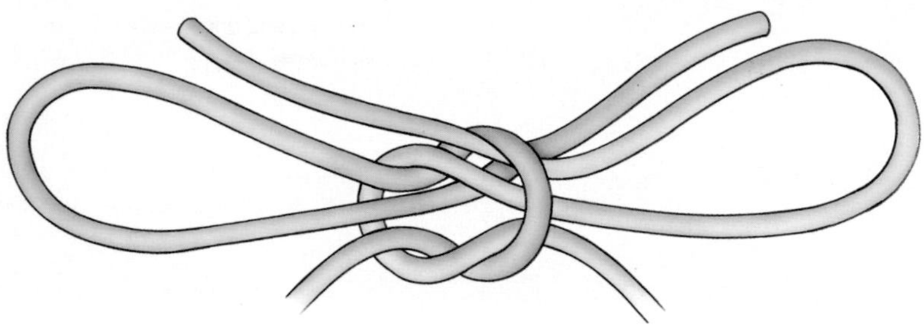

This is the traditional and easy-to-tie bow that is used for tying shoelaces or to secure a parcel. Surprisingly, many people still do not tie it correctly, and it has been included here for their benefit. When tied properly, it is a secure knot that has the added bonus of being very easy to undo. It also lends itself to being tied with different materials, such as ribbons, for a decorative look.

1 Start this knot in exactly the same way as a reef knot but use longer working ends.

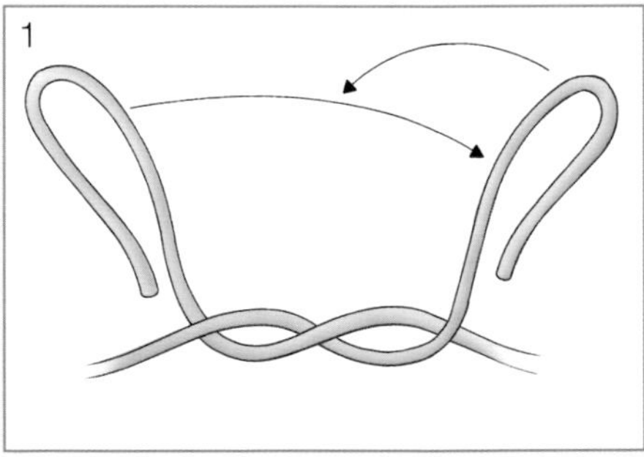

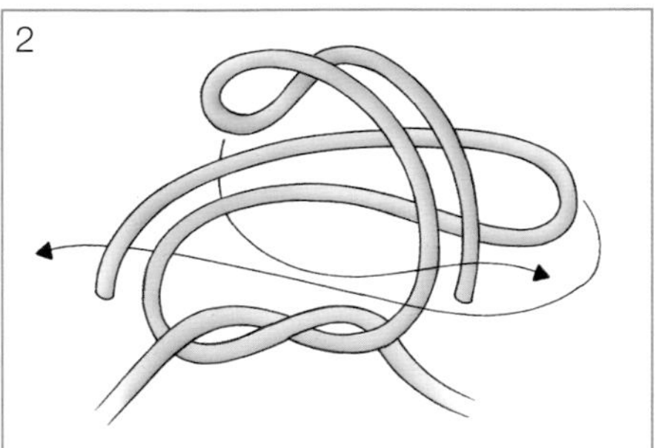

2 Once the first crossings have been made, form a bight in each working end and continue to tie the reef knot with the bights.

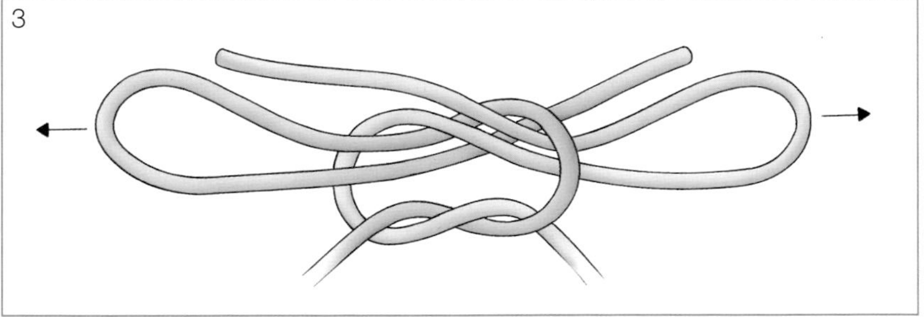

3 If the working ends are pulled when the bow has been tightened up, it will slip and come undone. If, however, the loops of the bights are pulled, the working ends will pass through the middle of the knot and you are left with a reef knot.

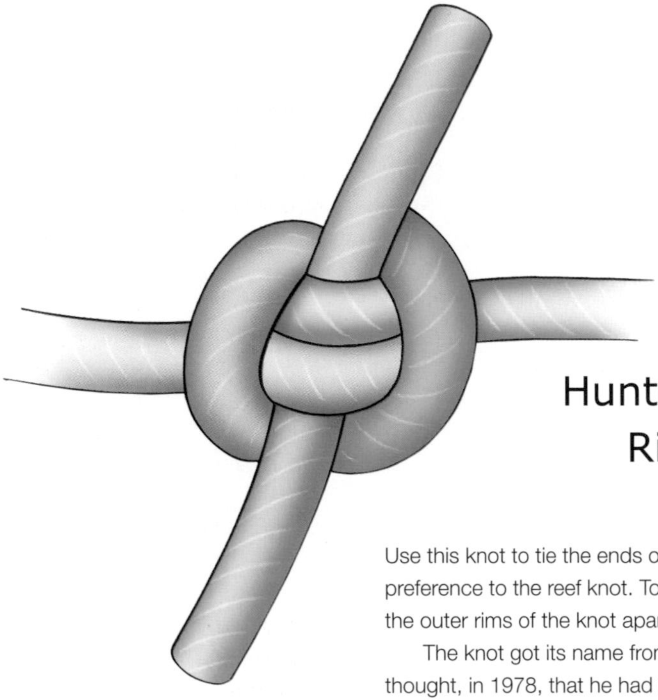

Hunter's Bend or Rigger's Bend

Use this knot to tie the ends of two cords together in preference to the reef knot. To untie it, you simply ease the outer rims of the knot apart and take out the ends.

The knot got its name from a Dr. Hunter who thought, in 1978, that he had invented a new knot. The discovery received a lot of publicity and the increased communication between knot tiers eventually led to the formation of the International Guild of Knot Tyers, which held its first annual meeting in 1982. A few years later an American, Phil Smith, wrote to say that he had included the knot in a book for mountaineers in 1953 and had called it a rigger's bend. In spite of his claim, the knot is widely known as the Hunter's bend, though it is just as useful no matter what it is called.

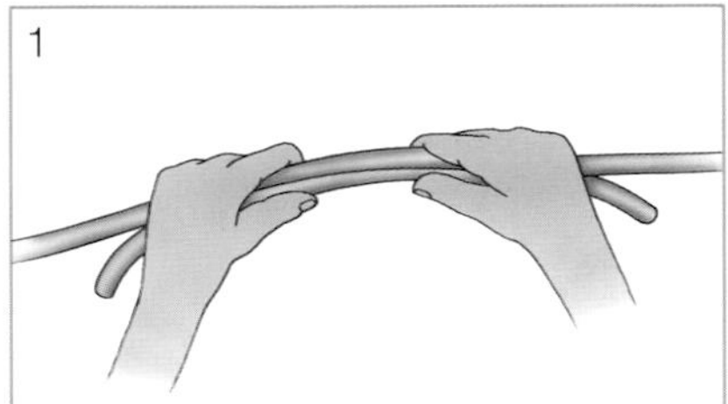

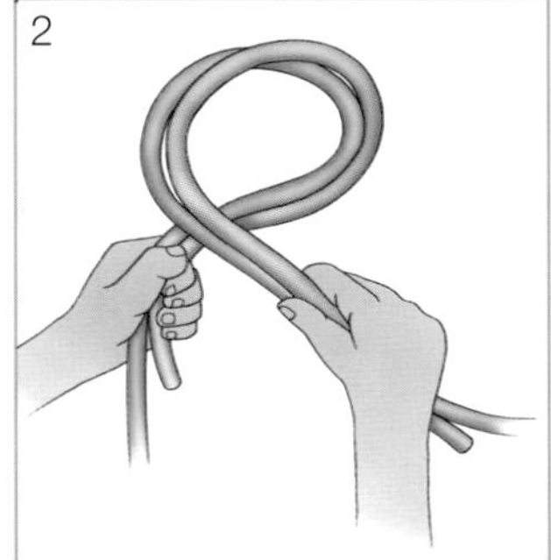

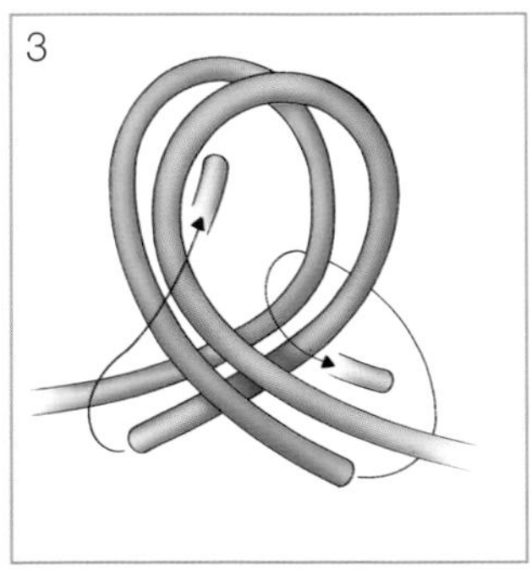

1 Take one rope in each hand and place them so the working parts are side by side but facing in opposite directions. Allow sufficient overlap to give enough cord to work with.

2 Keeping the ropes together, make a loop or crossing turn with the two cords. If necessary, rearrange the cords as in the third picture. There will be one working end lying beneath two cords and one working end lying on top of two cords.

3 Take the bottom end, bring it up, and pass it down through the loop formed by the crossing turn. Now take the other end, lead it under the cords, and bring it up through the loop. The knot is now formed and needs tightening. Hold one end and one standing part in one hand, the other end and standing part in the other, and gently pull. At this point it may not look very pretty, but with the pulling everything will fall into place and you get a symmetrical, secure knot that is easy to untie.

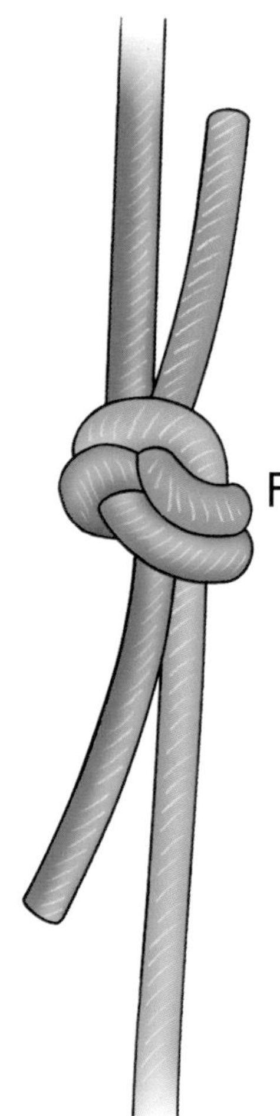

Fisherman's, Englishman's, or True Lover's Knot

This knot has been in books since the mid-1400s and was popular for joining the ends of fishing line. It is assumed that it gained its second name because it has traveled nearly everywhere that the British Empire has had a presence (though it might also be because it is such a simple thing to tie). It is only one of many knots that claim to be true lover's knots, but in this case the knot obviously owes this appellation to its similarity to two lovers snuggling up together.

1 Take the two ends and point them in opposite directions, allowing a reasonably long overlap. Tie a thumb knot with one end, but make it around the other cord.

2 Repeat this with the other end.

3 Gently tighten the thumb knots and then pull the two standing parts to make the thumb knots slide along the cord and butt up to one another.

Ideally, the two thumb knots will have been tied so that the finished knot will look like the picture on the opposite page. Even if this has not happened, the knot should hold. If you are not happy with it, it takes only a moment to pull on the short working ends to slide the thumb knots apart and retie one of them as you require it. Then, when all is correctly arranged, you may tighten everything up.

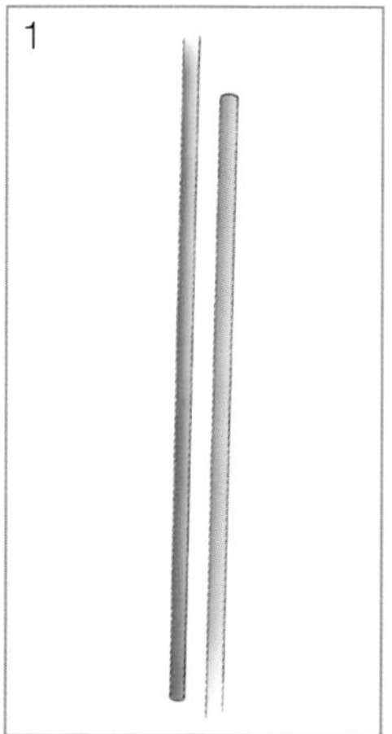

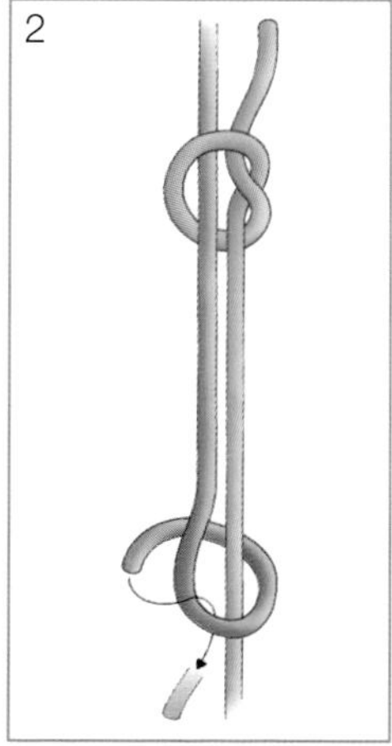

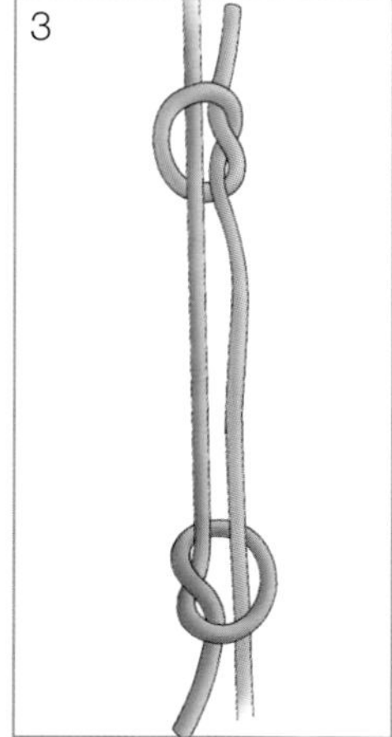

Double Fisherman's Knot or Grapevine

This knot is used to give greater security than the single fisherman's knot and is popular with climbers for joining their ropes. The illustrations for the next knot show an easy way to form this knot.

1 Start as for the single fisherman's knot. Instead of tying a thumb knot, take two turns around the cord, bring the end back over the turns, and then pass the end back under the turns to point in its original direction. Do the same on the other side. Again, the knots are worked up before pulling the standing parts. The knots will slide along as before and snuggle up securely.

Treble Fisherman's Knot

This knot forms a very secure connection between two ropes and is good for caving and climbing ropes when one rope on its own is not long enough.

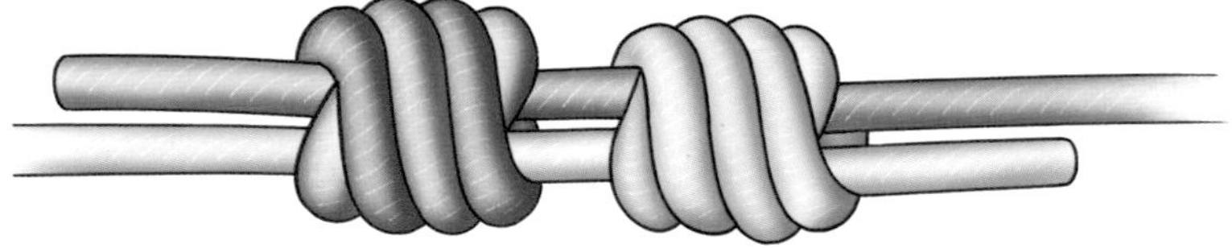

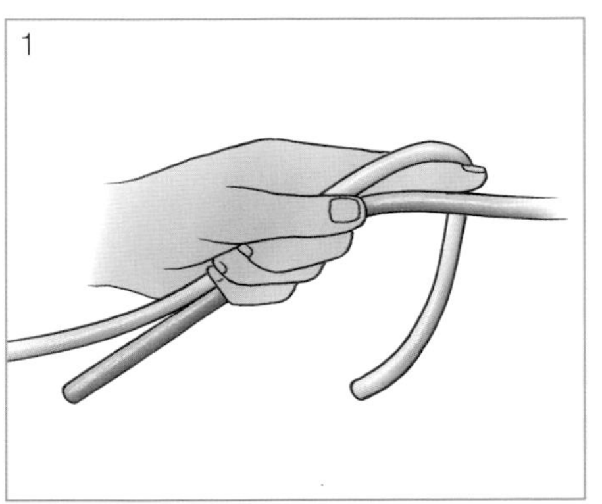

1 Prepare the ropes as for the previous knots; that is, parallel to one another with the working ends overlapping. Holding both the ropes in one hand, extend a forefinger along one.

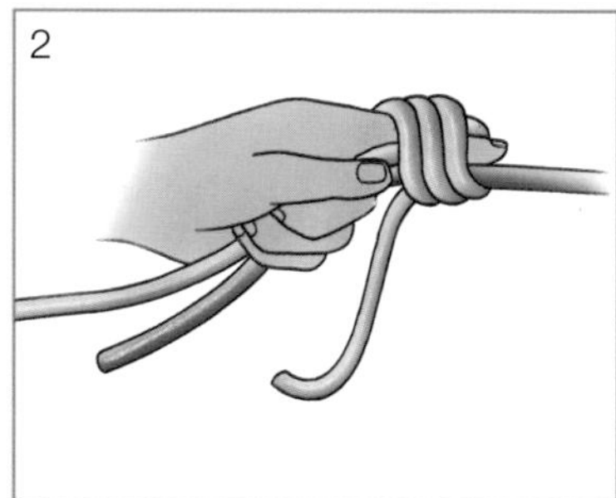

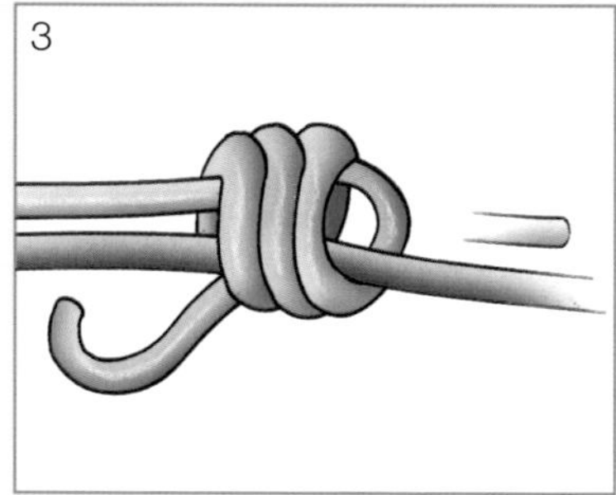

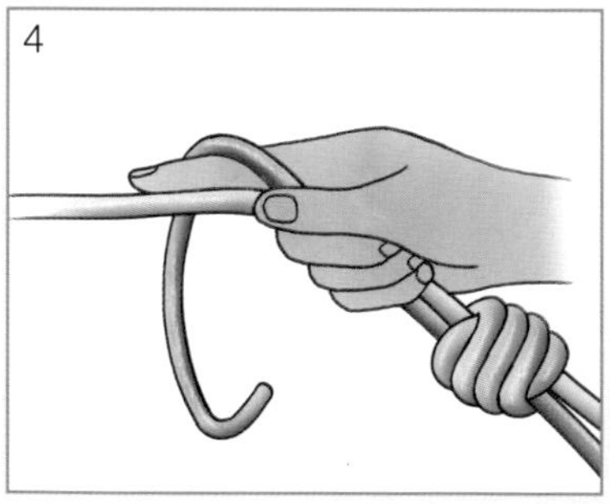

2 Wrap the other rope around your finger three times, working from the nail toward the palm. (Two wraps give the double version of this knot.)

3 Extract your finger from the coils and pass the end of the rope through the tunnel left by your finger.

4 Either change hands or turn the handful of ropes around and again extend the forefinger. Make three coils with the other rope and once more pass the end through the tunnel. Tighten these knots and then slide them along the ropes until they butt together.

To untie any of these knots, just pull the blood knots apart and then undo each one by easing the coils apart and removing the end.

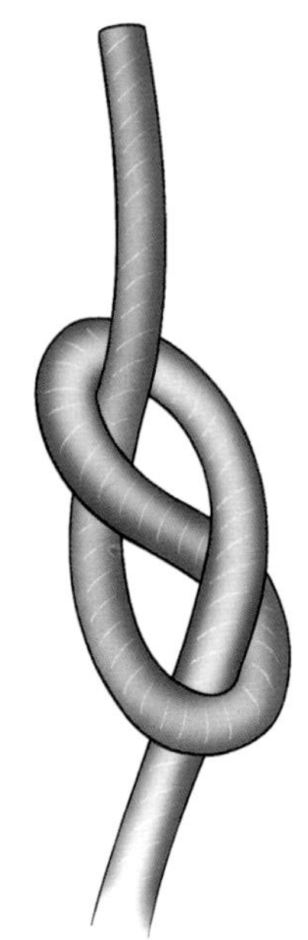

Figure Eight

In its simplest form, the figure eight is used as a stopper knot. Quick and easy to tie, it has more bulk than a simple thumb knot, which makes it more effective as a stopper and it is easier to untie, even after a load has been put on it.

1 Form a loop near the end of the rope. If your working end has passed over the cord, then lead it around under the standing part and back over itself and into the loop.

2 If the working end went under to form the crossing, the instructions are reversed.

1

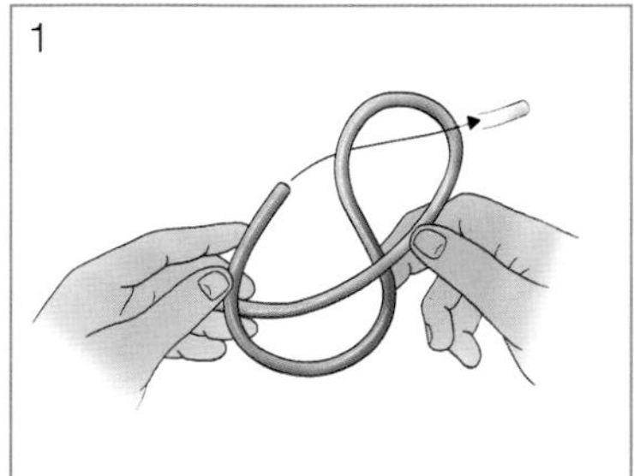

2

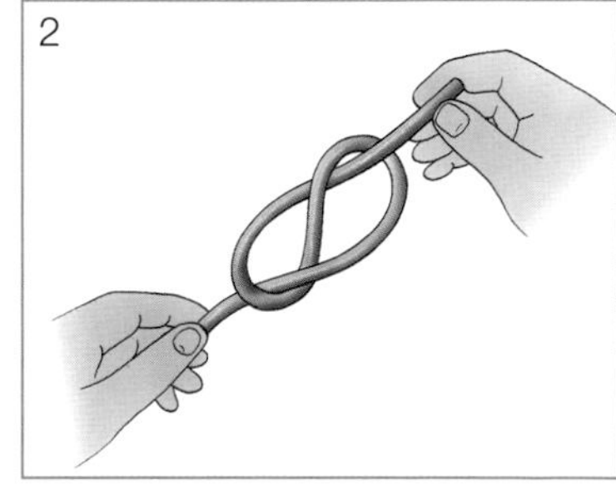

Figure Eight Loop

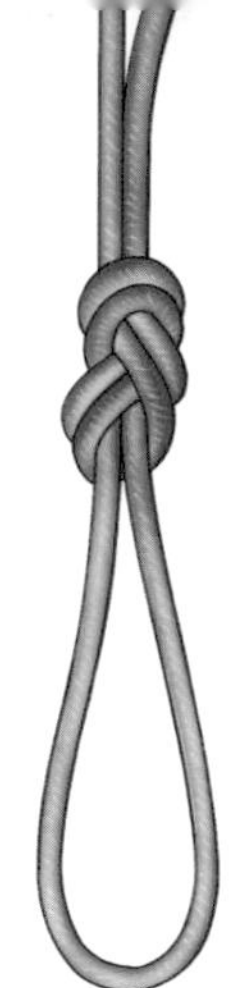

Also known as the Flemish loop, this loop is quite useful and has been widely adopted by climbers for the loop on the end of a rope. Because it is easy to tie and distinctively shaped, it is an obvious choice for those who need a reliable knot quickly. An added incentive is that, even when incorrectly tied, as an overhand knot it will still work to some degree, though it is not as effective and practice is advised so that it is tied properly at all times.

1 & 2 Make a long bight at the end of the rope and then tie a figure eight with the bight. Work the knot so that the strands lie flat and tidy.

3 The tail of the knot may be tied in a thumb knot around the standing part for added safety.

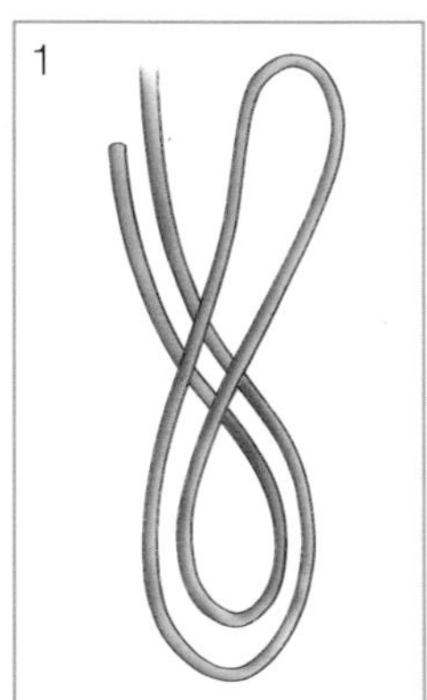

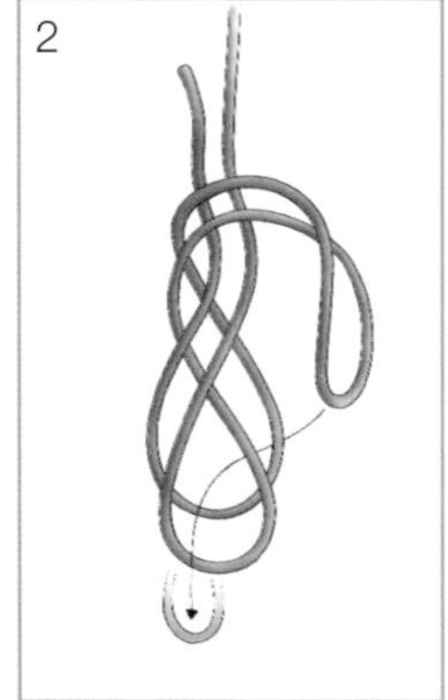

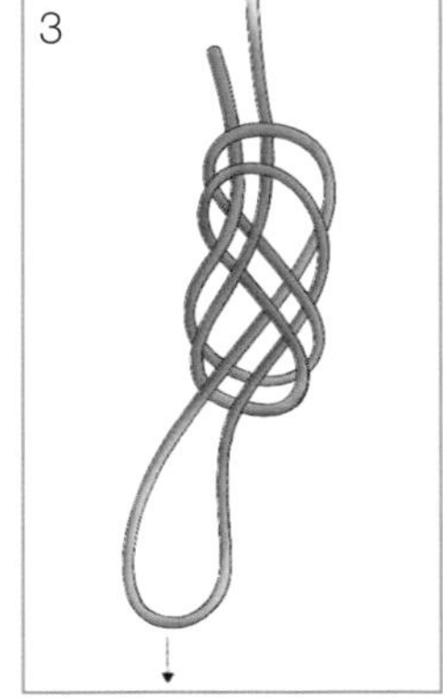

Figure Eight Loop: Threaded

If you want to tie a figure eight loop through a ring or something similar, then this is the technique to adopt. You will get the loop formed exactly where you need it.

1 Make a figure eight knot but allow a long working part. Do not pull the knot taut; leave it a little loose. Pass the working end through the ring and bring it back to the knot. Now simply thread the working end all through the knot, keeping parallel to the first strands. When the end emerges from the knot you can start to work everything up tight. Again, a thumb knot around the standing part is a good idea.

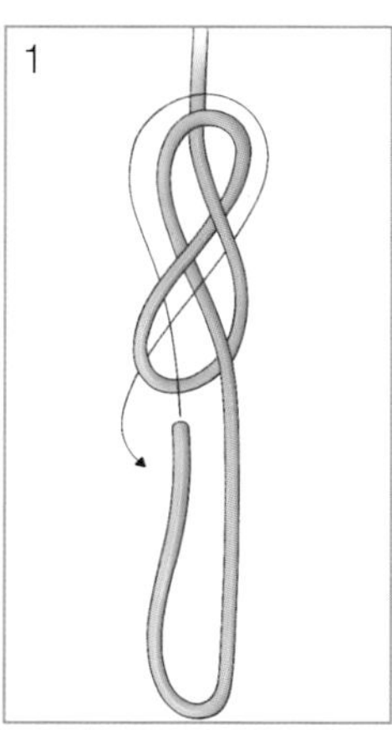

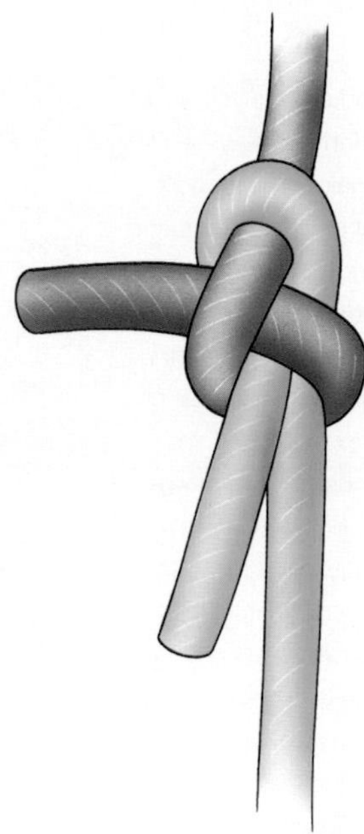

Sheet Bend

Because this knot is found in so many places and used for so many crafts, it has several names and is also known as a weavers' knot, a netting knot, and, when tied into a loop or bucket handle, is called a becket hitch. A piece of netting made using this knot has been dated to about 9,000 years ago, making this the oldest identified knot.

Tradition says that the sheet bend is only intended to join ropes of different thickness, but it works equally well when the cords are the same thickness. However, if there is any difference in the dimensions, the thicker cord must be used to make the initial bight.

1 Make a bight with the thicker cord. Lead the end of the other cord up into the bight.

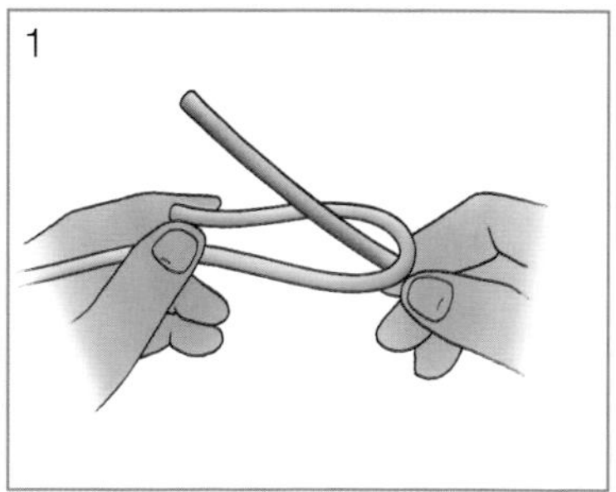

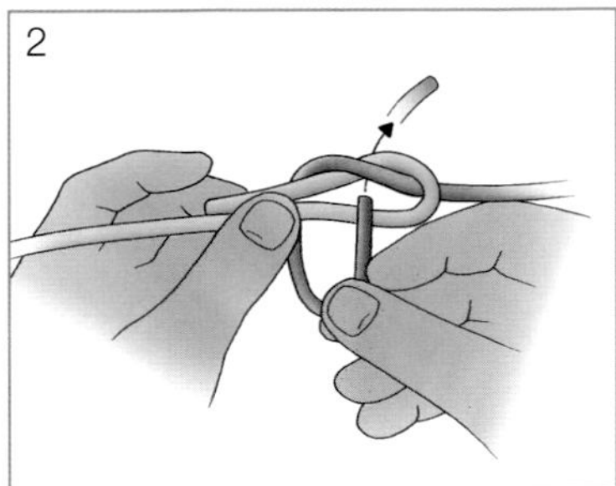

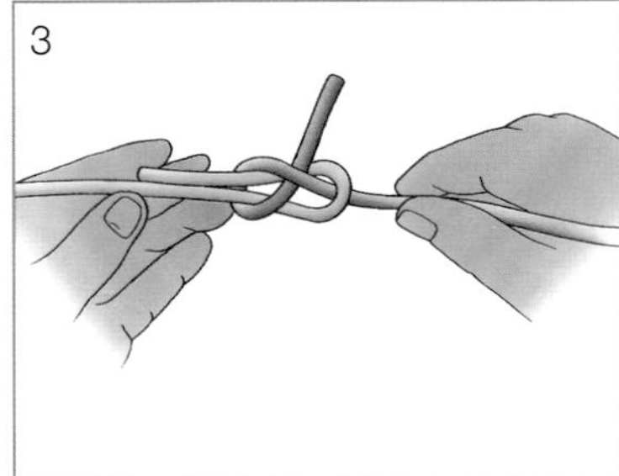

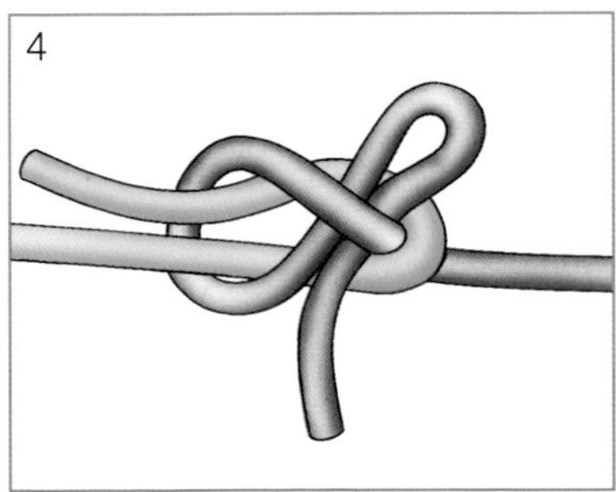

2 Take it around and down behind both parts of the bight. When it comes up again, pass it under itself and out on top of the bight.

3 Hold both sides of the bight and the working end together before you pull on the standing part of the other cord to tighten. The two loose ends should emerge on the same side of the knot to ensure security.

4 As a variation, if you pass a bight through in the last move you will get a knot that is easy to untie just by pulling on the loose end. This is known as a slipped sheet bend.

Double Sheet Bend

If the cords are slippery or there is a noticeable difference in size, then, for safety, a double sheet bend is recommended—the extra turn makes a big difference in terms of security. Always use the thinner cord to make the knot.

1 After passing the working end once around the bight, simply pass it a second time before bringing the end out as before.

2 Pulling the knot into shape must be carried out carefully to ensure that everything locks into place.

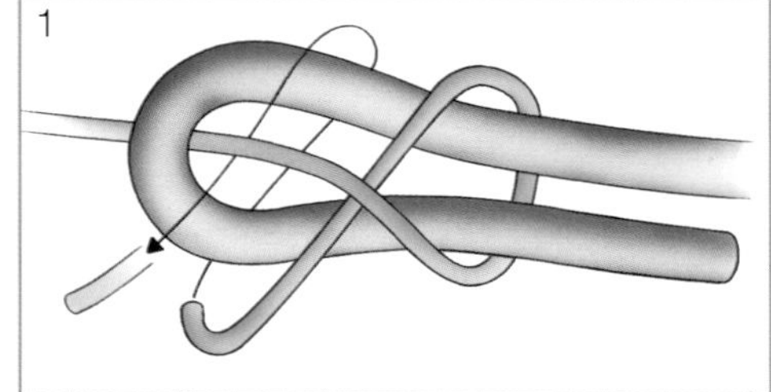

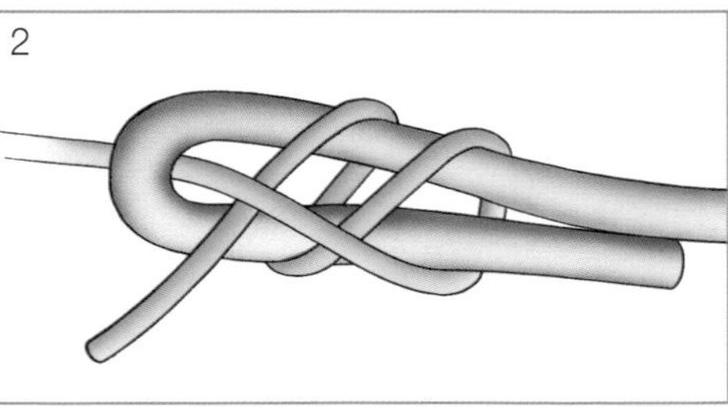

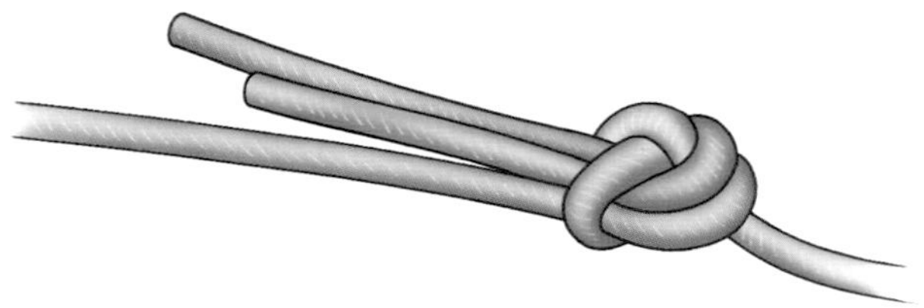

One-Way Sheet Bend

When a light line is used to pull a heavier one into place, perhaps up a cliff, through an obstacle filled with water, or along a pipe or tube, the protruding end of the light line could catch in an obstruction and cause the system to jam. The problem can be overcome by using this knot.

1 Lead the working end of the light line around itself and back through its own loop so it emerges facing the same way as the two ends of the thicker line.

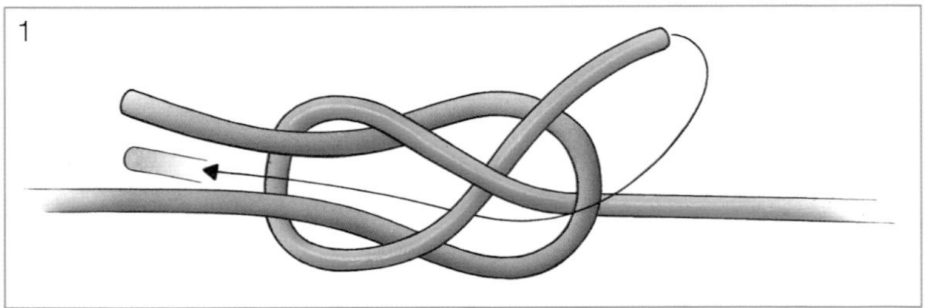

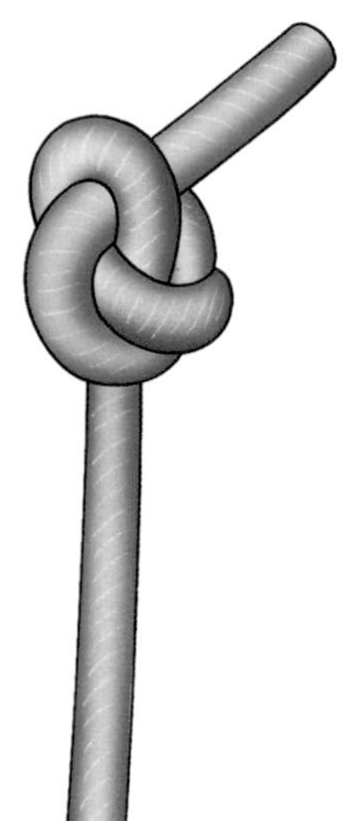

Ashley's Stopper Knot

This effective stopper knot was devised by Clifford Ashley, who tried to duplicate something he had seen and mistakenly came up with this knot instead.

1 Make a bight and tie a thumb knot around the standing part, as if making a simple noose.

2 & 3 Take the working end back into the loop of the noose and pull tight.

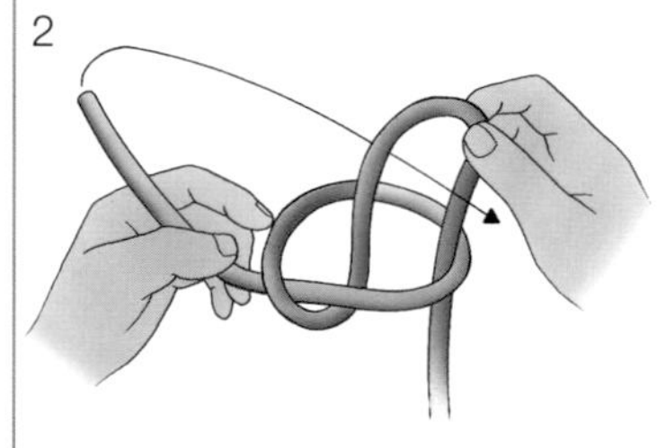

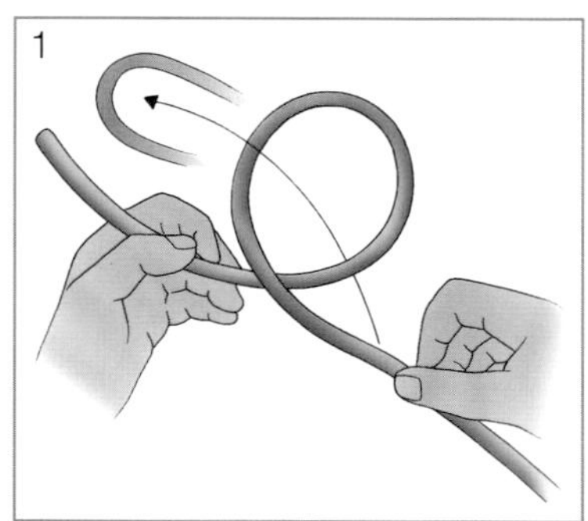

Round Turn & Two Half Hitches

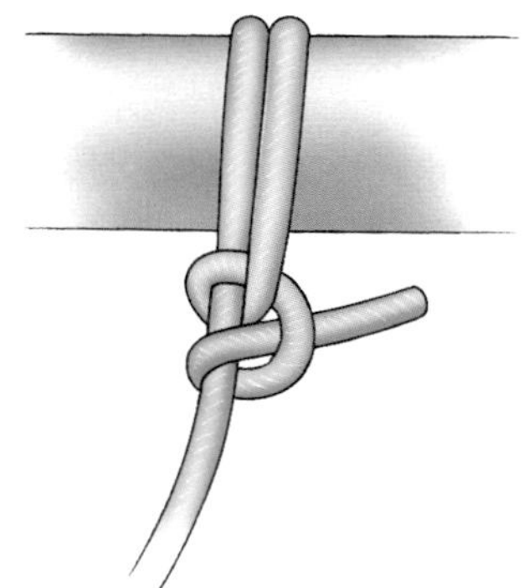

As discussed in the Terms and Techniques section at the front of the book, this is a good knot to moor a boat, but it has so many applications that it should be in everyone's inventory.

1 Pass the end of the rope over the pole (or through the ring) and then do it again to make a round turn. Lead the working end in front of the standing part, take it around the back, and return to the front through the space between rope and pole. This has created your first half hitch.

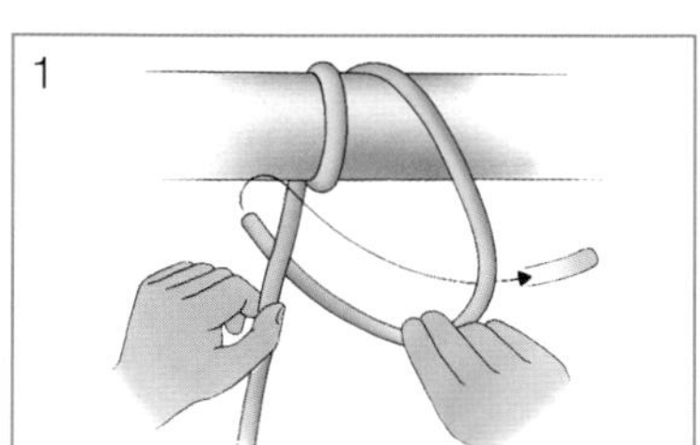

2 & 3 Copy this action around the standing part but below the first half hitch and pull taut to create a strong and reliable knot.

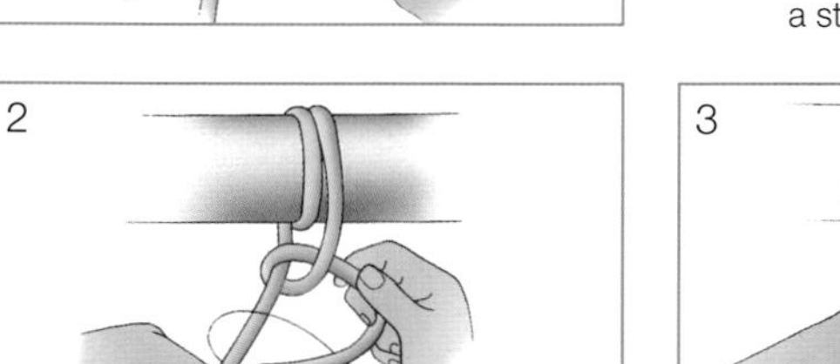

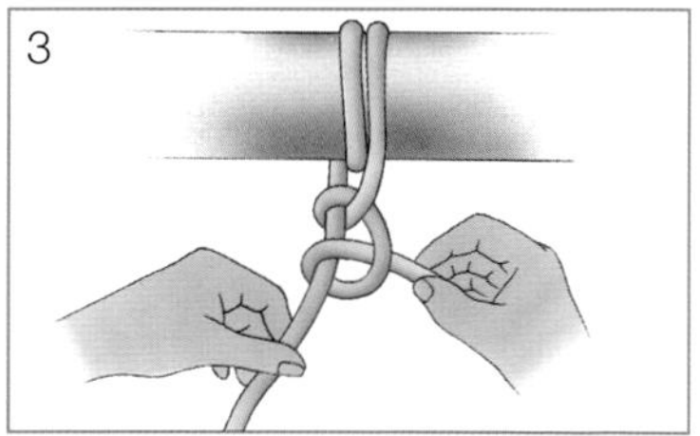

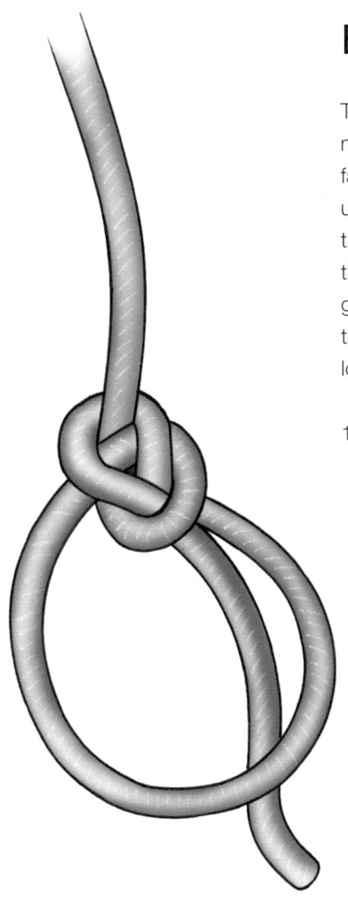

Bowline (1)

This knot, described as "the king of knots," has so many uses that it is impossible to try to list them. In fact, its only disadvantage is that it can be difficult to untie when the rope is under strain. With practice, the two hands act as a team and the knot can be tied on a climbing rope in under three seconds. It is a good idea to leave a long tail, which should be used to tie a thumb knot around the right-hand arm of the loop for extra security.

1 This is where the twist of the wrist mentioned in the Techniques section can be used. Take the rope and make a crossing turn to produce a loop.

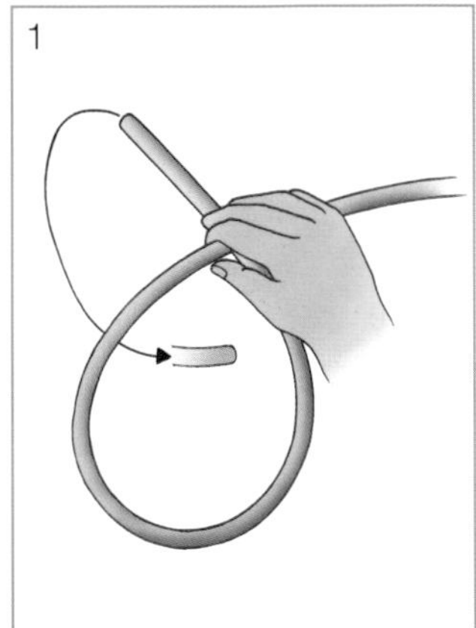

2 With your strong hand, hold the point where the working end crosses over the rope and twist your hand forward and down, and then turn your wrist away from your body.

3 The working end should now be poking up through a loop in the rope with a larger loop hanging below it. The illustration shows this using the right hand.

4 The other hand should be waiting behind the rope, ready to grasp the working end, pull it up around the back of the rope, and pass it down the small hole it has just left. It will be going down alongside itself. Hold the working part and the sides of the loop and pull on the standing end to tighten the knot. Depending on the purpose for which you have tied it, the dimensions may require adjustment before tightening.

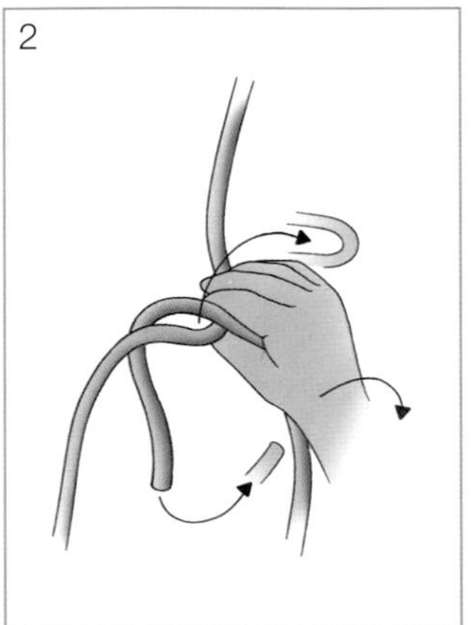

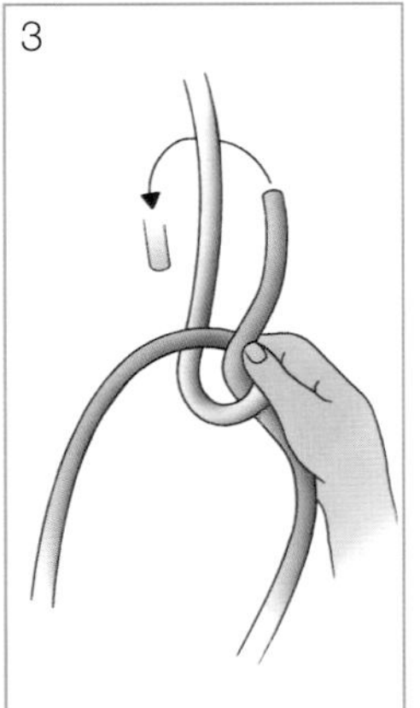

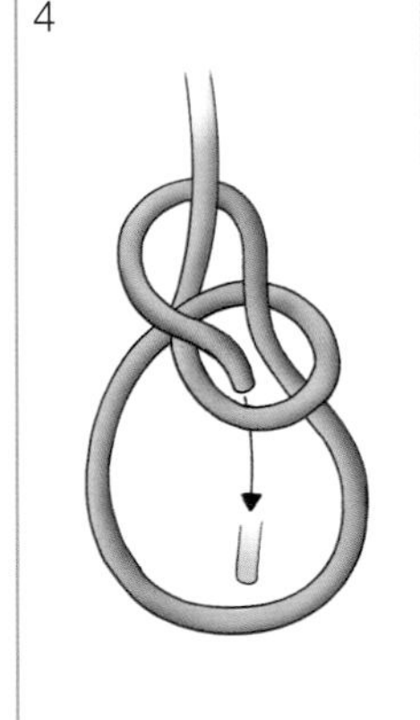

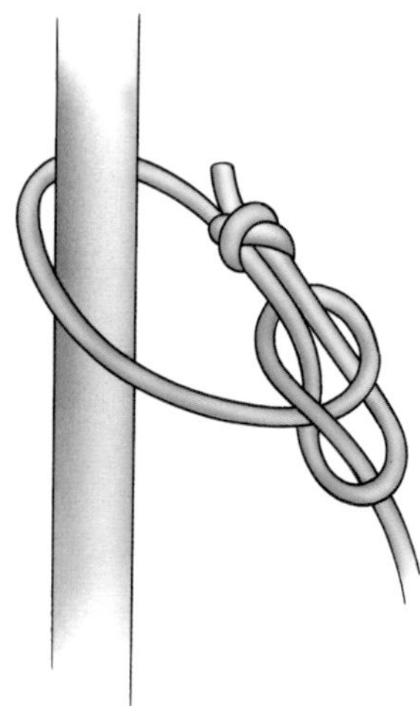

Bowline (2)

When you are facing the opposite way from that which you normally face to tie a knot, everything seems impossible and hands will not function as you desire. This method of tying the bowline shows how to approach it from the other direction and uses a method adopted by climbers to tie a bowline around their waists, but which allows the knot to be adjusted to fit. Again, a thumb knot around the right-hand side of the loop will give added security.

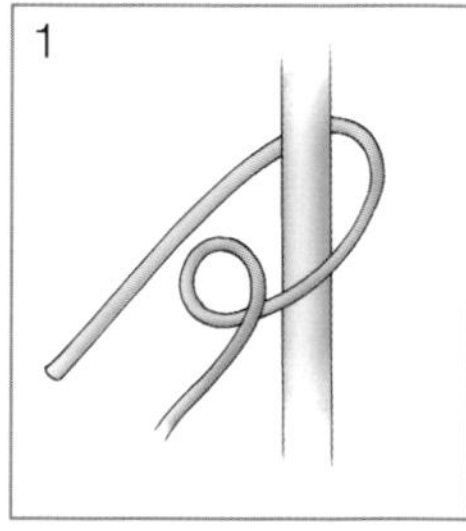

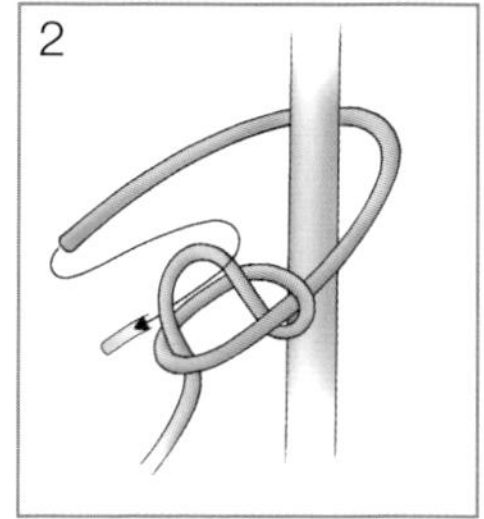

1 Pass sufficient rope around the post or through the ring. It could be passed on the other side of the post in the illustration; the direction has no significance. In the standing part of the rope, make a crossing turn. To get the correct turn it is easiest to hold the standing part in the left hand, back of the hand facing up and thumb toward the body. Turn the wrist away so the back of the hand is facing down.

2 Make a bight in the standing part and pass it up into the loop you have just formed.

3 Take the working end, feed it through the projecting bight, and hold on to it.

4 Pull the standing end and the knot should spill, leaving you with a perfect bowline. The pull on the standing end is usually more effective if it is a sharp jerk, rather than a steady pull. Sometimes things do not always go smoothly at this stage and then it helps to slide your hand over the knot to encourage it into the correct form.

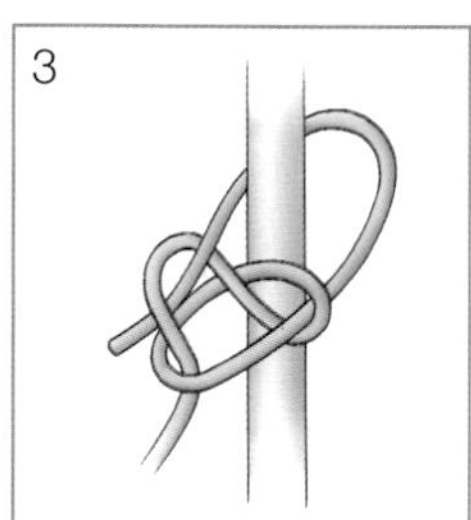

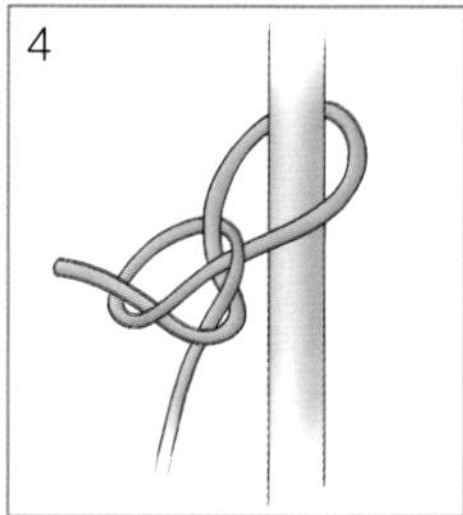

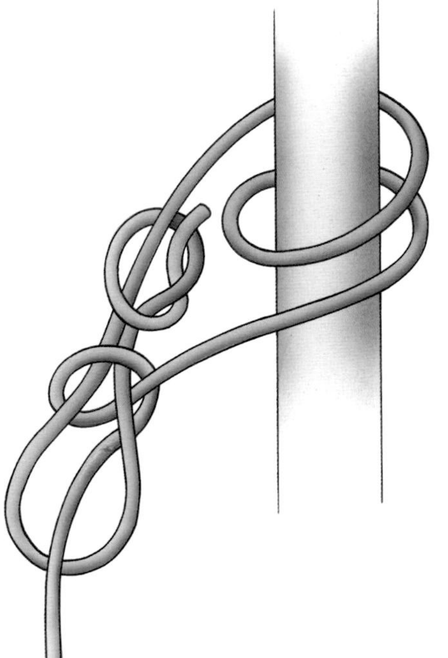

If there is time, you may want to pass the line twice around the post, forming a round turn before tying the knot. This can ease the strain on the rope as the extra area in contact with the post helps to spread the load. This will be called a bowline with a round turn. Tying the bowline around its own standing part, or feeding all the standing part through the loop, will give a running bowline, which is another form of noose.

Clove Hitch (1) on a Bar or Ring

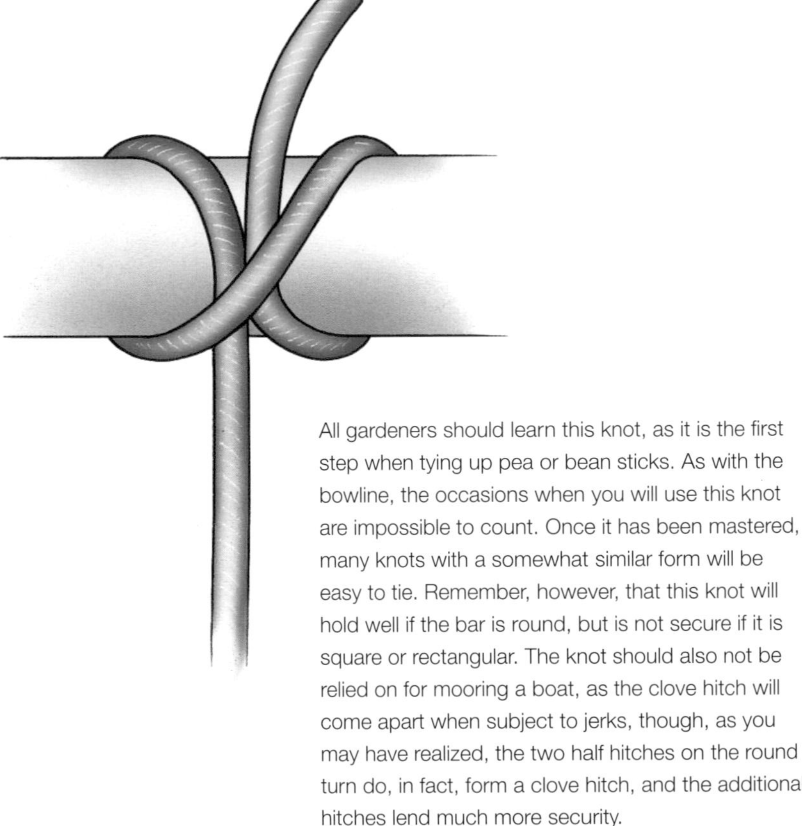

All gardeners should learn this knot, as it is the first step when tying up pea or bean sticks. As with the bowline, the occasions when you will use this knot are impossible to count. Once it has been mastered, many knots with a somewhat similar form will be easy to tie. Remember, however, that this knot will hold well if the bar is round, but is not secure if it is square or rectangular. The knot should also not be relied on for mooring a boat, as the clove hitch will come apart when subject to jerks, though, as you may have realized, the two half hitches on the round turn do, in fact, form a clove hitch, and the additional hitches lend much more security.

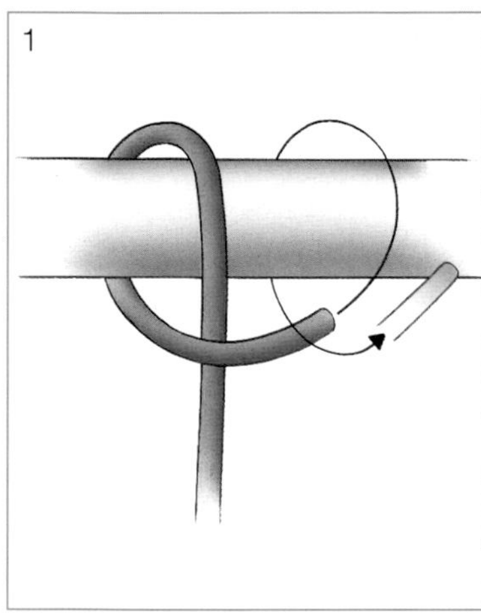

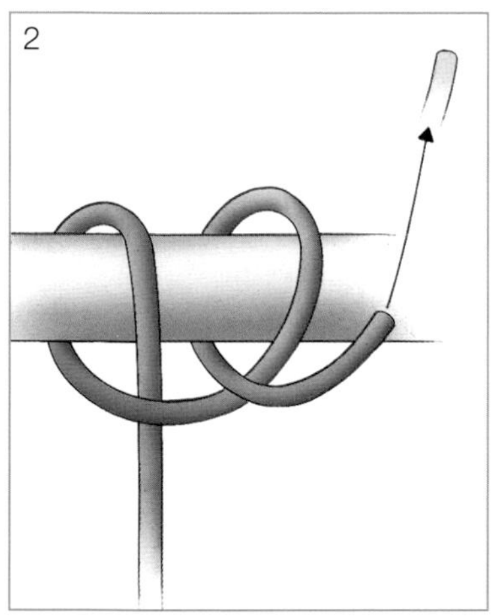

1 Pass the end of the rope over the bar or through the ring so that the short end hangs down at the back. Reach under the bar and bring the end forward at the side of the standing part. Lead it diagonally across the front of the standing part and pass it over the bar again, leaving a small loop hanging down.

2 The end is brought forward and up through this loop. Pull the rope on both sides of the knot to tighten it.

If you find it easier to tie when going the other way from that shown in the pictures, then do so (going from right to left rather than left to right). The knot will hold just as well.

Clove Hitch (2) over a Pin or Bollard

There may be times when the pin to which you are tying juts out, allowing access to its end. In this case you can quickly tie a clove hitch and drop it over the end by using this method.

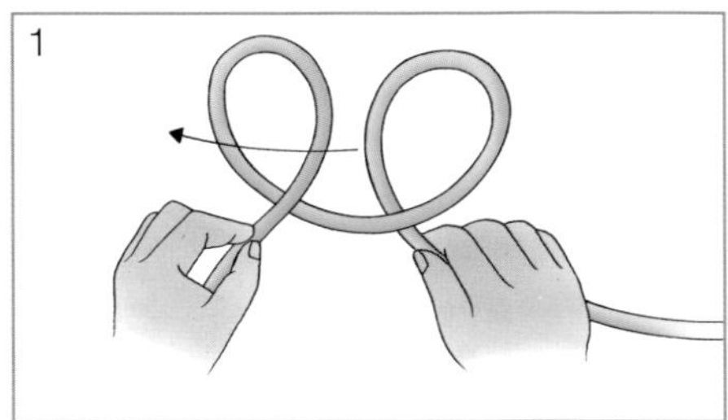

1 Form two loops side by side in the rope. They must both be of the same sort. Shown are two overhand crossing loops.

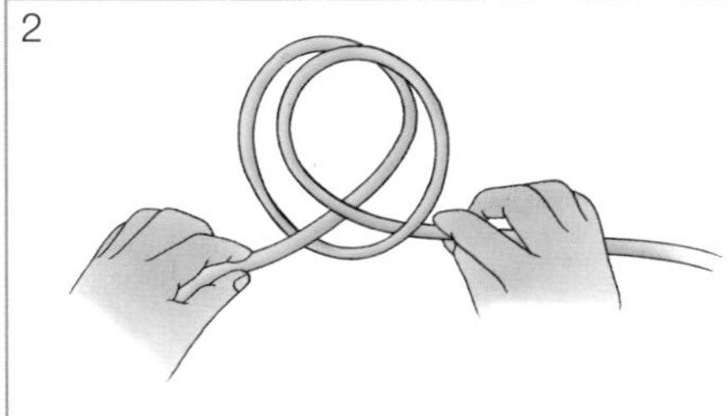

2 Slide the loops toward one another so that one sits on top of the other and the two ends come out between the loops.

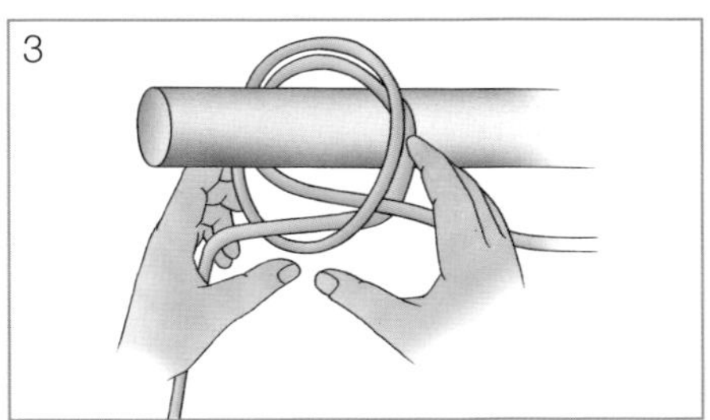

3 The two loops are then slipped over the end of the pin and pulled taut.

If you get the direction of either of the loops wrong, or do not get the ends to come out in the middle, the knot will fall apart and must be started again—with a little more care.

Timber Hitch

This is one of the simplest of knots and was once commonly used to secure the bottom end of a longbow string to the bow. It is also good, as the name suggests, for hauling logs or poles when wooding.

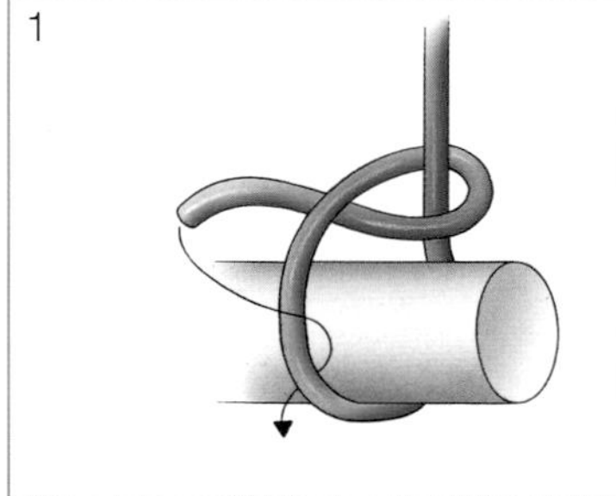

1 Pass the line around the log (or bundle of sticks). Take a turn around the standing part to make an underhand loop. The end crosses under the cord.

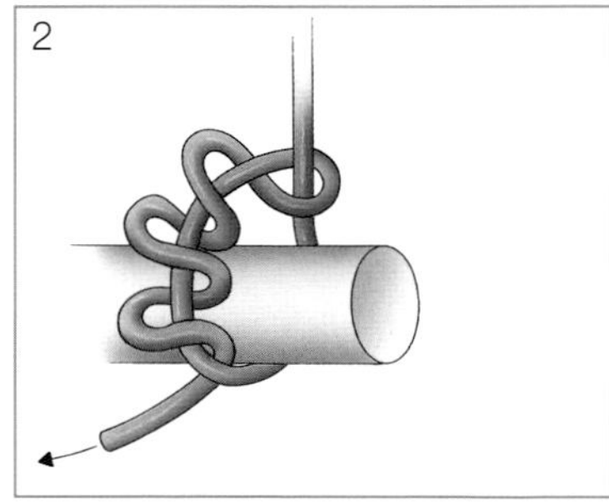

2 Now wrap several turns around the section of line leading away from the loop. Pull on the working end to remove slack. When a load is applied to the standing part it will tighten up and all the turns will lock into place.

Killick Hitch

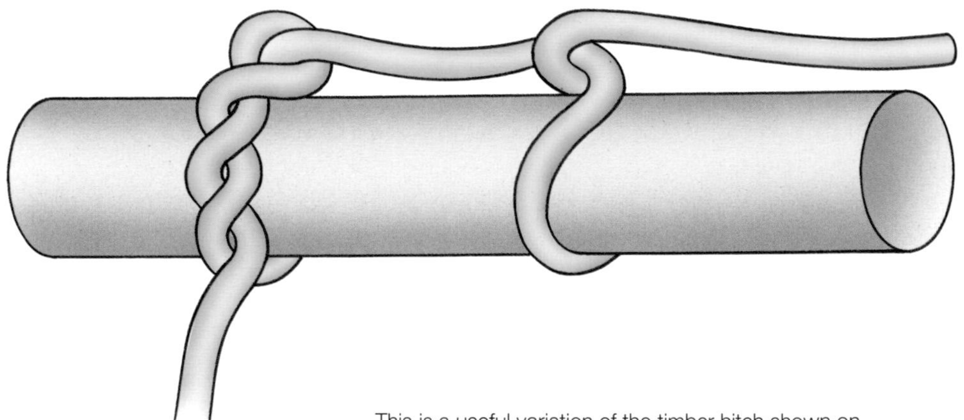

This is a useful variation of the timber hitch shown on the previous page. Sometimes the pole or bundle that you are dragging might be a little unwieldy. To overcome any tendency to go off course, the timber hitch is tied at the far end of the load and a half hitch is put on close to the near end. The load is applied at the near end and the additional guidance here means that the log will now behave perfectly.

The killick hitch can also be applied to a rock when used as an improvised anchor.

Honda Knot or Bowstring Knot

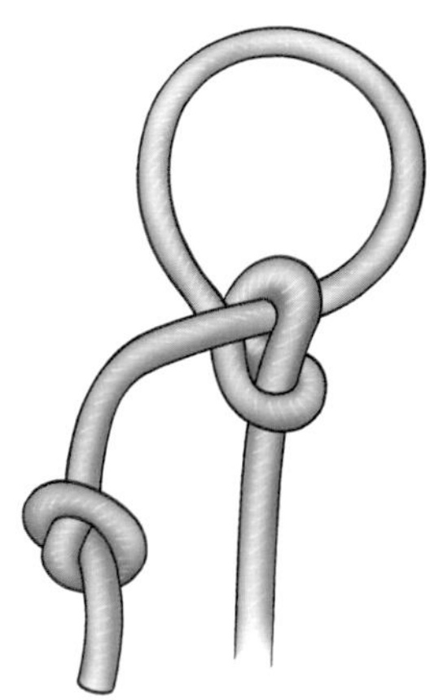

This knot was widely used at the end of the lariat to ensure that the noose slid easily when catching wild horses or cattle. It is used for the same reason when making primitive snares and traps.

It was also widely used as a bowstring knot (especially for the traditional English longbow), but in archery it was replaced many years ago by a formed eye in the bowstring. It can still be used if you need to improvise your own bow, or as a lariat.

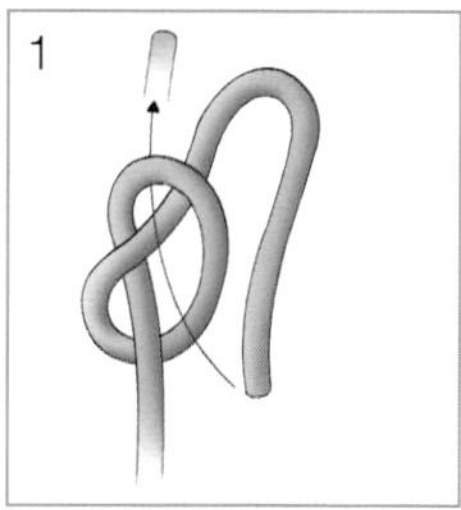

1 & 2 First tie a thumb knot. Do not pull tight, but feed the working end into the knot as shown. Tie a second thumb knot near the end of the working part and pull this one tight. It will act as a stopper to retain the end in place. Work the honda loop to give the size that is required and move the second thumb knot to jam everything tight.

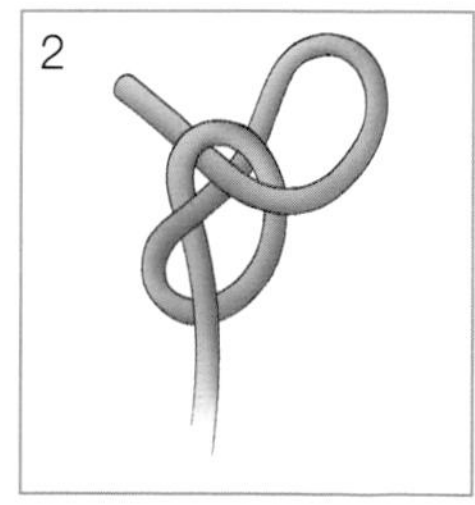

In order to make a lariat or snare, the rest of the cord must be fed through the honda loop. You will then know if the loop is too big or just right to slide. Remember that when in use the loop will come under tension, so adjust it accordingly.

Rolling Hitch

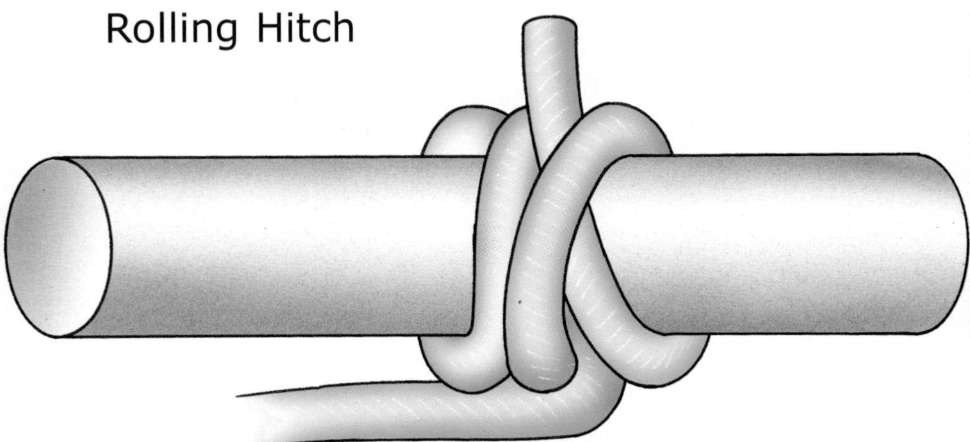

Occasions sometimes arise when a sideways pull has to be applied to a spar or rope, and for this task the rolling hitch is the first choice, though not the only one. This knot is designed to pull without slipping in one direction only, with the working part pulling hard down against the two turns, locking them in place.

This is another very old knot and a lot of debate has gone on among knot tiers about its origin. The name by which you are learning it may be the newest part of this knot.

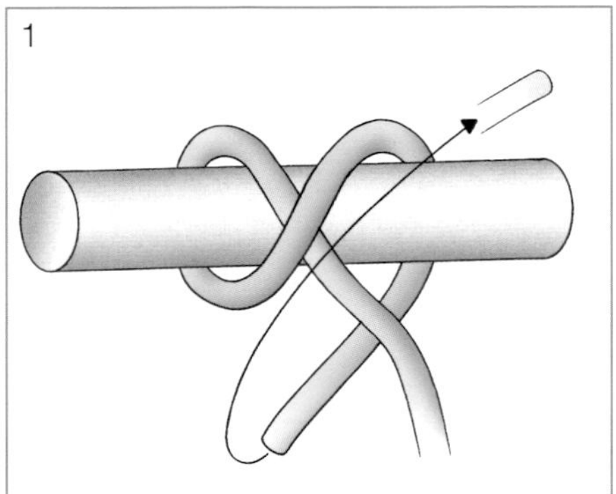

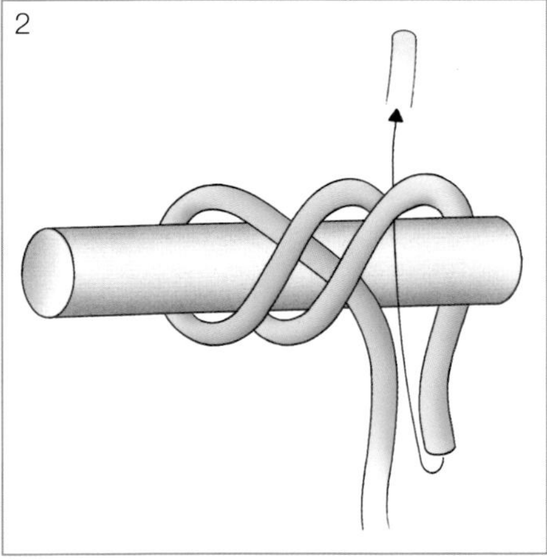

1 Start as for a clove hitch. Pass the end over the pole and bring it up alongside the standing part. Now pass it over again and once more bring it up alongside the standing part.

2 Pass the end a third time, but now bring it up on the other side of the standing part, as for a clove hitch, and take it under the last turn. Pull on the end to tighten the knot. The direction of pull must be against the two initial turns. Looking at the illustration, if you wanted to pull to the right, the knot would have to be retied with the first two turns on the other side.

Tundj

This is the Turkish way of fastening a bowstring, which differs substantially from that commonly used in the West, but it is interesting nonetheless. Applications for this knot are rare today, but it has been included in case you wish to experiment with it and to show how different cultures developed very different knots for the same needs.

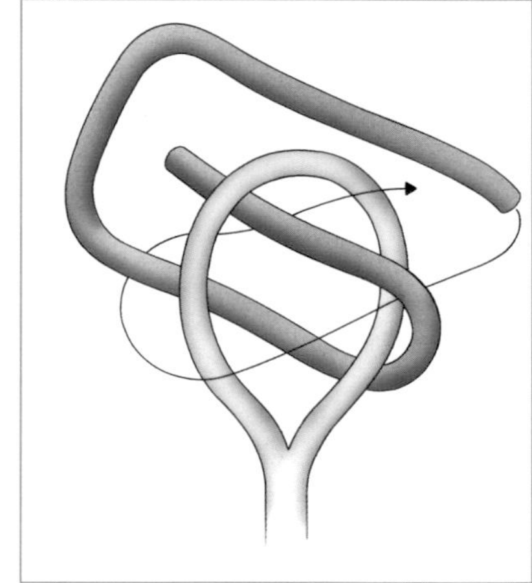

The secondary cord went through the eye of the bowstring and was tied as shown. Adjustments could be made to the tension by pulling or easing this cord. The secondary cord can be of thicker or stronger material than the bowstring, thus prolonging its useful life by reducing rubbing against the bow.

Clara

Another knot devised by Dr. Harry Asher, the Clara enables you to tie a thin line to a thicker line in order to pull on the thick line. You may have to do this more often than you would expect, so a working knowledge of the Clara will be beneficial.

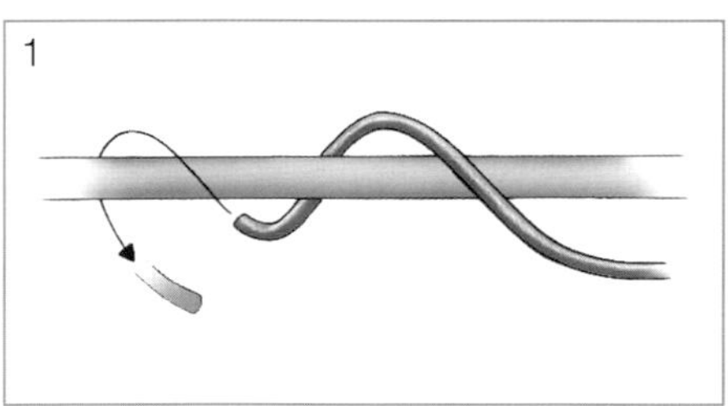

1 Make a full round turn along the length of the thicker rope. If it is a laid rope, follow the direction of the lay for the round turn. The load will come on the standing part, so make sure that you start your turn in the correct direction.

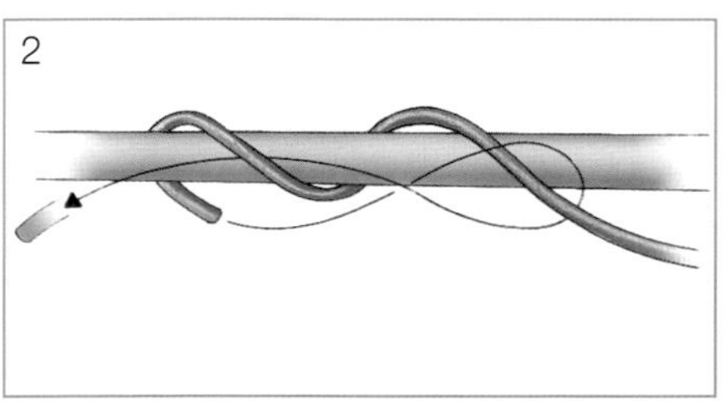

2 Bring the working end back toward the standing part and come over the standing part. Now reverse direction again, going under the standing part and finally, tuck the working end under the last crossing of the round turn.

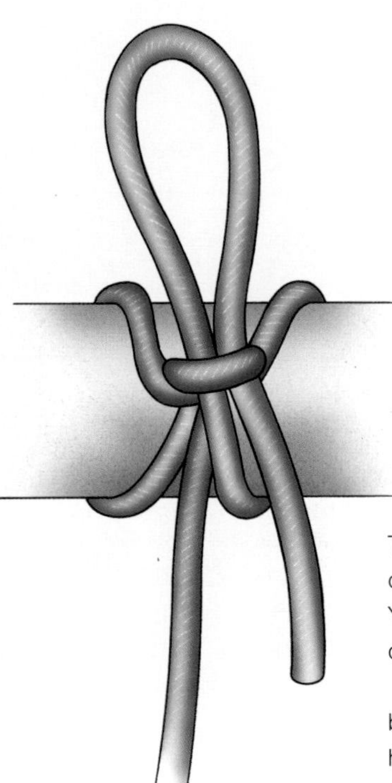

Highwayman's Hitch

The romantically named highwayman's hitch is a quick-release knot that has many applications. Young people love it because it can be made to disappear at the pull of a cord.

A deceptively complex arrangement of loops and bights, it derives its name from its supposed use by highwaymen who liked it because of the speed at which a horse could be untethered, making for a quick getaway when necessary. Today, it still works well for those who wish to tether a horse, as well as for mooring boats, though care should be taken that the load is taken on the correct end of the rope and that the hitch is tightly finished so that it will not accidentally untie itself.

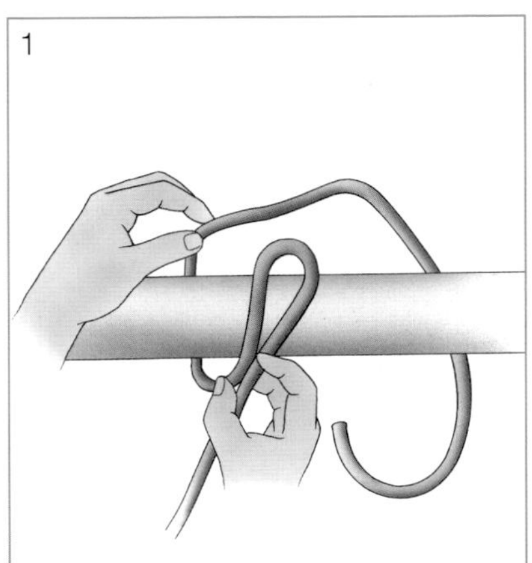

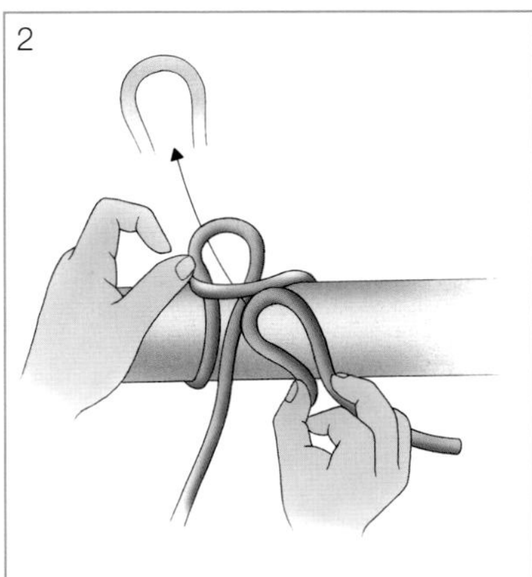

1 Make a bight in the rope some distance from the end. Pass the bight up behind the pole with the ends hanging down. Hold it in place. Make another bight in the side of the rope that will be under load (the horse). Usually, this will be the long end. Bring this bight up in front of the pole and feed it through the first bight. You can then let go of the first bight, as the second one will keep it from falling.

2 Now form a third bight in the short end hanging from the first bight. Bring this up and feed it through the second bight. Pull on the long end (horse) to lock the third bight. When the third bight is secure, the knot is complete.

To undo, give the short end a quick tug. It will come out of the second bight. The horse will pull, taking the second bight out of the first bight, which falls away from the pole. Only trial and error will show you how far along the rope you must make the first bight.

Constrictor Knot

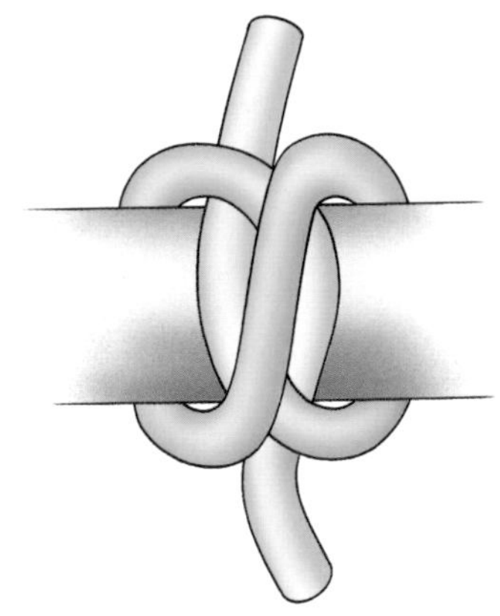

The constrictor knot holds firmly and will not normally slacken off. Indeed, if tied with soft cord around a hard object, it can grasp so firmly that it may have to be cut when the time comes to remove it. It is very handy in a number of everyday situations, such as tying up garbage bags.

There are several ways to tie the constrictor. Shown here are the two variations that I have found most useful.

1 With the first of these variations, start by tying a clove hitch. Pass the cord over the pole (or neck of the garbage bag), cross it over the front, over the pole again, and up under itself.

2 The end is now taken over and then under the first turn of the clove hitch before being tightened.

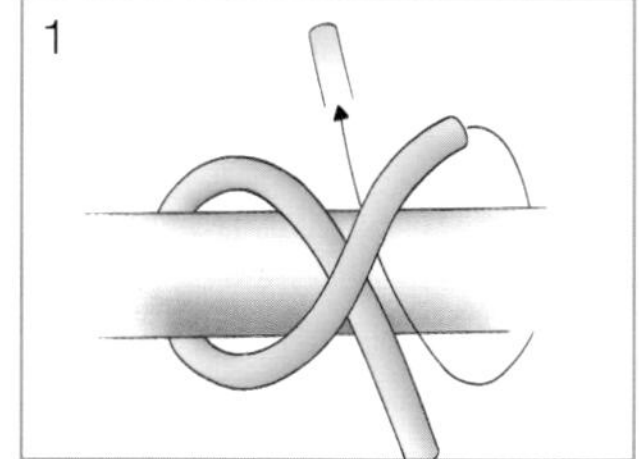

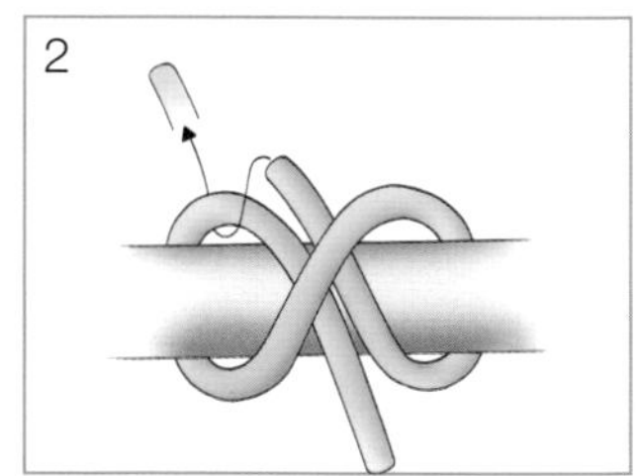

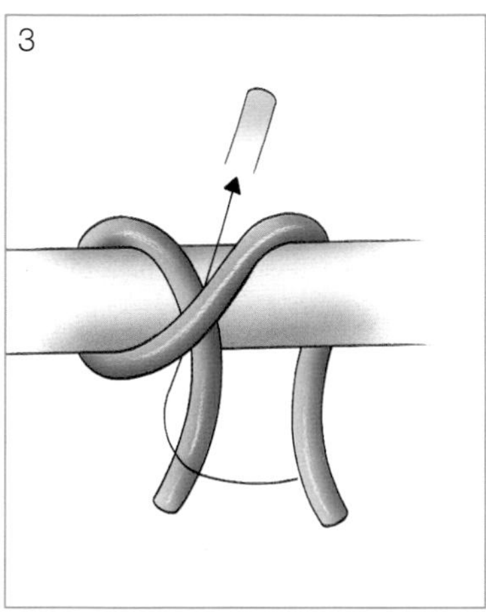

3 The other way to make this knot is to start by making the first half of a clove hitch. After passing the cord over the pole for the second time, lead it in front of the standing part and bring it up under the crossing. When this is pulled tight, it will form a constrictor knot.

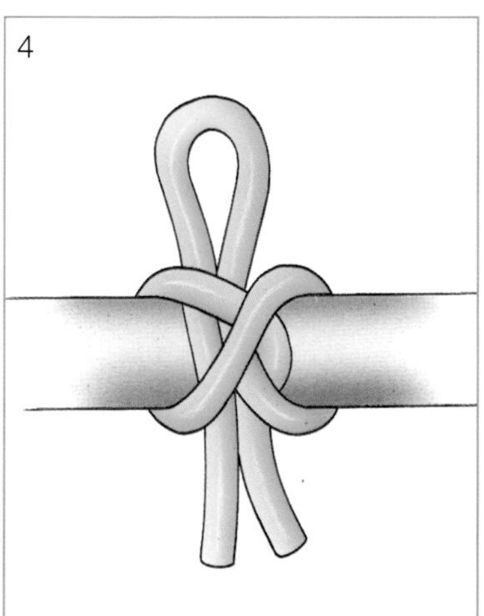

4 The last variation on this knot enables it to be undone much more easily. If you pass a bight when making the last tuck, you make a slipped constrictor knot, which will hold securely but is simply removed by tugging out the bight.

Boa

This is a development of the constrictor knot that holds even more securely and is very useful when a tight temporary whipping is needed on the end of a rope.

The method shown to tie this knot can also be applied to a single loop to tie the constrictor.

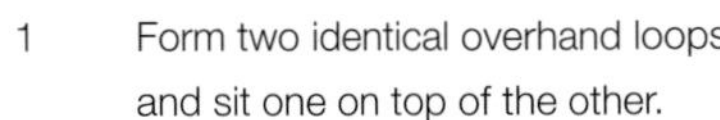

1 Form two identical overhand loops and sit one on top of the other.

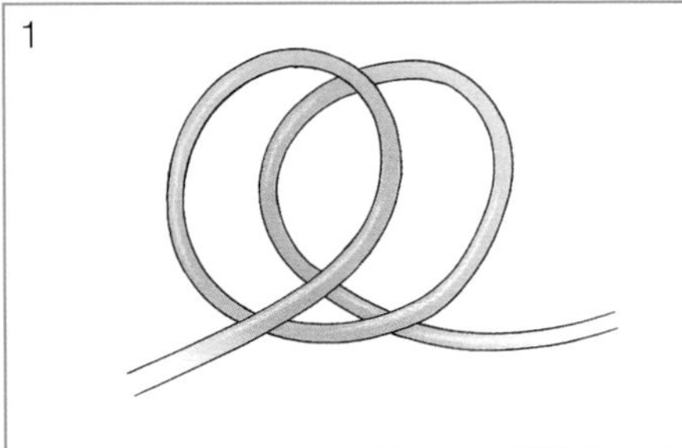

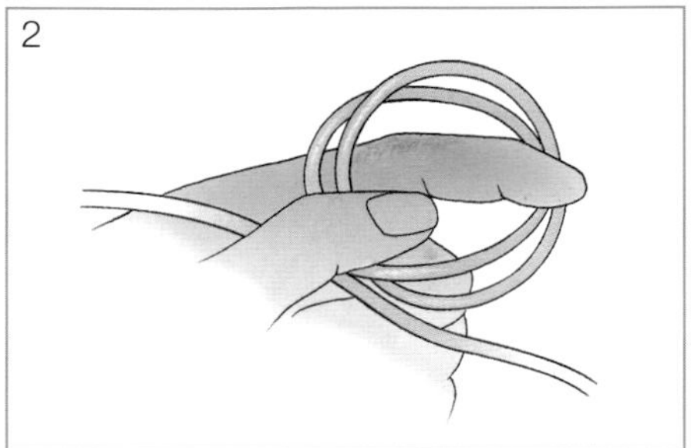

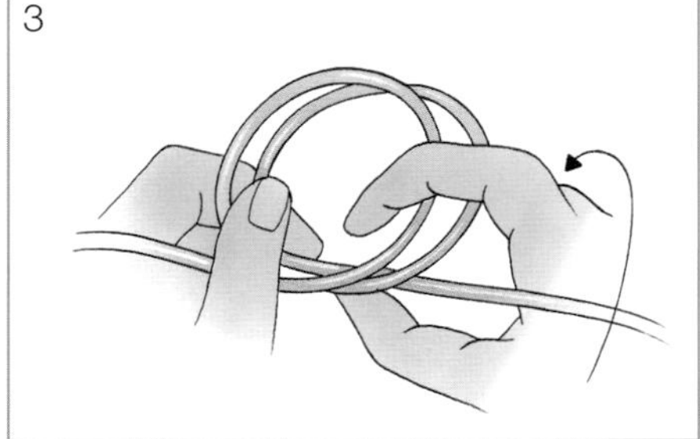

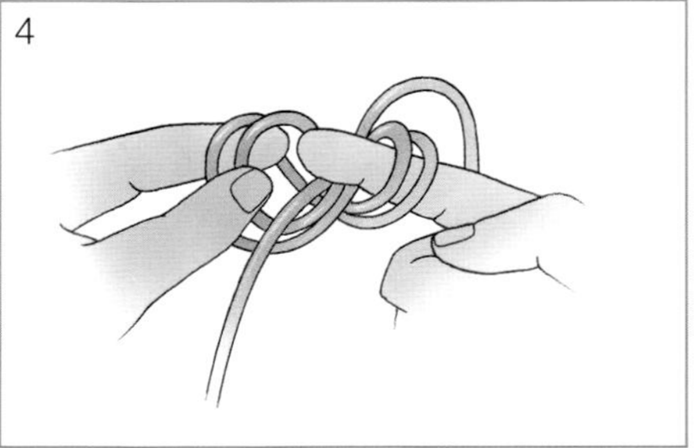

2 & 3 Push your left forefinger up through the loop and your right forefinger down through the loop.

4 Twist the right wrist away to bring both fingers facing up, as in picture 4. Then remove the left forefinger and slide the right forefinger into the space this creates. The complete knot may then be slipped over the end of the item to which the tie is being applied and pulled tight.

Marlinespike Hitch

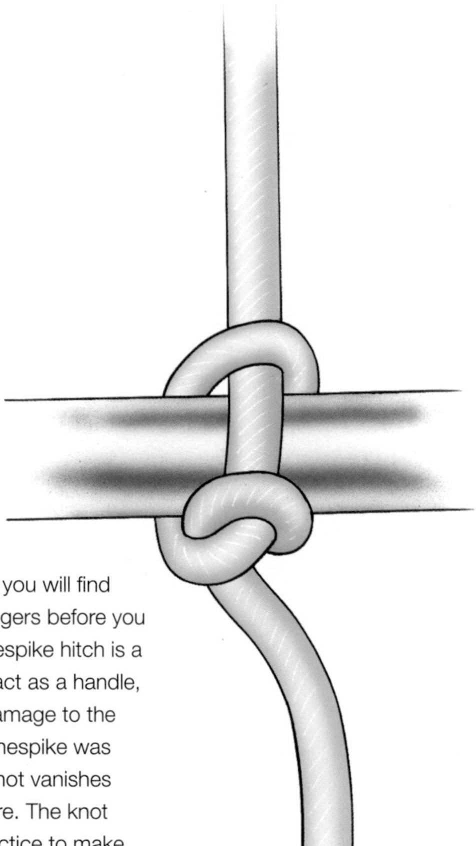

When you have to pull on a length of line you will find that thin cord can cut the skin on your fingers before you have achieved much tension. The marlinespike hitch is a means of fitting an object to the rope to act as a handle, allowing you to heave strongly without damage to the fingers. On removal of the object (a marlinespike was commonly used, hence the name), the knot vanishes and may be reapplied wherever you desire. The knot can only be used in one direction, so practice to make sure that you can tie it the right way the first time.

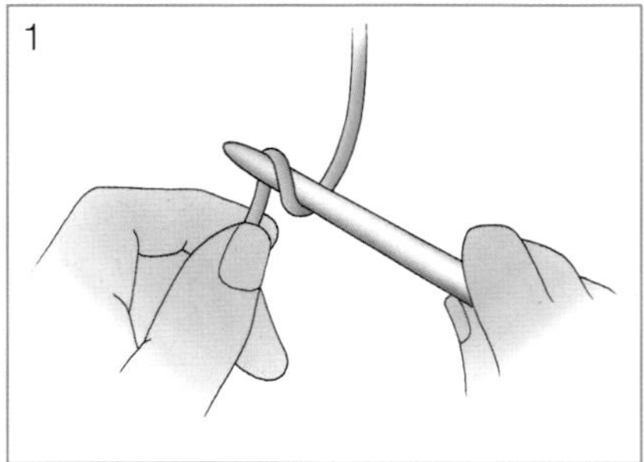

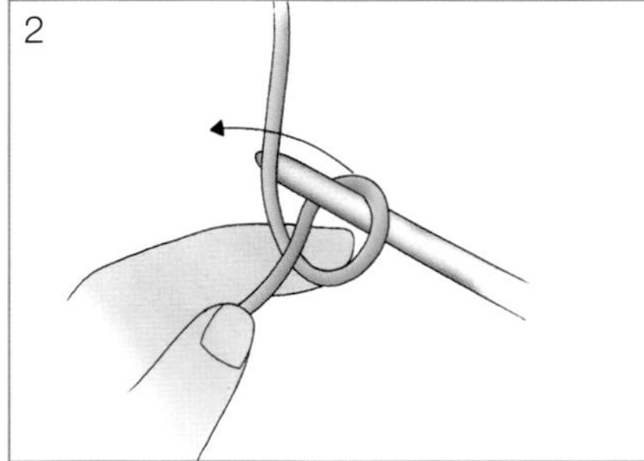

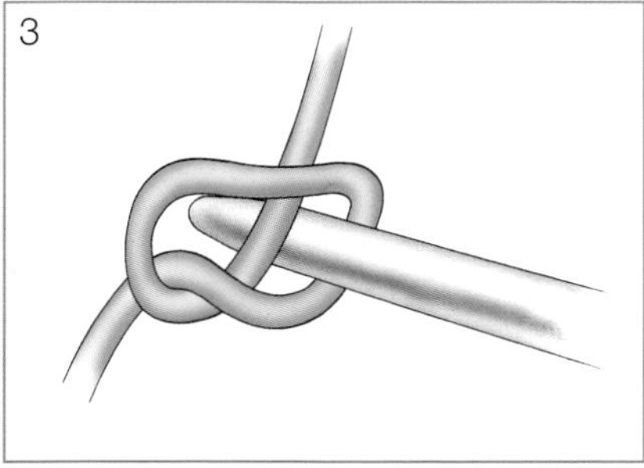

1 Take your marlinespike (or stick, screwdriver, or whatever you are using as a handle) and place it across the rope. Using the same sort of twist as for the bowline, rotate your wrist. This should give you the position shown in the illustration.

2 & 3 Gently remove the spike and turn the loop to rest on top of the cord that you intend to pull.

Ease the knot tight and you have a firm grip with which to apply tension to the cord. Don't forget that you are only able to pull in one direction—downward—in these illustrations. With only a little practice, this knot takes about three seconds to apply and can be very useful.

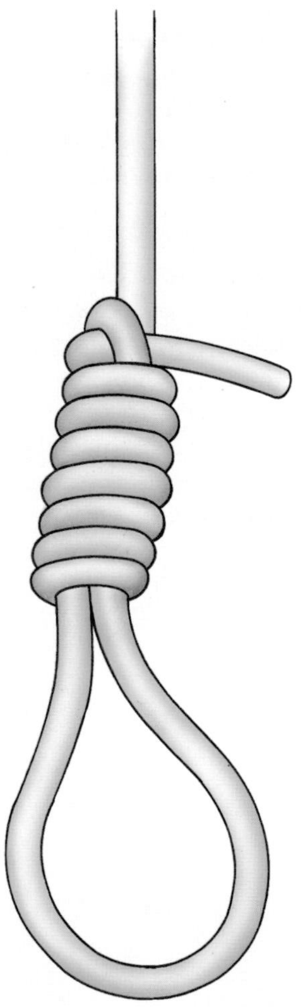

Hangman's Knot

There is usually some dispute about the inclusion of this knot in books of instruction, as the fear exists that the knot might be misused. As any ten-year-old with the time and inclination can work out how to tie it, I do not believe that leaving it out would deter anyone who has unsociable tendencies. Although it has a rather grim history, it is a useful noose with many variations, and the principles involved in its construction are applied in many other knots, especially in the fishing section. Practice with larger cord will help you to understand the moves with fishing line.

1 Some distance from the end of the rope, make a bight. With the working part, make a second bight, leaving a long working end.

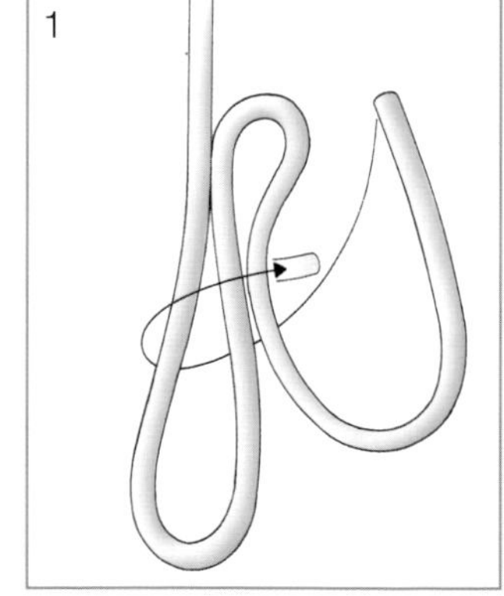

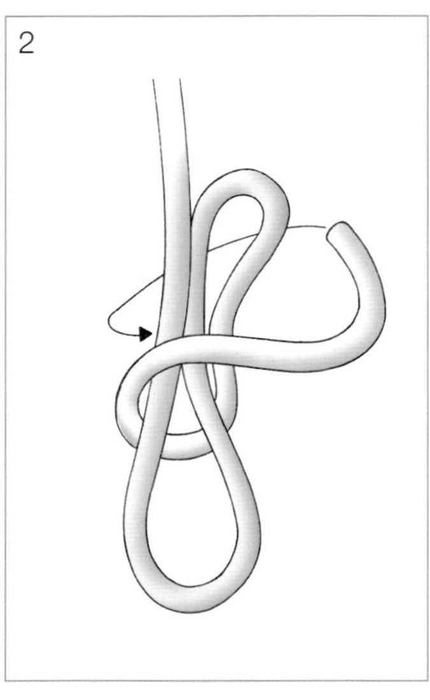

2 Wrap the working part around the three sections of rope, moving away from the loop of the first bight.

3 Continue to wrap the working part until you get near its end.

4 Pass the end through the eye of the second bight that is protruding from the coils. By pulling gently on one of the two cords emerging from the other end, the eye can be closed, trapping the working end and securing the knot. The size of the noose may now be adjusted.

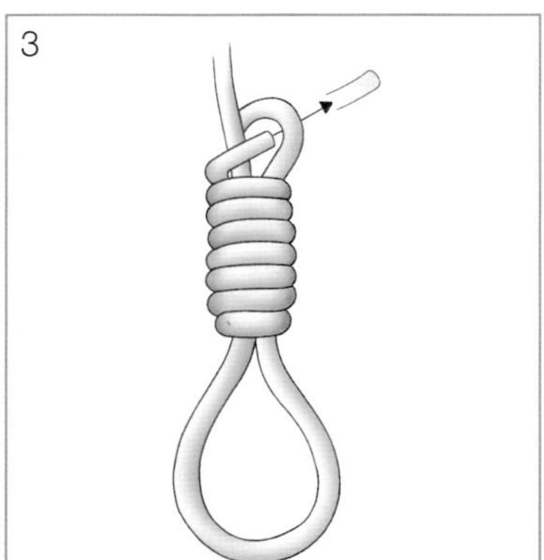

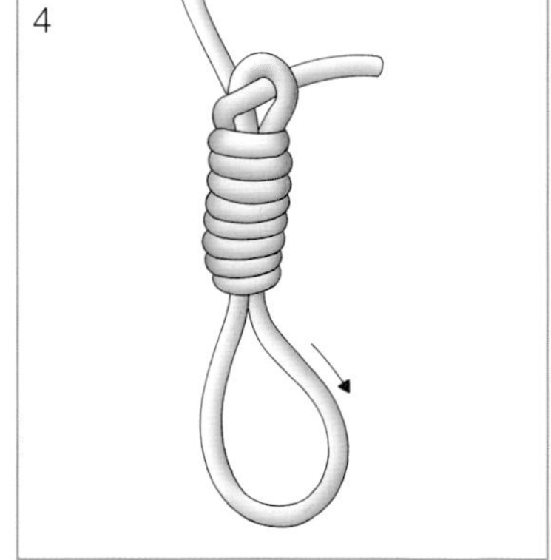

Hangman's Knot: A Fishing Application

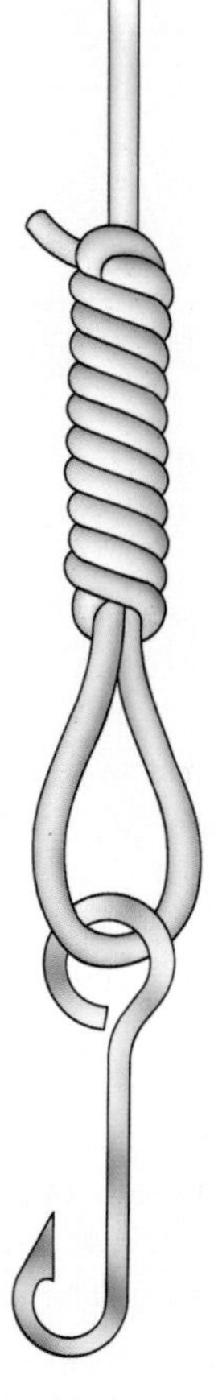

To help clear the reputation of the hangman's knot, a demonstration of its usefulness has been included here—securing a hook to a fishing line couldn't be less grisly. Other uses might include making a simple swing for a child (just insert a rounded piece of wood instead of a hook and tie the other end to a sturdy branch) or securing an anchor to a line.

To use the knot in this way, simply pass the end of the line through the eye of a fishhook before forming the two bights and applying the wrapping. This will need to be snuggled down securely before attempting to catch fish.

It is worth noting that if the end of the cord is passed through the first bight before starting to wrap the coils, it will lock off the noose, thus stopping it from being pulled out. When the knot is pulled taut with the noose closed and locked, it makes a very effective heaving line knot.

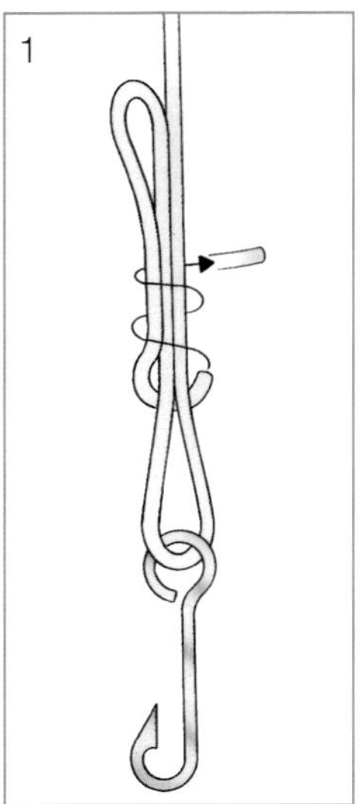

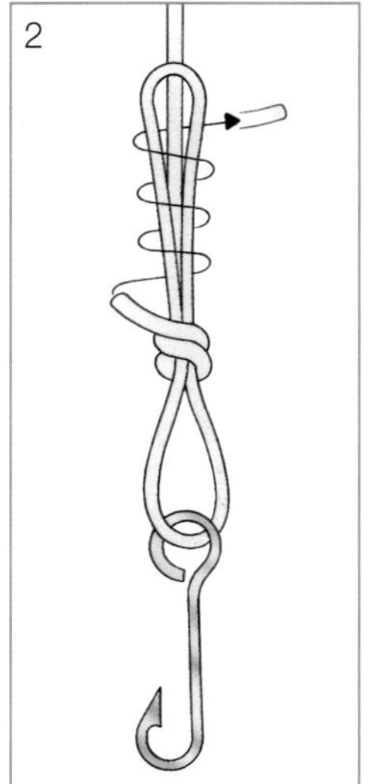

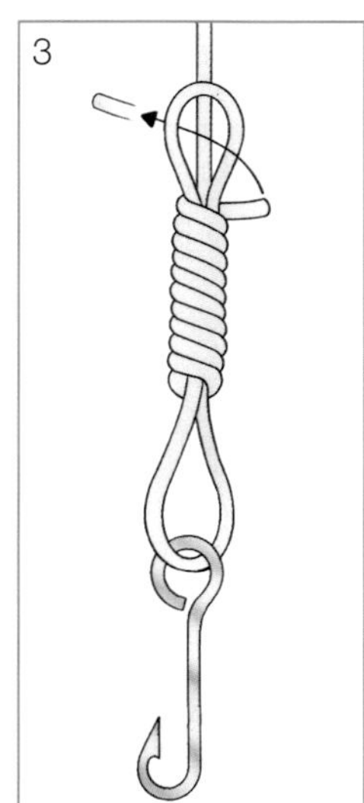

1 Thread the line through the eye of the hook and, as before, make a bight some distance from the end of the line. With the working part, make a second bight, leaving a long working end.

2 Wrap the working part around the three sections of line, moving away from the loop of the first bight.

3 Continue to wrap the working part until you get near its end. Pass the end through the eye of the second bight that is protruding from the coils. By pulling gently on one of the two cords emerging from the other end, the eye can be closed, trapping the working end and securing the knot. The size of the noose may now be adjusted.

Monkey's Fist

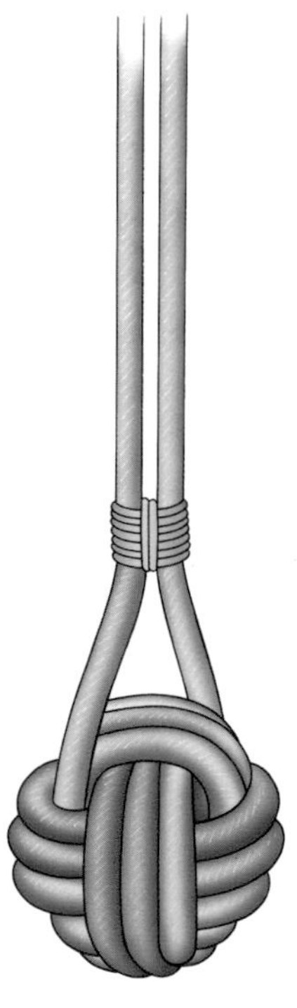

Throwing a rope across a gap is made easier if the end of the line is weighted. The monkey's fist is a traditional heaving line knot that can be tied around the fingers. At one time, a weight was inserted into the center of the knot to aid its flight, but this is now frowned upon for safety reasons (however, a plastic ball may be used to firm up the center when the knot is being used for decorative purposes).

The monkey's fist is tied in a light heaving line, the other end of which is fastened to the heavier rope that you wish to get across the gap. Today, the knot is often replaced by a small sandbag that has weight but will not hurt if caught awkwardly. However, even if you use it only rarely, it is worth knowing; at the very least it is an attractive knot and can be used for decorative purposes.

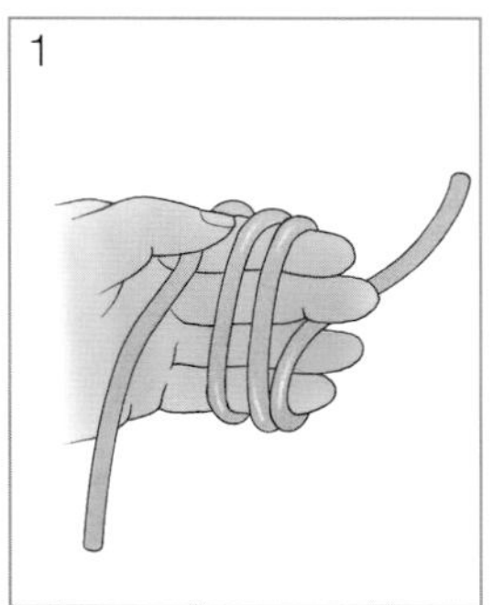

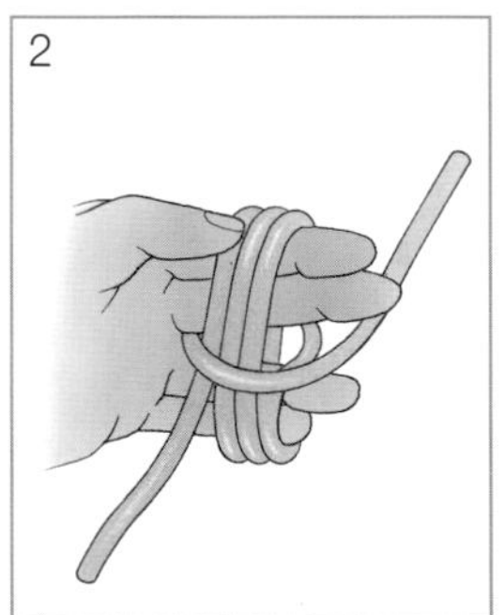

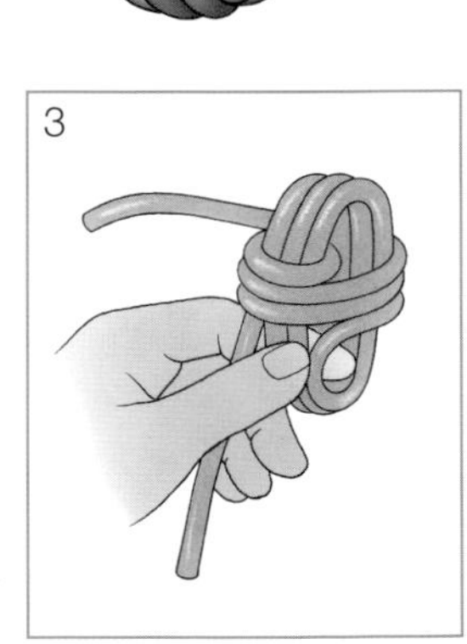

1 Wrap the cord three times around the spread fingers of one hand, leading the working end out between the gap in the middle.

2 Spread your fingers to enlarge the central gap and pass the working end around the first three coils. This is repeated twice to give three turns, which can be pulled fairly tight around the first coils.

3 & 4 Carefully remove your fingers. At this point a weight or plastic ball can be added.

5 Then make three more turns through the spaces where your fingers used to be. These should also be pulled tight. Working back toward the start, remove any slack and arrange the coils tidily.

6 By having already pulled the previous coils fairly tight, you only have to manipulate the first three coils in reverse order to tighten and complete the knot. The working end may be spliced into the standing end to form a permanent end to the heaving line.

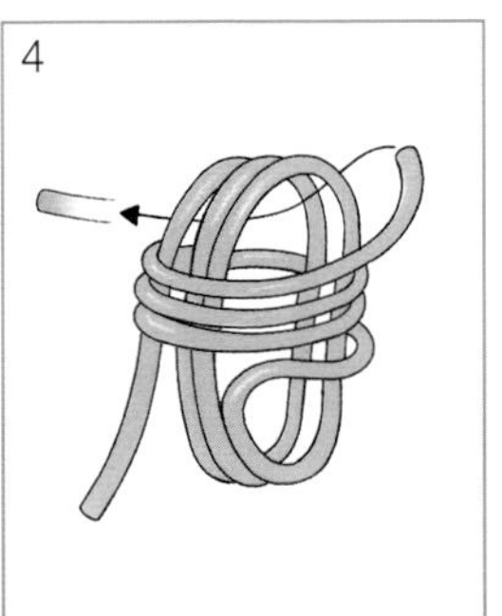

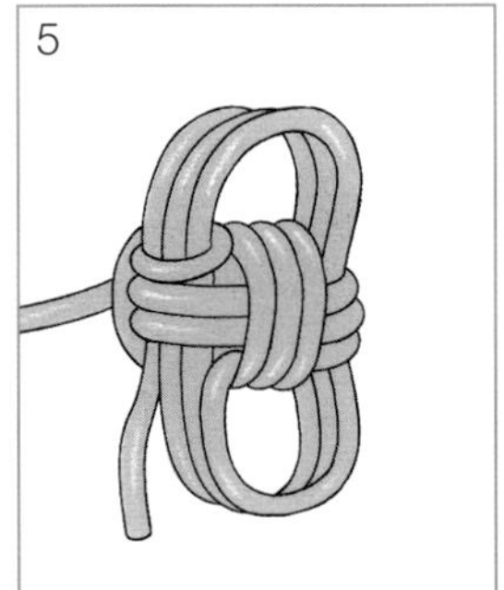

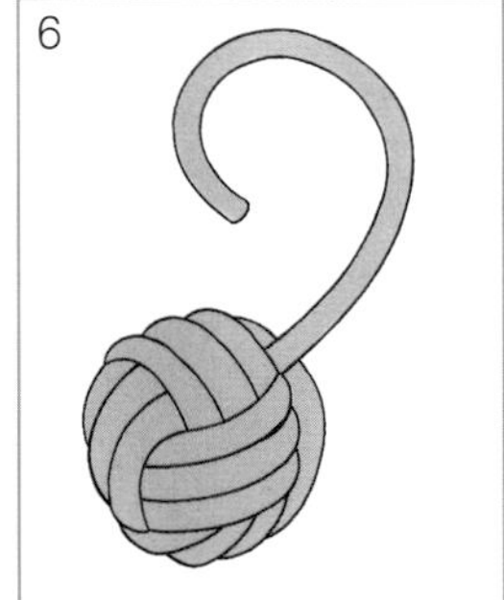

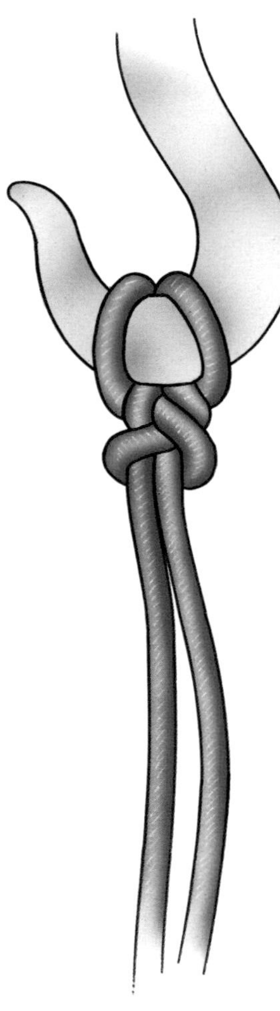

Cat's Paw

Merely looping a sling over a hook is not the safest way to hang a load; the cat's paw, however, is the perfect knot for this function. It is usually tied in the middle of a sling with the load hanging down beneath it. It also has uses in some fishing knots.

1 Take a bight at the center of the sling and allow the top of the bight to fall back behind the two uprights.

2 Twist the wings thus formed in opposite directions three or four times. Pass the hook through the tops of the wings and pull the two uprights to close up the knot.

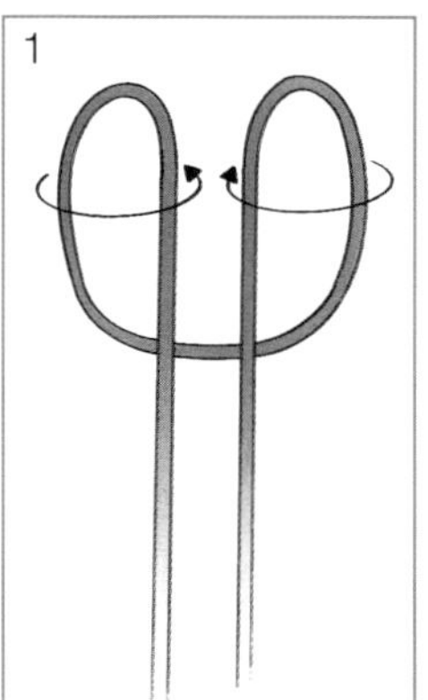

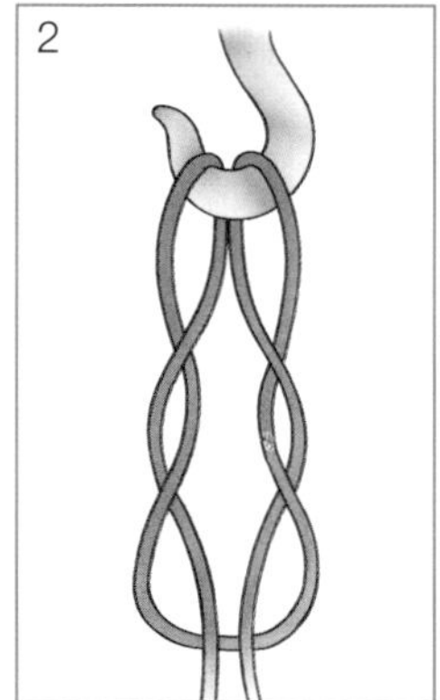

Single Cat's Paw

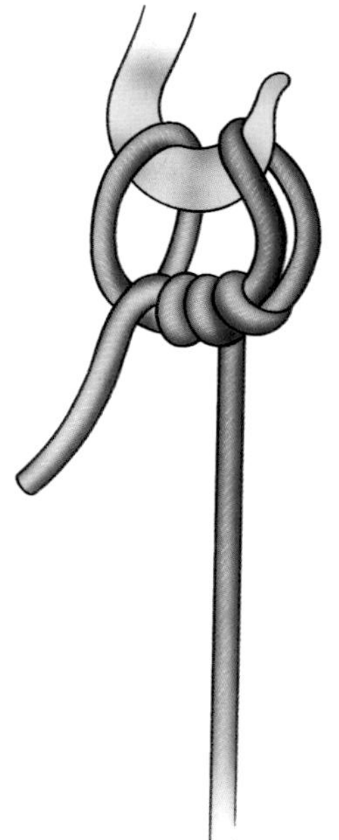

Sometimes the load needs to be slung from a single line. This requires a single cat's paw tied in the end of the line.

1 Make a bight in the line a little way from the end. Double the cord back in a similar fashion to the hangman's knot. Take at least three turns around the three parallel cords, leaving a decent-sized loop at each end.

2 Bring the two loops up and fit them over the hook. Work the loops tight. When the load is applied, the single cat's paw will hold firmly.

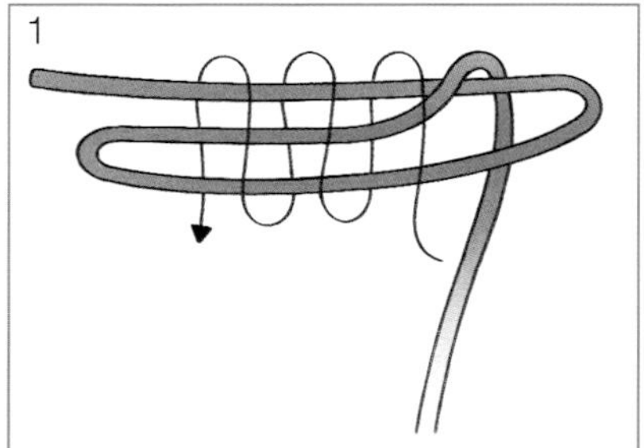

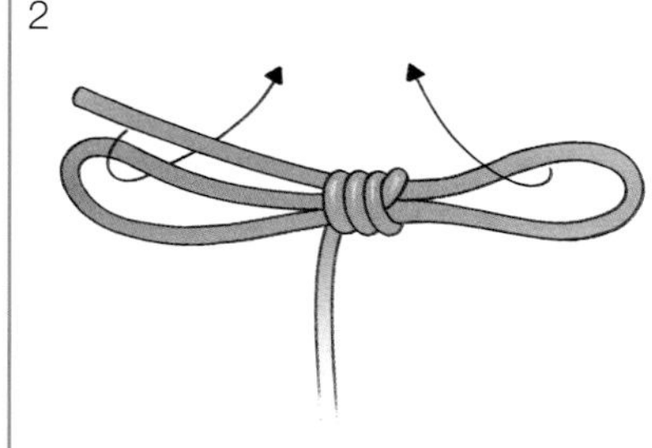

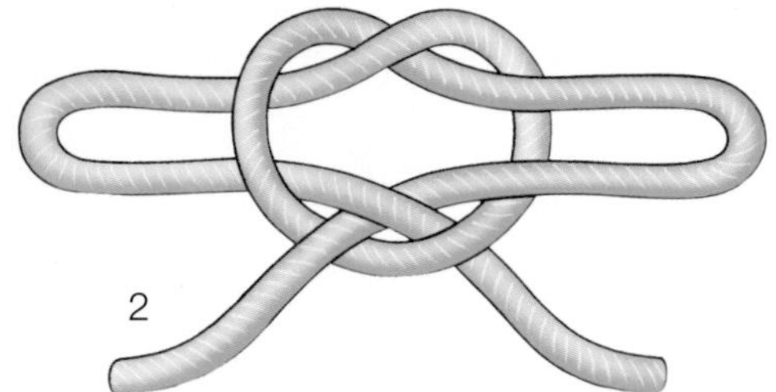

Handcuff Knot

As the name suggests, this knot is used to form improvised restraints but should not be relied upon to hold someone captive for very long.

1 Make two overhand crossing loops and bring them together so that they overlap, bottom over top, just as though you were tying a clove hitch by method two. Reach down through the right loop and grasp the side of the lower loop. Reach up through the left loop and grasp the side of the top loop.

2 Gently pull the loops partly through one another. When used as handcuffs, the hands go through the side loops, which must be pulled tight by the ends, which, in turn, have to be tied to secure the prisoner.

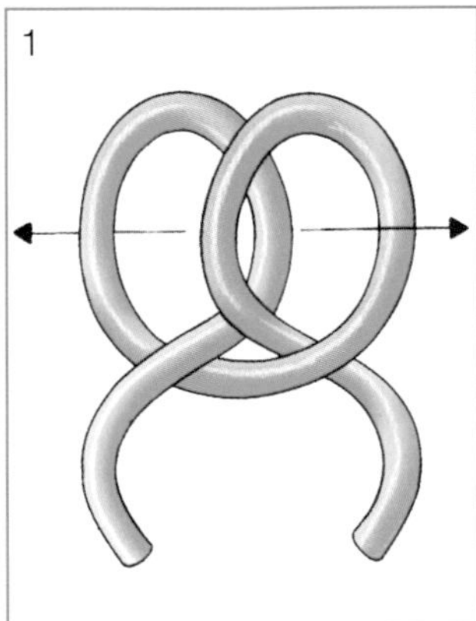

Tomfool Knot

At first glance, and often second or third glance, this is the same as the handcuff knot. It does not, however, have the same crossings and careful study shows that it is different.

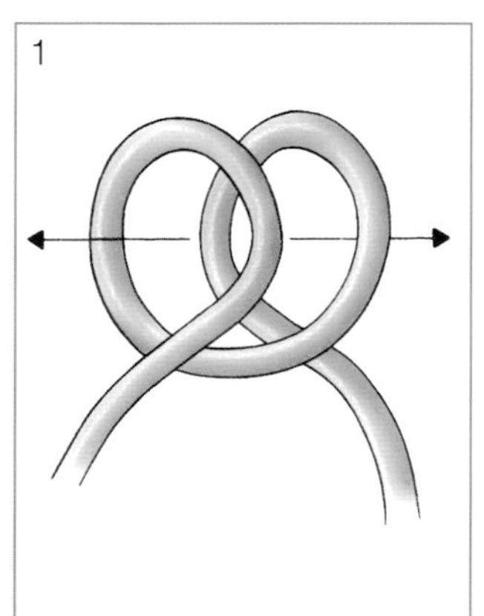

1 Make two overhand crossing loops and bring them together, top over bottom. Pull a bight of each loop through the other loop and the knot is tied.

Fireman's Chair Knot

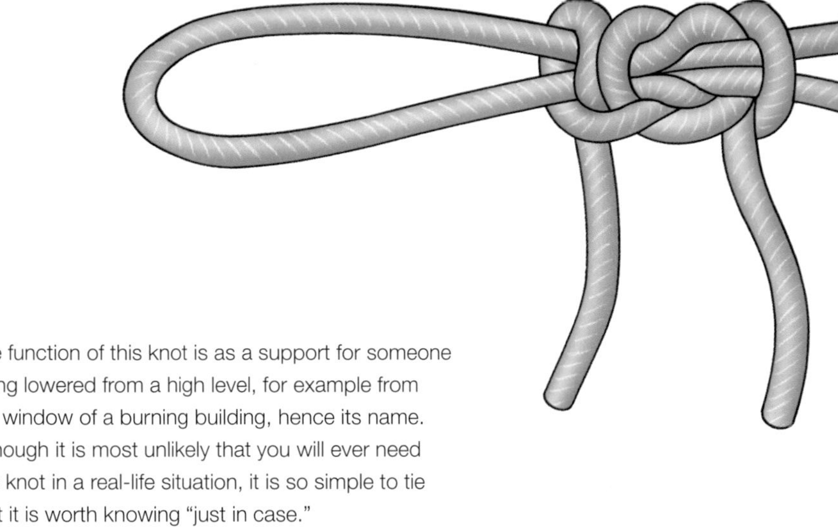

The function of this knot is as a support for someone being lowered from a high level, for example from the window of a burning building, hence its name. Although it is most unlikely that you will ever need this knot in a real-life situation, it is so simple to tie that it is worth knowing "just in case."

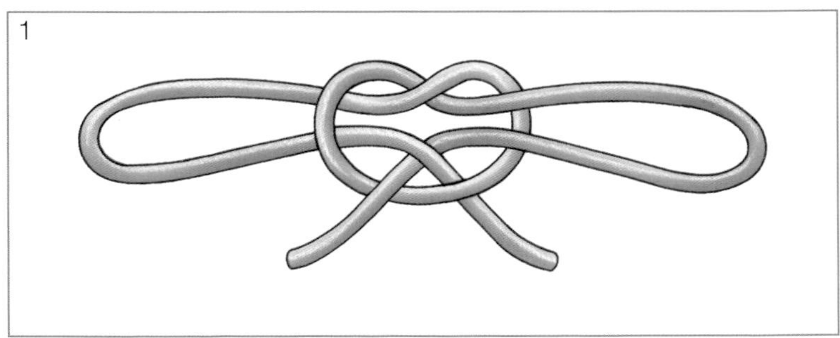

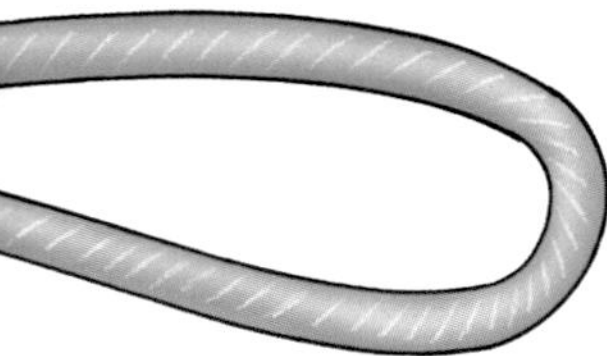

1 Start with either a handcuff knot or a tomfool knot in the middle of a long line. Adjust the loops so that the upper loop (when lowering) will fit around the chest under the armpits, and the lower loop will accommodate the legs.

2 Make further crossing loops on either side of the starter knot and pass the newly adjusted loops through them. Pass the new crossing loops, which have now become half hitches, up to the central part of the knot and work everything tight. Half of the rope is lowered to someone on the ground, who can prevent the person in the harness from bumping into the wall or cliff, while the other half of the rope is used for the actual lowering. Make sure the rope is long enough or there could be a further accident.

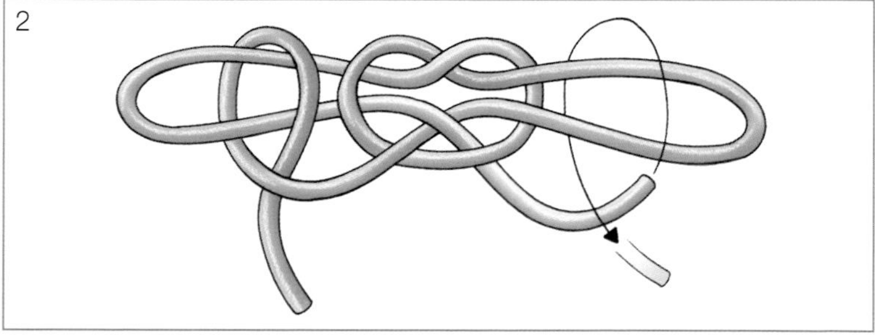

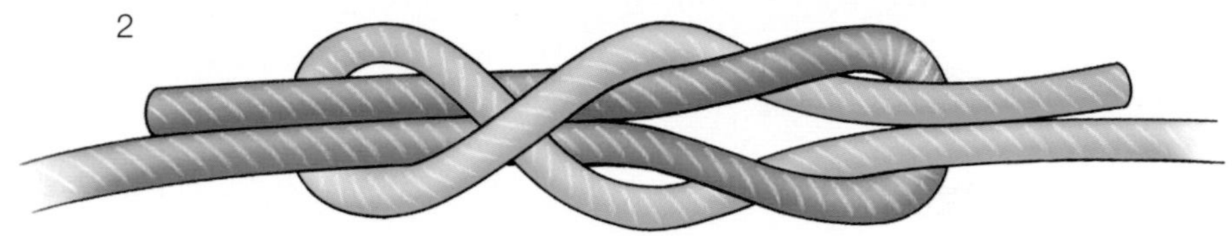

Simple Simon Over

This knot, and the two that follow, was devised by Dr. Harry Asher as an improvement on the sheet bend when using slippery synthetic cords.

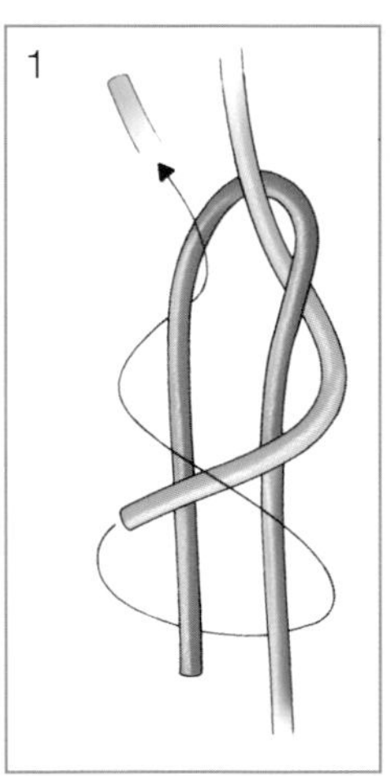

1 Make a bight in the thicker of the two lines to be joined. Bring the other line into the bight from the top, lead it down, under one side, and bring it up to cross the bight completely. Here the line goes under the side of the bight and reappears alongside itself at the point of entry.

2 Tighten carefully, working the knot gently into the form shown.

Double Simple Simon

This is especially useful as it holds well even if the cords are slippery and of different diameters.To tie it, simply follow the method for a Simple Simon but add an extra turn around the bight.

Simple Simon Under

This knot is virtually the same as a Simple Simon over, but the returning cord is passed under itself rather than over. It takes a moment longer to tie, but the extra tuck adds a little more security.

Single Strand Diamond or Simple Lanyard Knot

This appears to be the most complicated of the knots yet encountered, but is, in fact, quite easy to master. It also teaches you control of the cord, the basic idea of over one, under one, over one, and you will end up with a most attractive knot, from the loop of which you may suspend keys, knives, whistles, etc. It works best in cord that is firm but not too stiff and not too thick.

1 Ensure that the line will be long enough and find the middle. Place the cord over your left hand and let it hang so that the midpoint of the cord is roughly centered at the back of your fingers. Take the cord at the back of your hand and bring it up in front and over your thumb.

2 Slip the thumb out and use it to hold the loop you have formed.

3 & 4 With the end of the cord that hangs at the front of your hand, weave it over and under the cords,

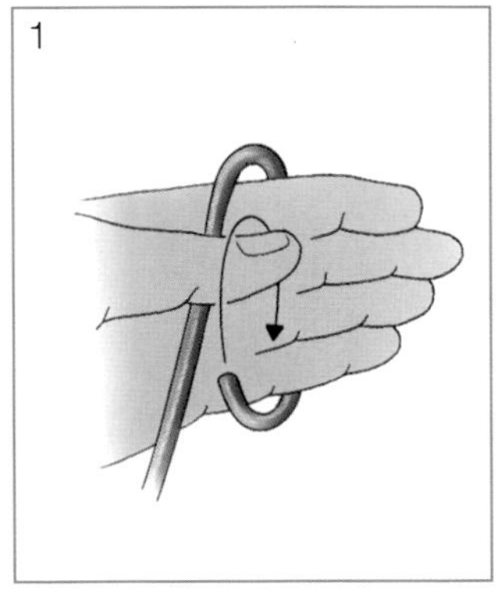

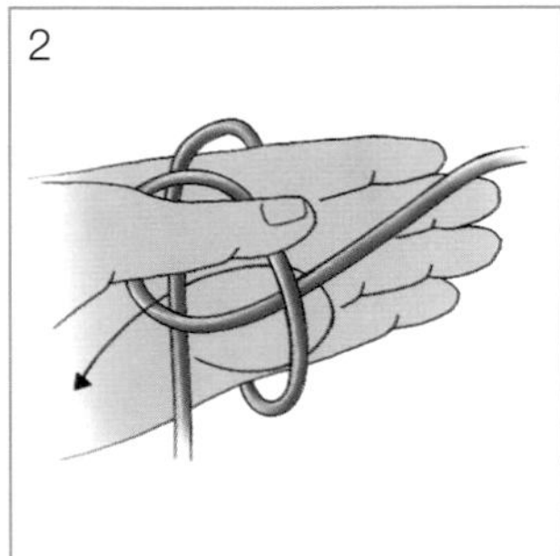

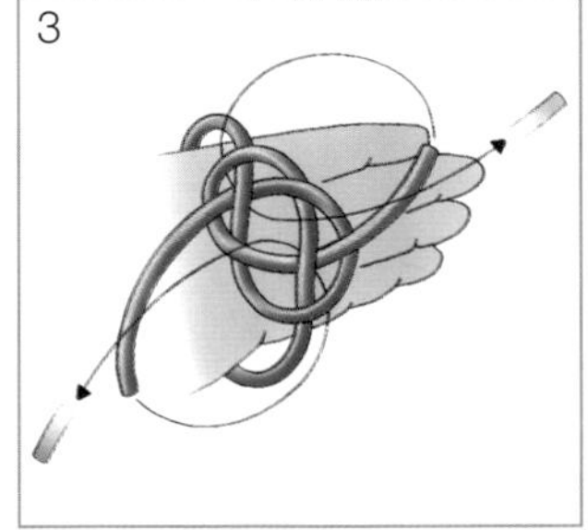

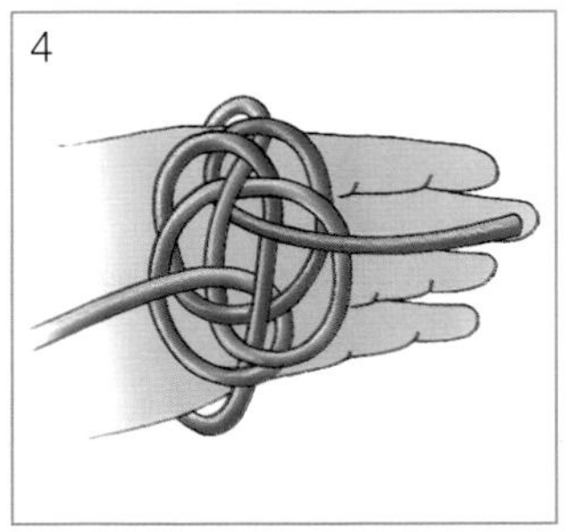

crossing your fingers. It is a simple sequence of over one, under one, over one, under one, but you will need to check the illustrations to ensure that you start and stop in the correct places. You now have an attractive carrick bend sitting in your hand. Take one of the working ends (for this knot you have two working ends), lead it around the outside of the knot, pass it under the edge of the knot, and bring it up into the little square center of the carrick bend. Do the same with the other working end, but making sure that you go in the correct direction.

Holding the two working ends, gently remove your hand and work the knot up into its final shape. One way to do this is to gently pull the loop while simultaneously pulling on the working ends. At the same time, hold the knot and gently rub it or squeeze it to persuade it to adopt its final form. Since you do not have three hands, hook the loop over a door handle or other projection and you can then pull with one hand and manipulate with the other. Teeth are a very useful tool in a situation like this, but you cannot always see what you are doing. Do not pull too tight at first. If all goes well you will be delighted with your lanyard knot, but if it does not work out as you expect, do not despair, undo it and start again. It will only take a minute and next time it will probably come out perfectly.

Camping Knots

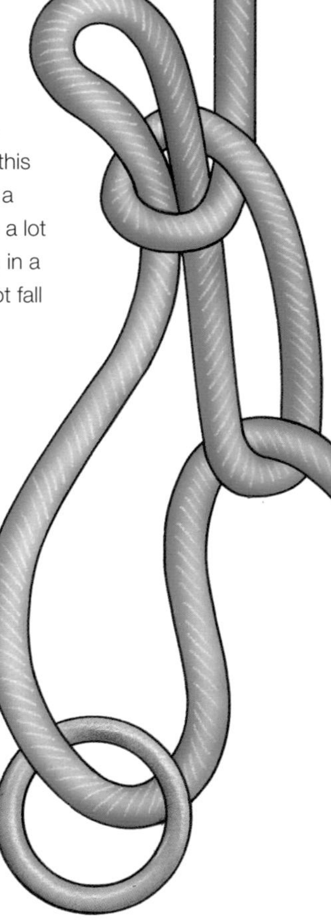

I have camped in a variety of places over the past fifty years and cannot remember an occasion when I did not have to tie something down or fix up a clothesline to dry the laundry. You will not often need all of the knots contained in this section for a quiet vacation in the countryside, but if you are a more adventurous camper, you may need to construct quite a lot of camp furniture or put up picket lines for animals. Sleeping in a hammock will be more enjoyable if you are sure that it will not fall down during the night!

As with all knots in this book, there is no single use and these camping knots can be used in many other situations.

Contents of Camping Knots

Slipped Figure Eight 100
Slipped Zigzag Hitch 102
Speir Knot 104
Sheepshank 106
Strangle Knot 109
Transom Knot 110
Pile Hitch 111
Pipe Hitch 112
Camel Hitch 113
Icicle Hitch 114
Jug or Bottle Sling 116
Asher's Bottle Sling 118
Lapp Knot 119
Jury Masthead Knot 120
Tent Pole Hitch 122
Rope Ladder 124
Lark's Head or Cow Hitch 126
Pedigree Cow Hitch 127
Midshipman's Hitch 128
Miller's Bag Knot 129
Waggoner's or Trucker's Dolly Knot 130
Crown Knot 132
Back Splice 134
Eye Splice 136
Short Splice 138
Square Lashing 140
Diagonal Lashing 142
Shear Lashing 144

Slipped Figure Eight

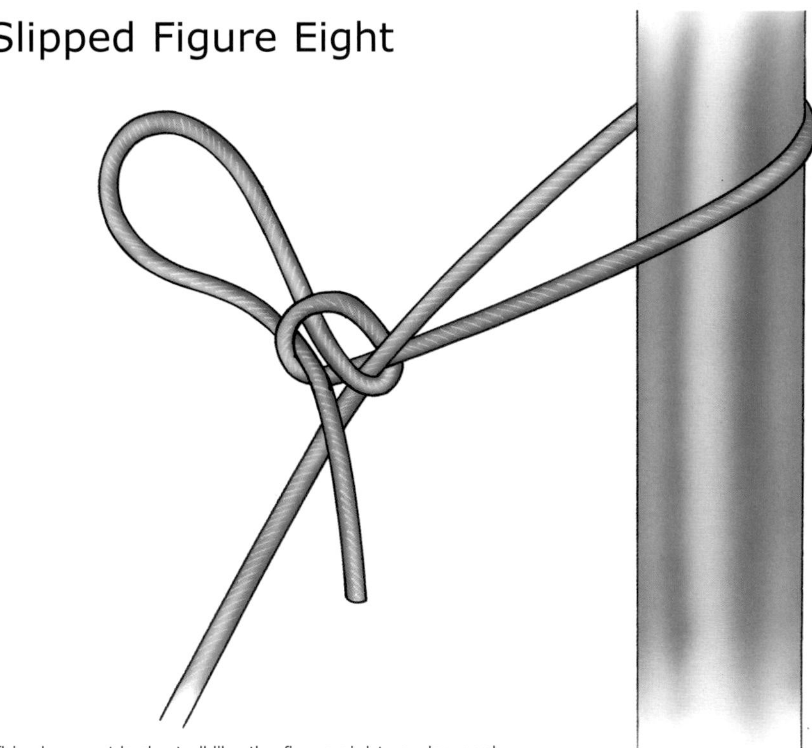

This does not look at all like the figure eight you learned in the earlier section, but if you include the loop around the tree as part of the shape, then it starts to make sense. Use this knot at one end of your hammock or the support for a large banner. It will slide up and lock in place against the tree and can be released by pulling on the projecting tail.

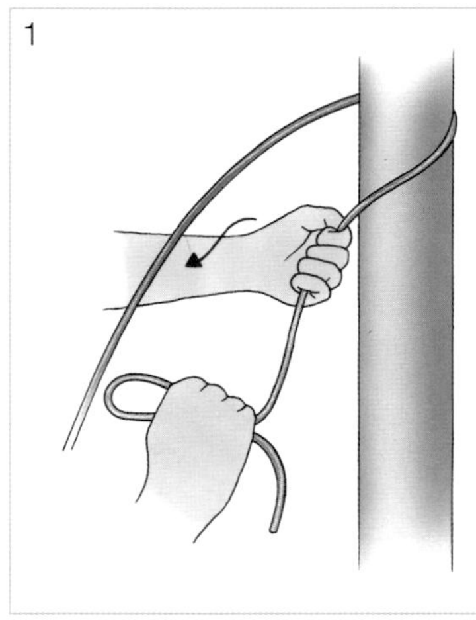

1 Lead the line around the tree or pole, getting it as high up as you can reach while still being able to work on the knot. Reach over the loaded line and take a bight of the working part with the right hand, with the palm down. Then reach under the loaded cord with the other (left) hand, grasping the working part with the palm upward.

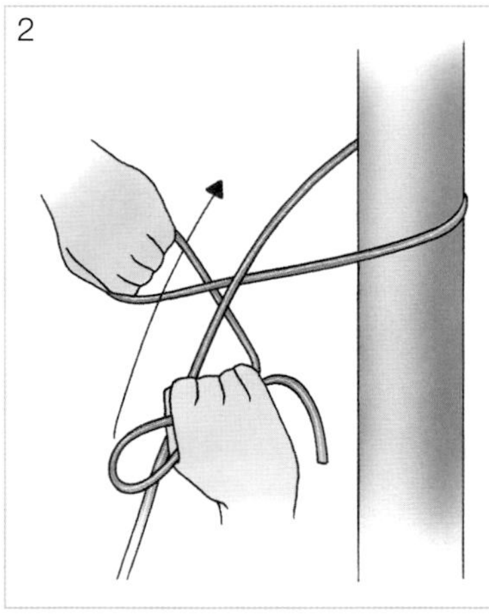

2 Pull the left hand back and turn it toward you and down, creating a loop. Bring the bight in your right hand over the loaded cord and pass it through the loop. You now have a trapped loop as in the highwayman's hitch. The weight of the load will cause the knot to slide up to the tree and lock. If you are setting up a hammock, it should be tensioned with a different knot at the other end.

Slipped Zigzag Hitch

The zigzag hitch is one of a number of hitches that can be used to string a line along a series of posts to act as a temporary barrier and it is very easy to tie. Pulling on the working end applies tension to the standing end and tightens the line, so this is very useful to get hammock lines tight, though in that situation it is best to make it a slipped knot, allowing it to be undone rapidly.

If you are tying this on a tree, it helps if you have a clear area of trunk for the cord to rest against and you may want to put a pad down to protect the bark and reduce the environmental impact of your visit.

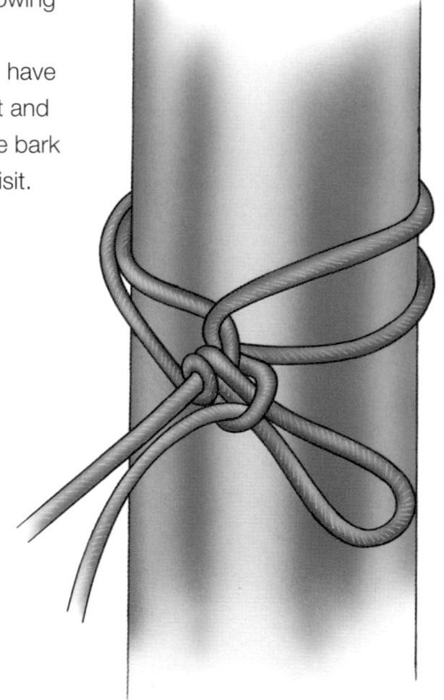

1 Pass the rope around the tree as high as you can manage (remember that if you are tying a hammock, you want it to be roughly level). Bring the end over the standing part, lead it down, and pass it back around the tree just below itself. At this stage you pull on the rope and work it tight to get the tension you require.

2 Taking a bight at the working end, come under the standing part, and lead it back over the rope and between the working part and the tree.

3 Keeping this first bight in place, make a second bight in the working part and feed it through the first bight. Again, it is reminiscent of the highwayman's hitch. Everything will lock up securely and the trailing end serves as a quick release.

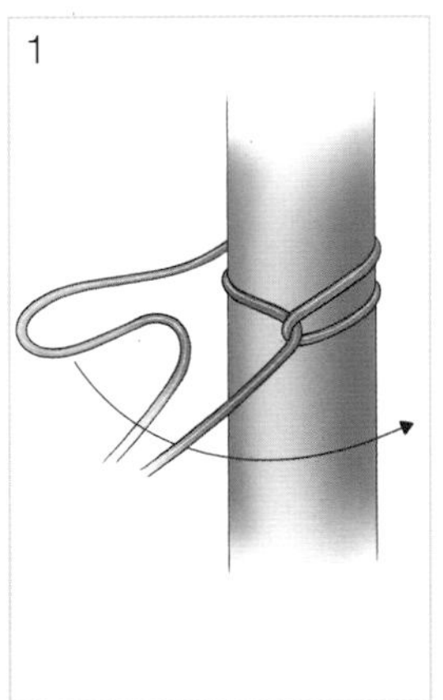

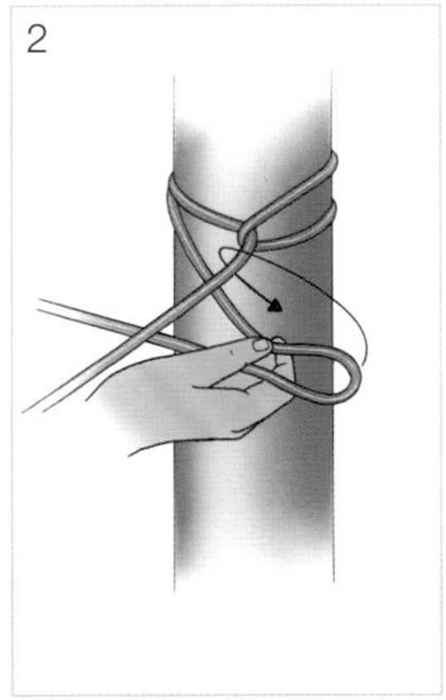

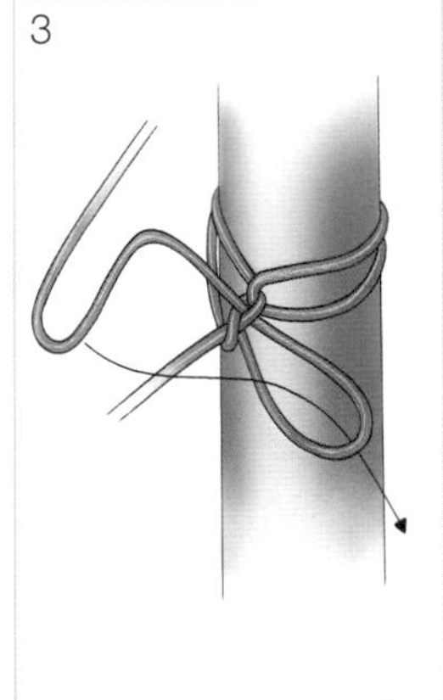

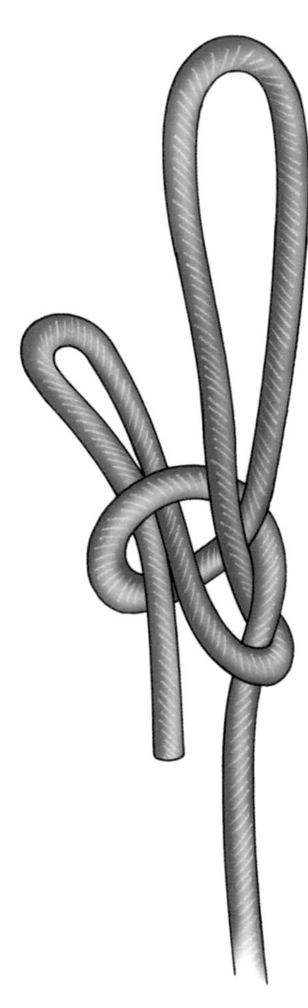

Speir Knot

This knot is taught in the United States but is not seen so often elsewhere in the world. It is another quick-release knot, very similar to the slipped figure eight on page 100, but it gives a fixed loop rather than a sliding one, so it has different applications.

1 To begin, pass the rope around the pole or tree, which has not been shown here.

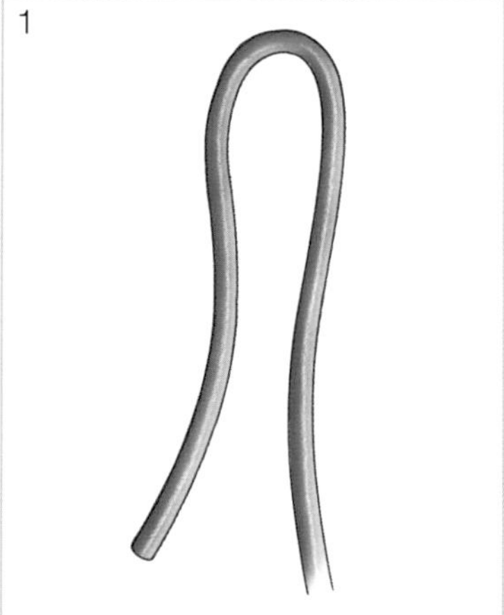

2 Push a bight of the working part under the standing part, and at the same time pull a bight of the standing part under the working part.

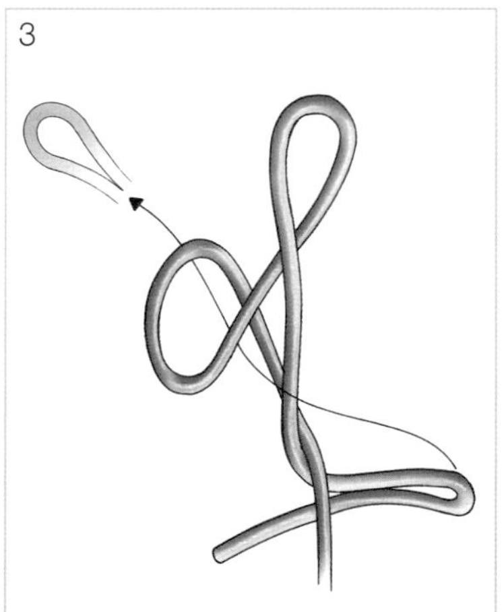

3 Twist the standing bight into a loop and pass the working bight through it. Finish the knot by working it taut.

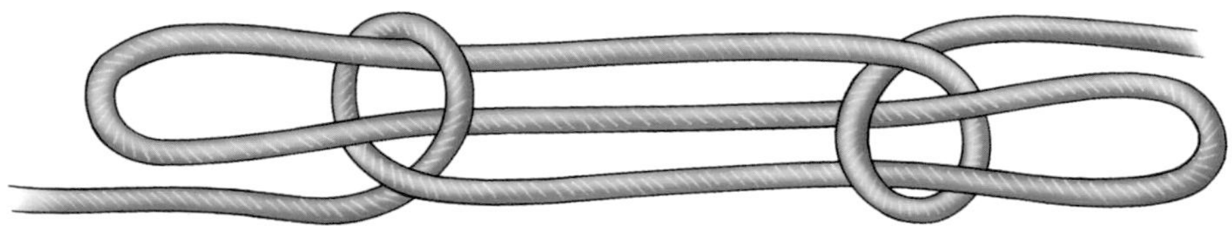

Sheepshank

This is traditionally taught as the knot used to shorten a line without using the ends. You may use it only rarely. In over fifty years I have only had to tie it twice, to shorten the guy ropes of my tent on an awkward pitch, but on those very rainy occasions, knowing how to tie it saved me a soaking. Otherwise it provides good practice at digital dexterity. There are many variations, some of them attractive.

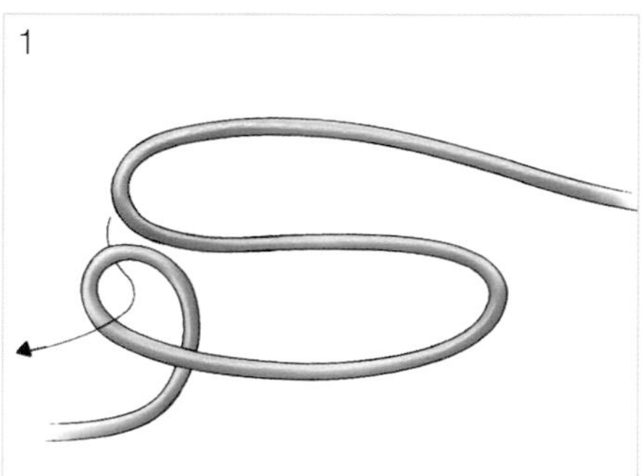

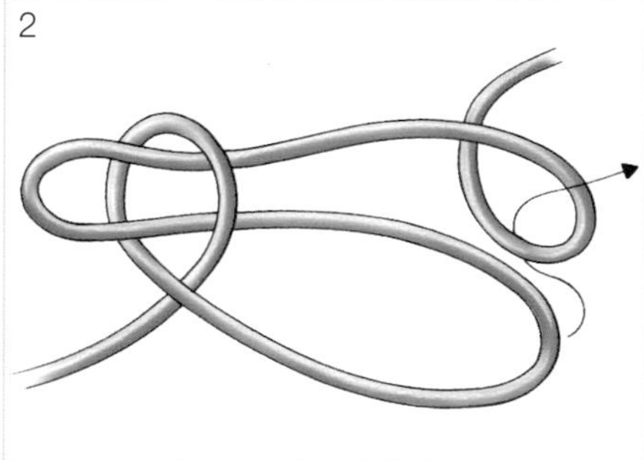

Method One

1 Lay the rope out in a rough *S* shape. Make a loop in the rope just below one bight of the *S*. Pass the bight through the loop in a direction that will lock it. You have put a half hitch on it.

2 Go to the other end of the *S* and repeat the process, passing the second bight through its loop to lock in place. If you take one of the bights of the *S* and lay it across the line, by performing the twist that you did with the bowline you will form the half hitch in one move and this can be repeated for the other half hitch. This technique will also be used for the waggoner's hitch later.

Method Two

1. Again, lay the rope out in the form of a flattened *S*.

2. Take the bight at one end and wrap it around the standing part. Pull firmly on the end of the bight and the standing part will spill to form the half hitch.

3. Repeat this at the other end and the knot is complete.

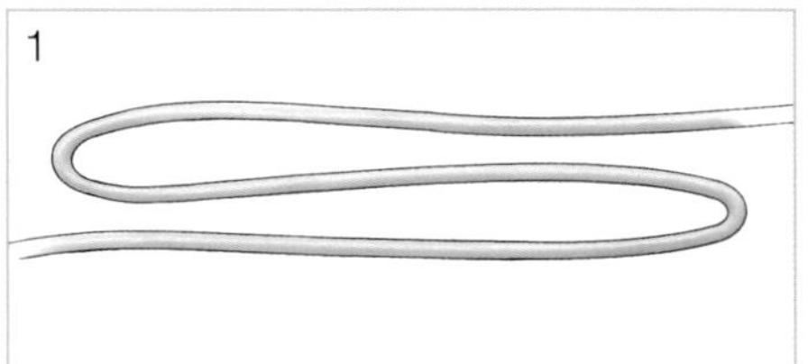

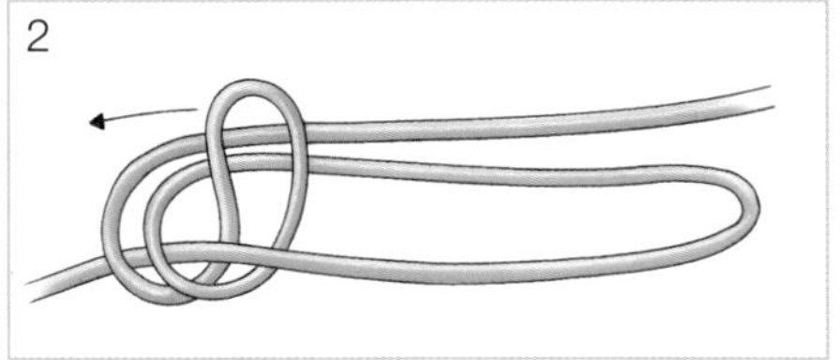

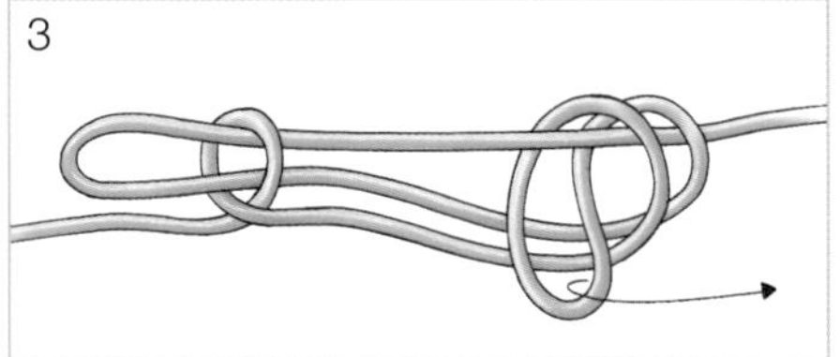

Should you have a damaged rope and not be able to replace it, a temporary solution is to make a sheepshank with the damaged part in the central straight section of rope. The outer two sections then act like a splint to support the damaged section.

To ensure that the knot does not fall apart if the load is removed, the end loops may be seized to the standing parts, a toggle may be passed through each bight to trap the standing part, or a second half hitch may be made at each end of the sheepshank.

Strangle Knot

This knot and its variant, the transom knot, provide good knots for securing bundles. You might find that it is useful for tying up your tent poles or rolled-up sleeping bags. It is basically a double thumb knot tied around the bundle.

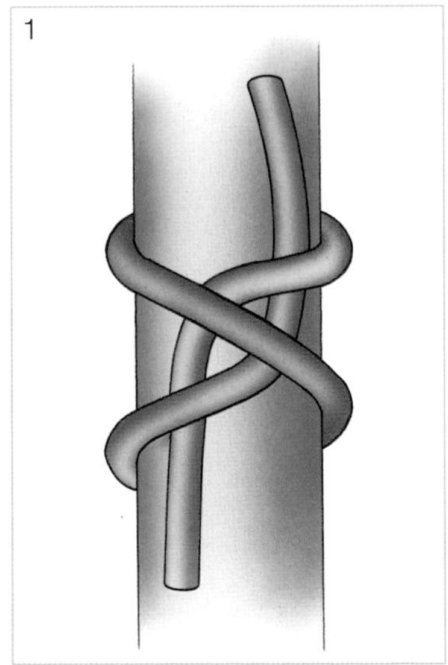

1 Pass the line twice around the bundle so that the second crossing traps the end of the cord. When the working end comes up, lead it under the two turns and pull tight. This will not grip quite as well as the constrictor but is a very useful binding knot.

Transom Knot

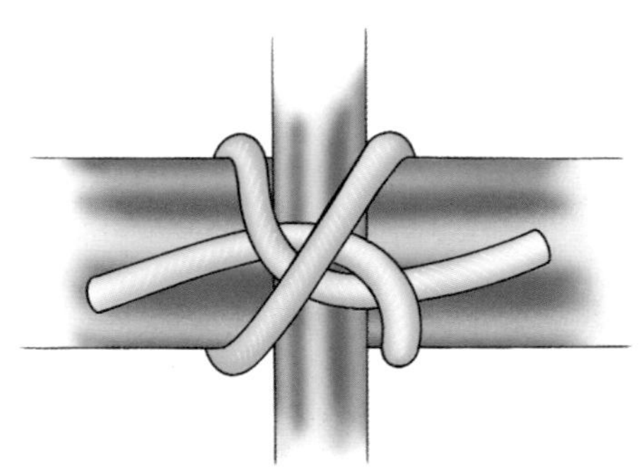

When the strangle knot is tied so that a second spar lies at right angles to the first, it will hold the two together. This can be convenient, for example, when building a kite, as the joint is firm but flexible.

1 Tie as before but ensure that half the knot (the first turn) lies on one side of the second spar while the second turn lies on the other side of the spar. The locking crossing is done on top of the second spar.

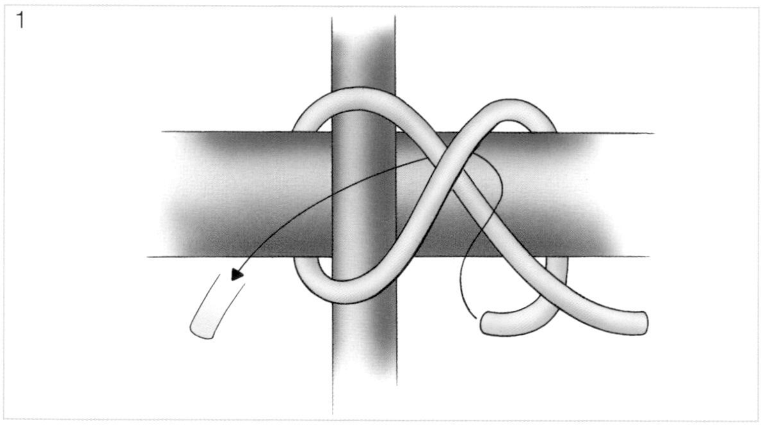

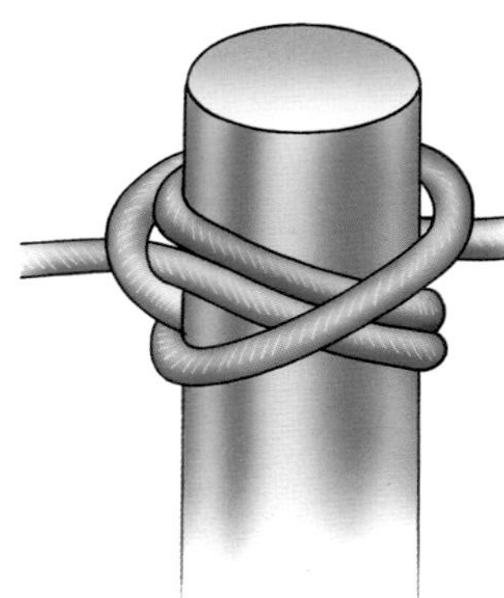

Pile Hitch

As previously mentioned, there are several knots suitable for a line between posts, and the pile hitch is one of the quickest and easiest. Providing the posts are secure, it allows a tethering line for animals to be erected rapidly.

1. Wrap a bight of the rope around the post and bring the bight under itself.

2. Reverse direction and lift the bight up over the top of the post. Work taut and proceed to the next post.

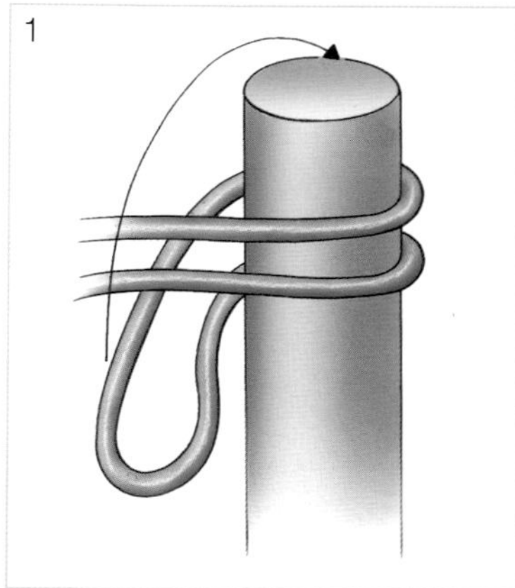

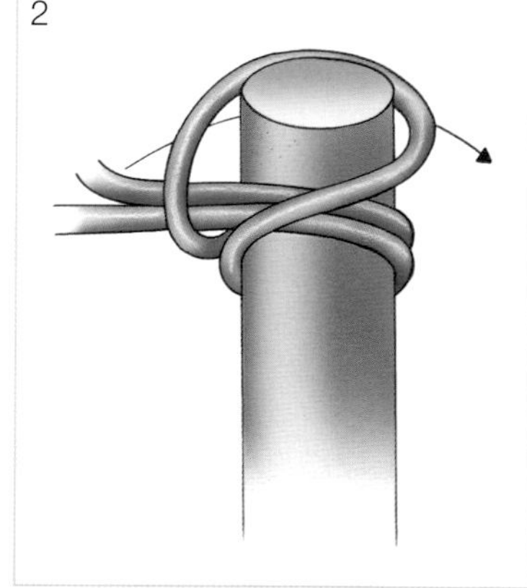

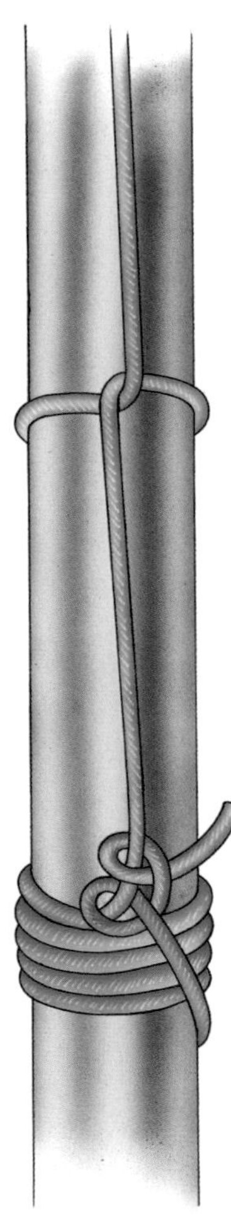

Pipe Hitch

While camping, you may have to lift a length of tube or a log lengthwise. This knot has long been used for that task by oil well riggers and is simple but effective.

Using what you have learned previously, this is a very easy knot to tie and will not need a step-by-step guide. Take a half hitch around the pipe near the top to act as a stable base when lifting.

A little way below the half hitch, wrap the rope firmly around the pipe, taking sufficient turns to be secure. A lot will depend on the type of rope and the pipe. Probably four or five will be enough, but be prepared to stop the lift and start over again if there is any chance of slipping.

Bring the working end up from the last turn and secure it to the standing part coming from the upper half hitch with two half hitches.

Camel Hitch

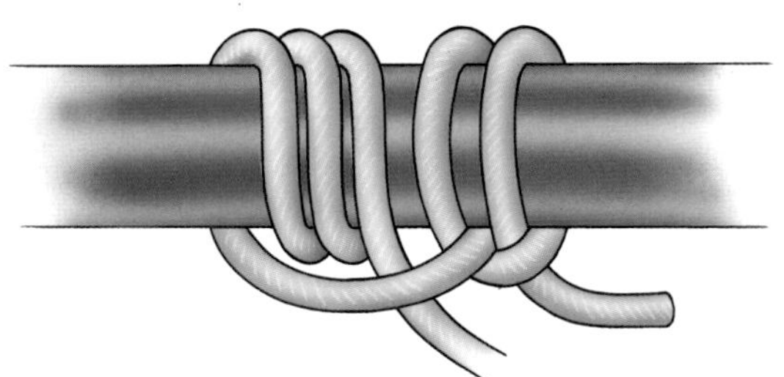

This rope is so named because camels tend to drool a lot when contemplating the world and the slobber makes their tether ropes slippery and liable to come undone. Although most people will not need to tether a camel, this knot will enable you to confidently tie with cord that may become slippery for whatever reason.

1

1 Take three turns around the post, winding away from the loaded standing part.

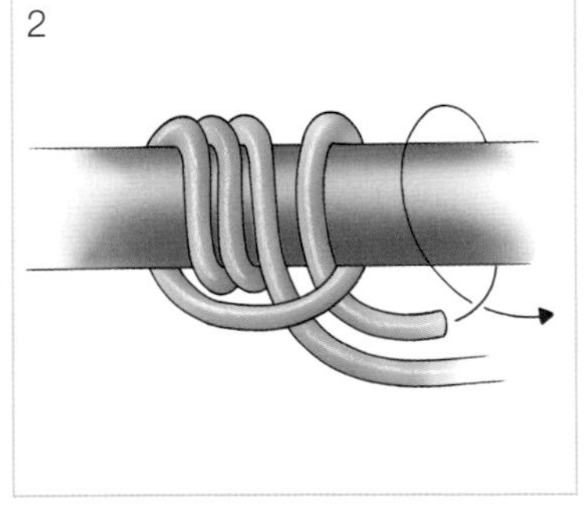

2 Bring the line across in front of the standing part and take it behind the pole to make a half hitch on the other side of the standing part. Make another half hitch alongside the first and work tight. The knot should stay secure in any circumstance.

Icicle Hitch

John Smith of the International Guild of Knot Tyers devised this knot to withstand a steady pull along a narrowing taper of a polished pole, something hitherto considered impossible. Two methods of tying the knot are shown, one with both ends of the rope available and the other with only one.

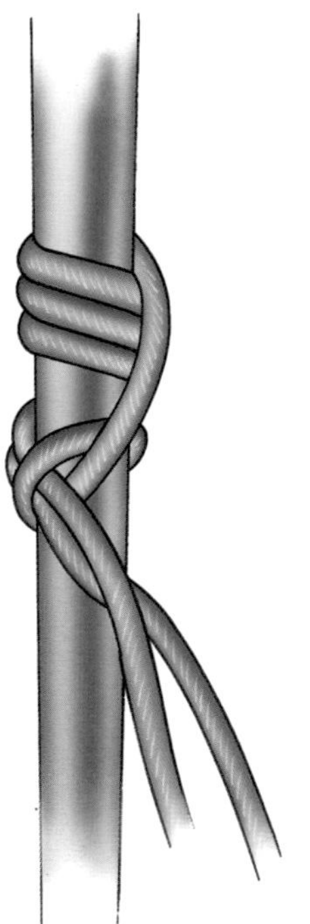

1 With both ends of line free, wrap several turns of cord around the core item. This will leave one end closer to the direction of pull, which we assume to be toward the point of the tapering pole.

2 Bring the far working end back across the turns and give it a twist to make a loop. Take the loop over the back of the core. Bring both ends of the line up and through the loop. Work all slack out carefully, then apply the load slowly and without jerking.

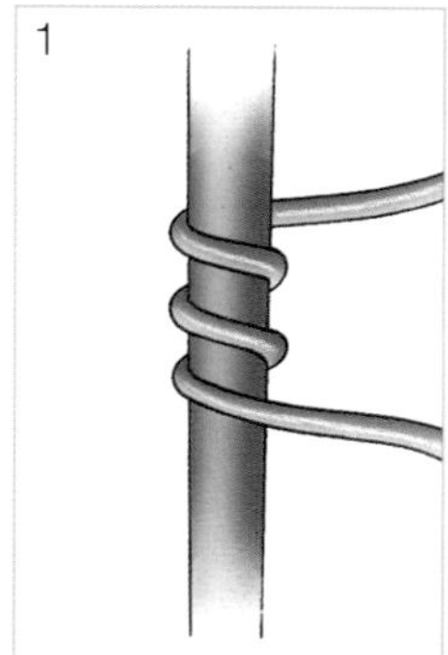

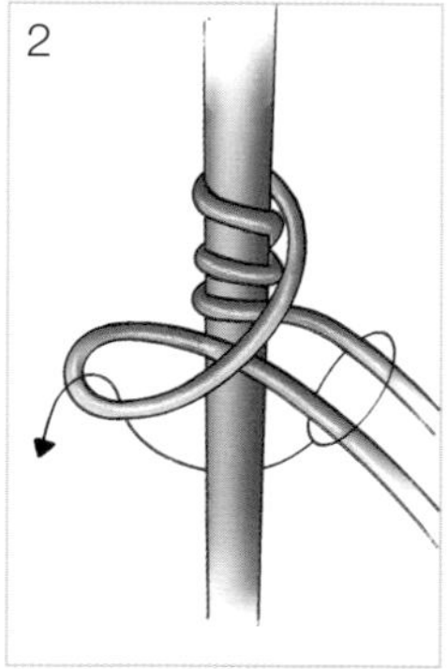

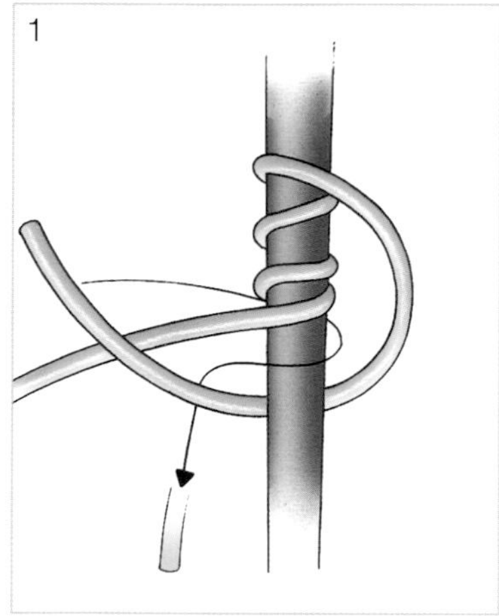

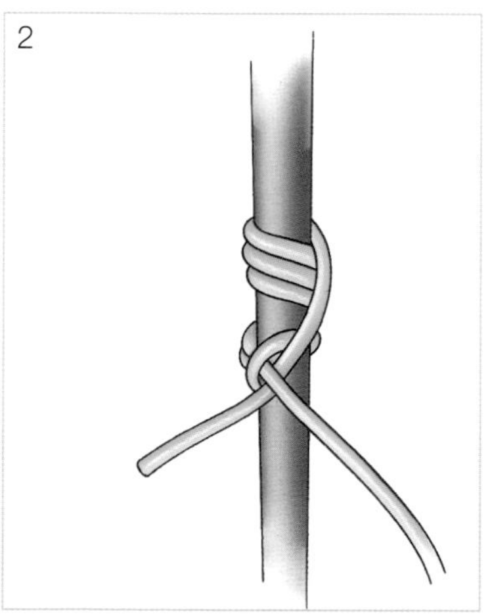

1 With only one end of line free, (we will assume that one end of the line is fixed to something already), lead the line to the core and take several turns leading away from the narrow end, or direction of pull. When there are enough turns, bring the working end across the turns and lead it down behind the pole and then back up again. The working end now crosses in front of the fixed part, goes down again, and comes back up to pass between the fixed part and the standing part. Work tight.

2 A steady pull on the working end will show if it is going to slip. If slippage does occur, then undo the knot and retie using more initial turns.

Jug or Bottle Sling

Bottles can be awkward items to carry, especially when full, but by tying this sling around the neck, they can be easily suspended for transport. A soft cord will pull up and grip well. Some of the moves are confusing at first, but persevere, as this is the perfect way to hang your bottles in the river to cool on a hot summer day.

A slight rim is required on the bottle to keep the knot from slipping off.

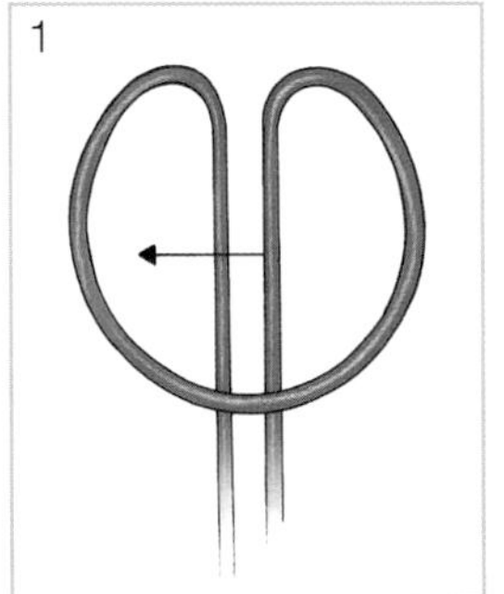

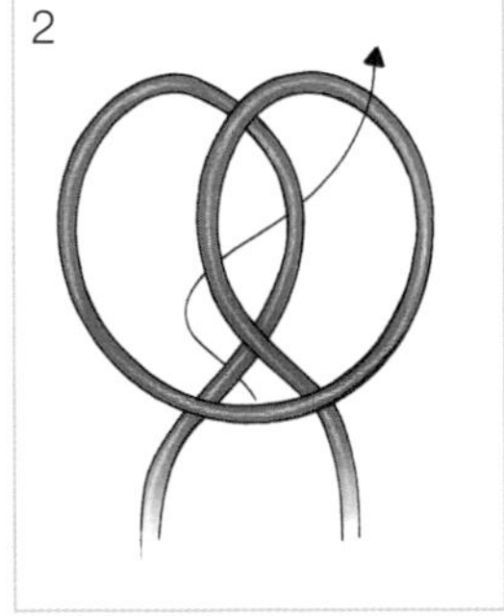

1 Form a bight and let it drop forward to make two loops or wings. Take the right-hand wing and pass it in front of the other so that two crossing loops are formed.

2 & 3 With some care, take the bottom of the front loop and weave it through the crossings of the other two side loops. Go first to the left, then come up and move diagonally across to emerge at the top right. Slightly distort the cords until the shape in picture 3 is formed.

4 Now we let the back loop (A) drop down behind the knot to the position in picture 4.

5 Loop B is brought forward to the position in picture 5. The neck of the bottle must be fitted through the diamond-shaped gap in the center of the knot and then the cord is worked tight to grip the bottle. The loose ends are tied together to match the other loop for suspension purposes.

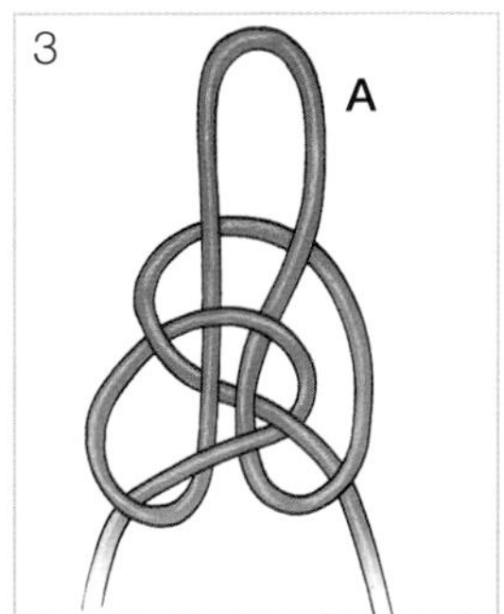

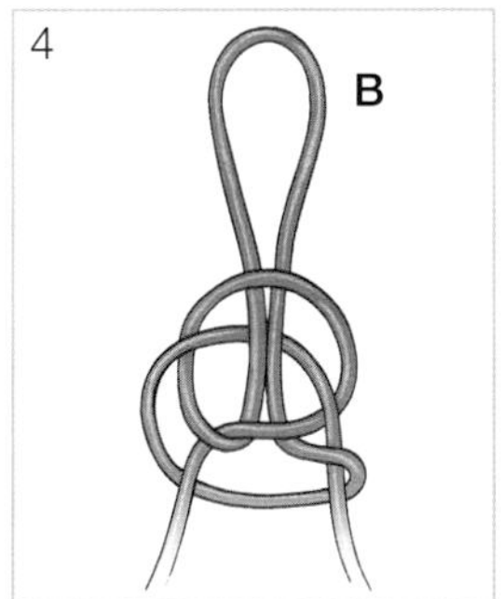

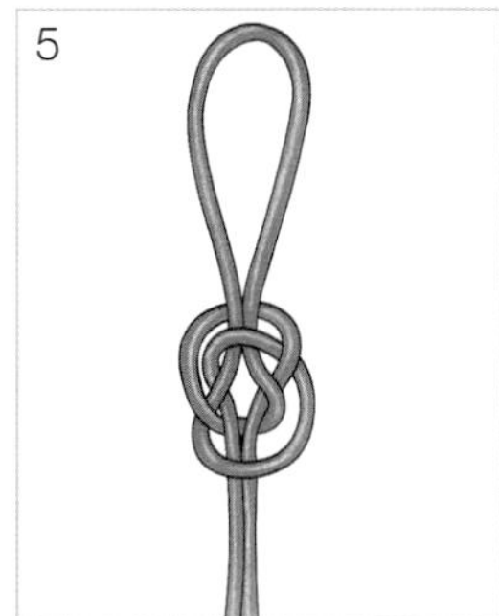

Asher's Bottle Sling

Your bottle may be lighter in weight and the previous sling too hard to remember. This sling, another knot devised by Harry Asher, will do the job just as well.

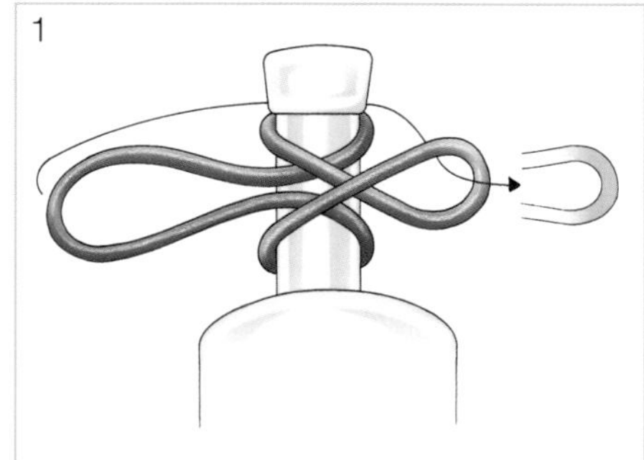

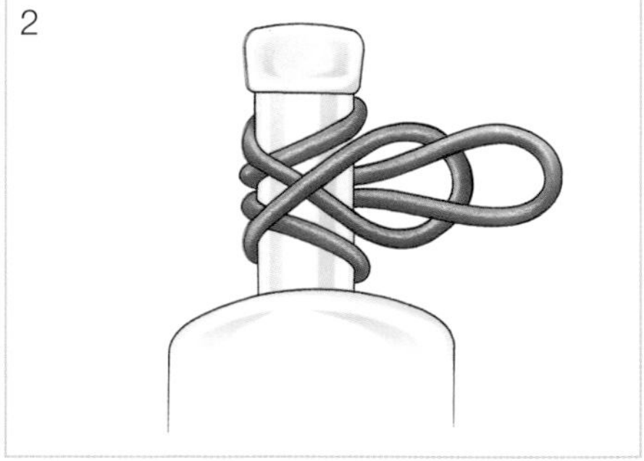

1 Take a closed loop of cord or tie the ends of your cord together. Place the neck of the bottle across the loop near the middle. Bring the sides of the loop up around the neck so that one end passes through the other. Give the loop that is on top a half twist, forming an overhand loop.

2 Take the other end on around the neck and up through the overhand loop. Pull it taut and the sling is formed.

Lapp Knot

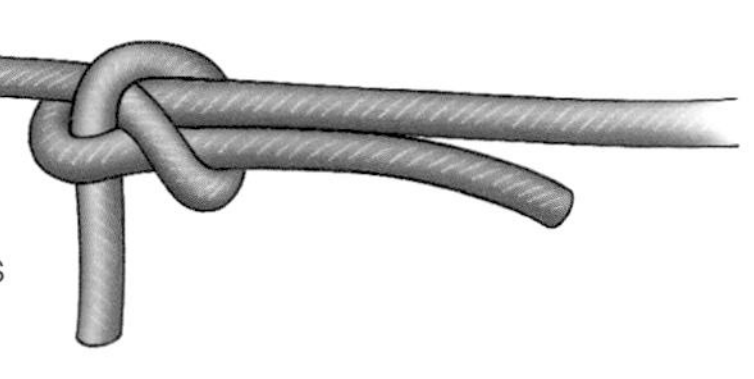

This simple knot has been found among many so-called "primitive" societies. It has numerous uses and is perfect to tie the two ends of a cord together.

1 Take a bight in one end and lay the other end across it.

2 Lead the end around under the bight and pass the end through the loop of the bight.

3 Pull to tighten.

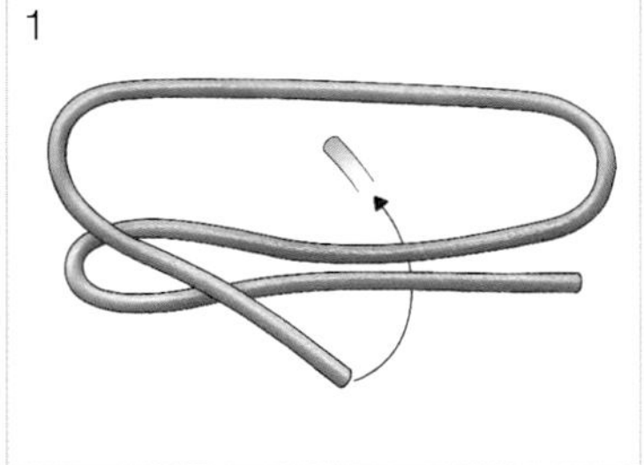

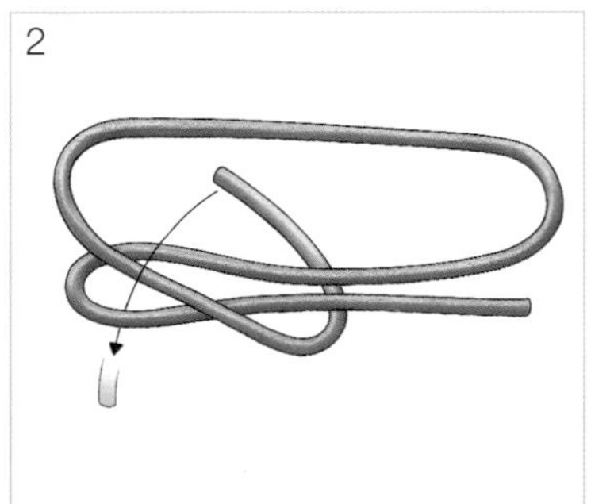

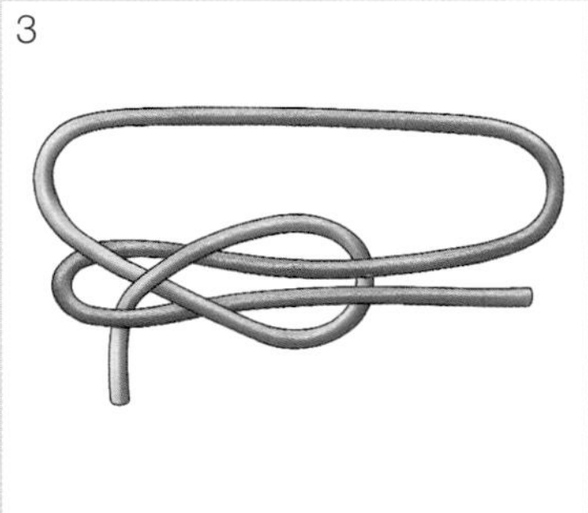

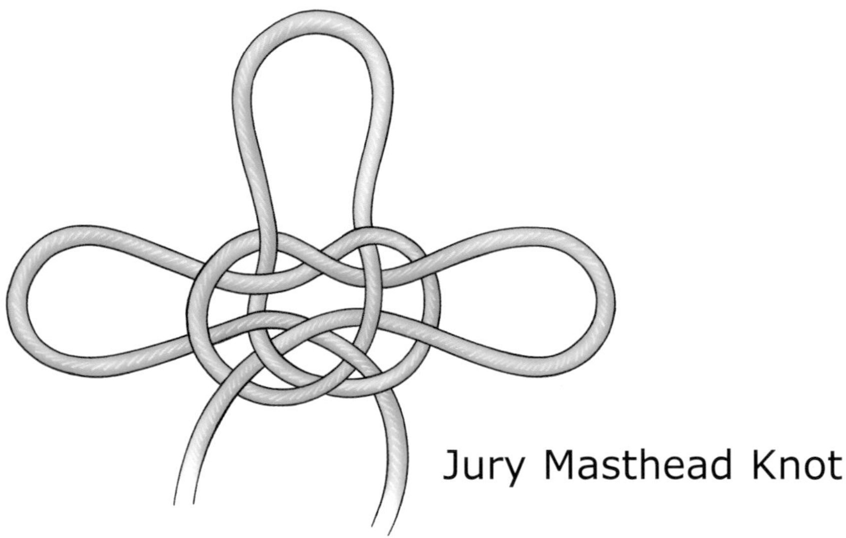

Jury Masthead Knot

This is a most attractive knot and is often seen ornamentally in needlework. Its practical use was at the top of an improvised (or jury) mast, where the stays and shrouds are tied into the loops of the completed knot. It can also be used on a flagpole.

While it is unlikely that it will be needed today for its original purpose, it is a beautiful knot and one that is worth knowing.

There are several variants of the jury masthead knot, but the one I recommend follows a technique you will have already learned from some of the previous knots and saves you from having to remember a new method.

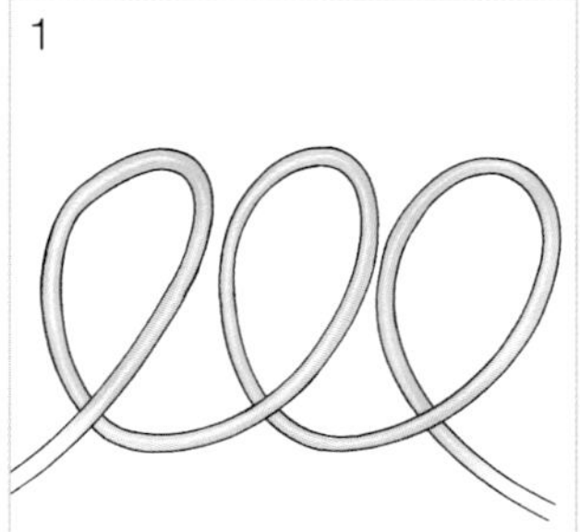

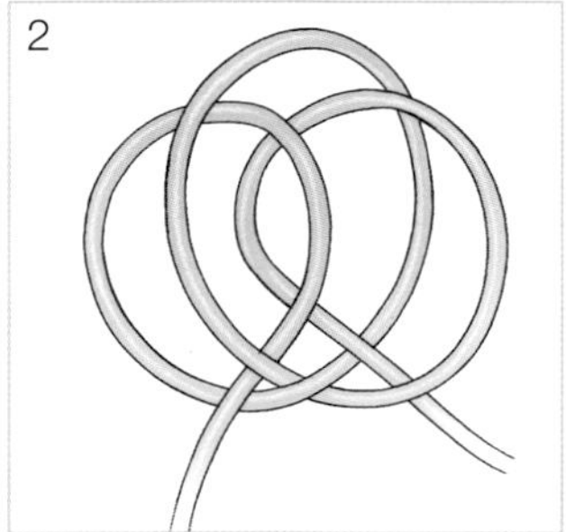

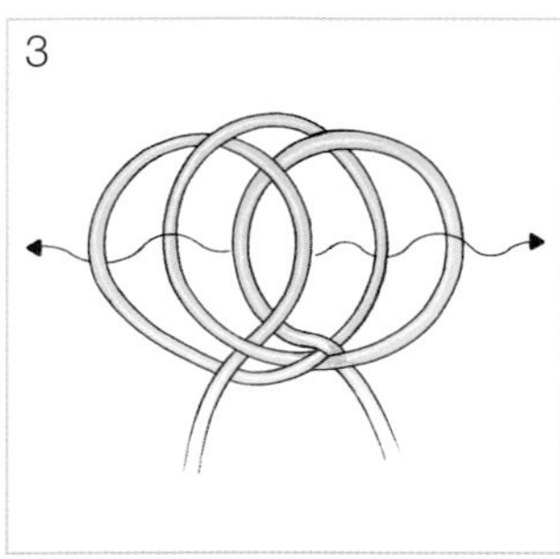

1 Make three identical overhand loops. The middle loop can be a little larger than the other two.

2 Overlap them in the same way you did when making the clove hitch by method two.
Now overlap the left loop a little over the right loop as in the illustration, the overlap lying inside the middle loop. It may be easier to place the loops on a flat surface for the next move, which involves some weaving.

3 Reach under the extreme left loop, over the left side of the middle loop, and grasp the left side of the right loop. Pull this through, following the path your hand took. From the right-hand side, reach over the outside loop, go under the right side of the middle loop, and hold the right side of the left loop. Pull this back through. The illustrations show the paths taken by the loops and the positions of the hands. At the same time, the top of the slightly larger central loop is pulled outward. Work the knot into shape. The masthead fits in the little diamond in the center of the knot. As with many knots, it is far easier to do it than to read about it.

Tent Pole Hitch

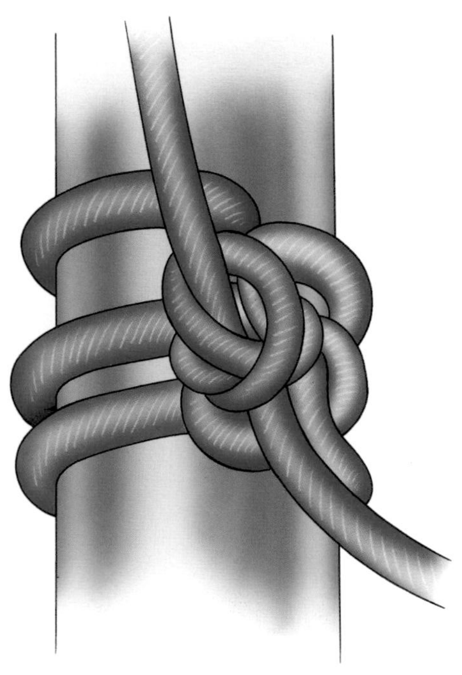

This simple knot is used to tie a bundle of sticks such as tent poles or bean sticks. It may also be used when slinging a plank.

1 Lay your cord in an *S* shape and place the bundle of sticks across it.

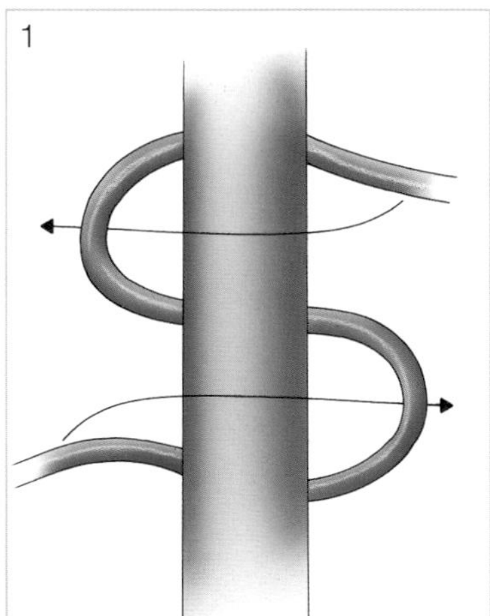

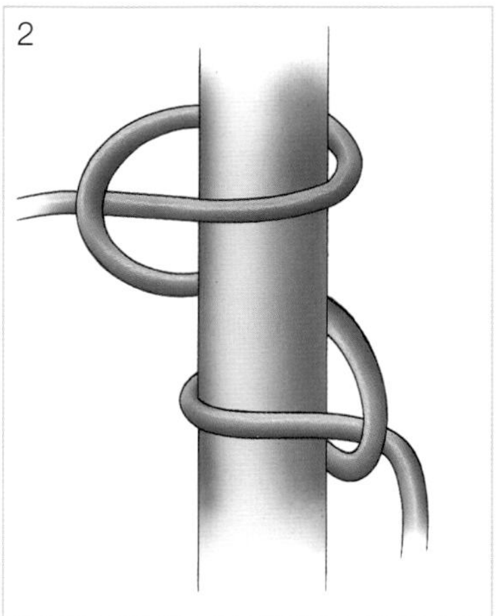

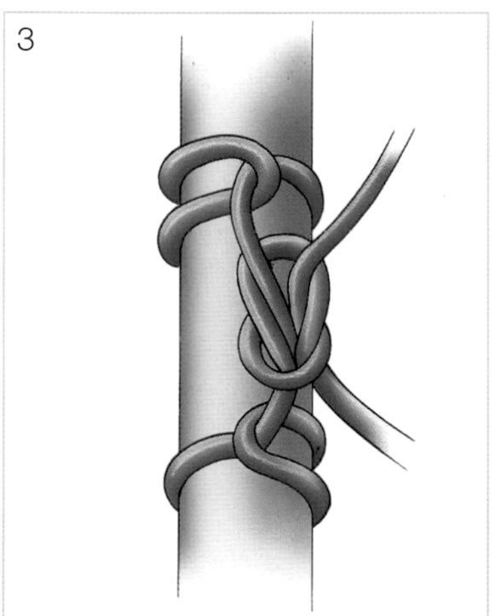

2 Take one end, lift it over the bundle, and pass it through the *S* bight on the other side. Repeat this with the other end, but in the opposite direction into the other *S* bight.

3 Haul taut and tie the ends. A square knot could be used here. Do the same at the other end of the bundle or everything will spread apart and be awkward to carry.

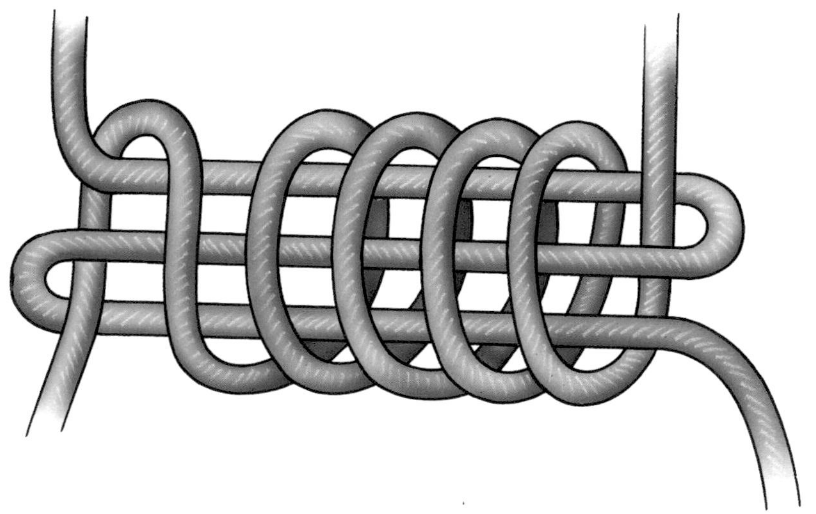

Rope Ladder

This knot uses a lot of rope, but looks most impressive. It is also practical, and in tying it you will be applying ideas learned from other knots. If you have enough rope (and enough time), it can be used to make an entire ladder from scratch, or just a single stirrup. It is best to use fairly stiff rope.

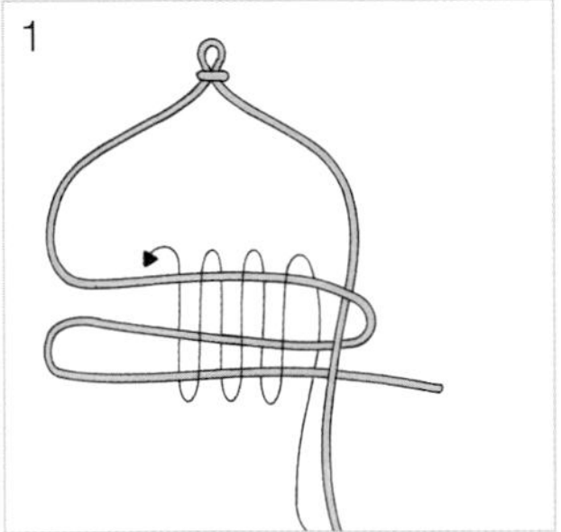

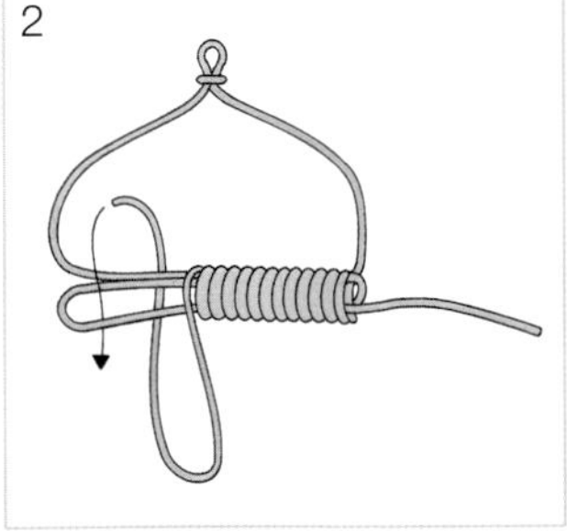

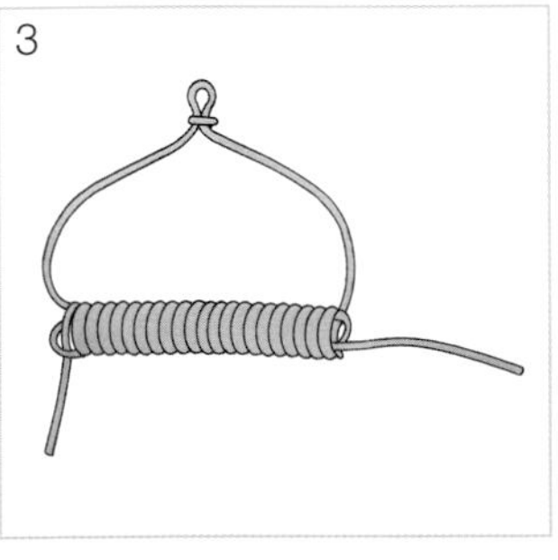

1 Middle the rope. (You might want to put a seizing on the middle to form a suspension eye.) With the left strand, make a *Z* a little way from the top. Ensure that the other strand goes through the top bight and then wrap it several times around the three branches of the *Z*.

2 & 3 Finish off by passing it down through the left-hand bight of the first *Z* and working the rung up taut. You may need to feed cord in or out of the *Z* in order to make both arms of the suspender an equal length.

Repeat the process exactly until the ladder is as long as you need. At each step, pull the rung taut, as this saves a tremendous waste of time trying to adjust every rung at the end of the tying. You should ensure that the distance between the rungs stays the same and that they are always level. This is a fairly difficult task for those making their first attempt, but patience and practice will pay off.

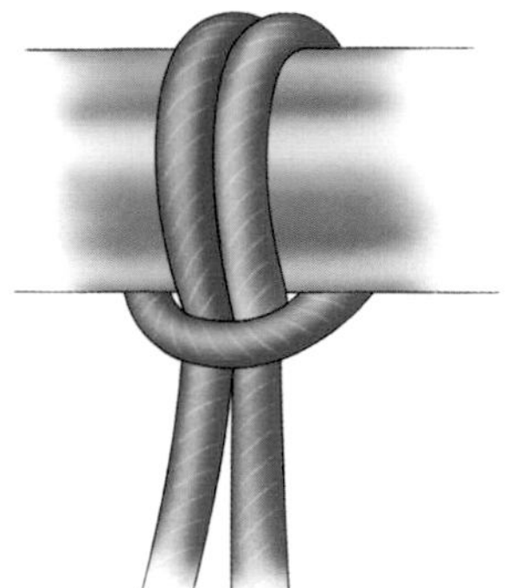

Lark's Head or Cow Hitch

We have already seen this when a square knot was spilled, but this time we want to make it. It is used to fasten things onto a line or through rings when it is not necessary to undo them in a hurry. Despite its name, it should not be used for tethering cows!

1 Make a bight and let the top of the loop fall forward to give two wings or ears.

2 Slip the pole through the ears and pull taut. Alternatively, pass a bight behind the pole and let it drop down in front. Feed both ends through the bight and tighten. You may also tie this by following the lead of the knot. Come up and over the pole, around, and cross in the front. Go up and over again, then back down through the front crossing.

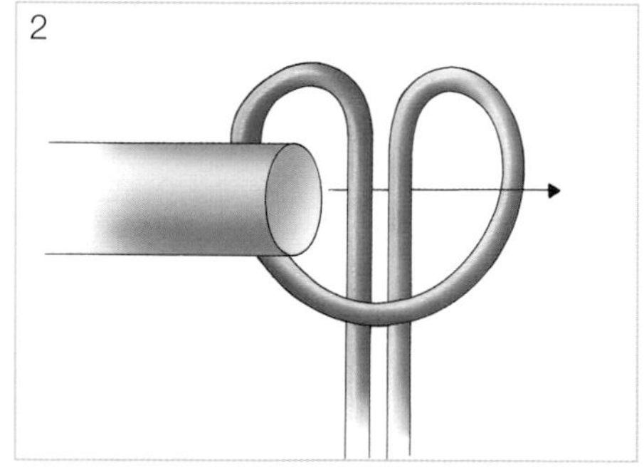

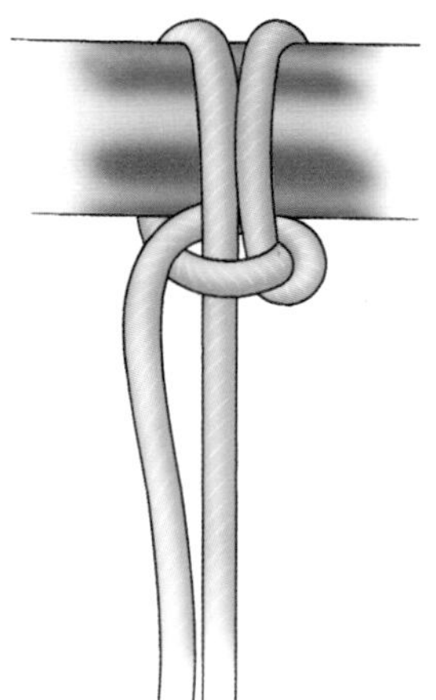

Pedigree Cow Hitch

If, after forming the knot, you take one end and pass it through the gap between the pole and the cords, you will have produced the pedigree cow hitch. This is slightly more secure if there is a load on the other end of the rope, but can take longer to undo. The name was given in fun, but it stuck. The illustrations below are self-explanatory.

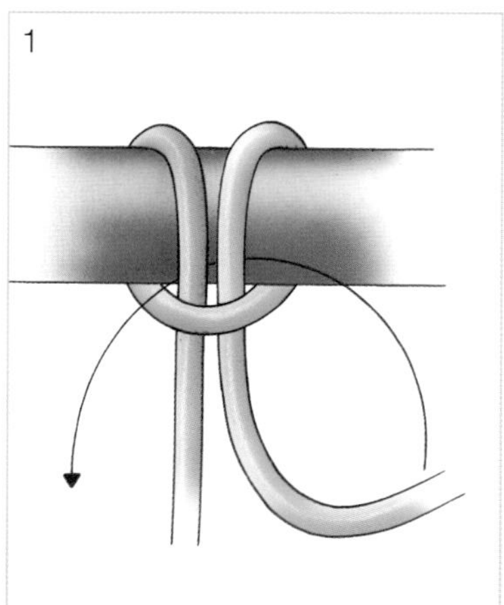

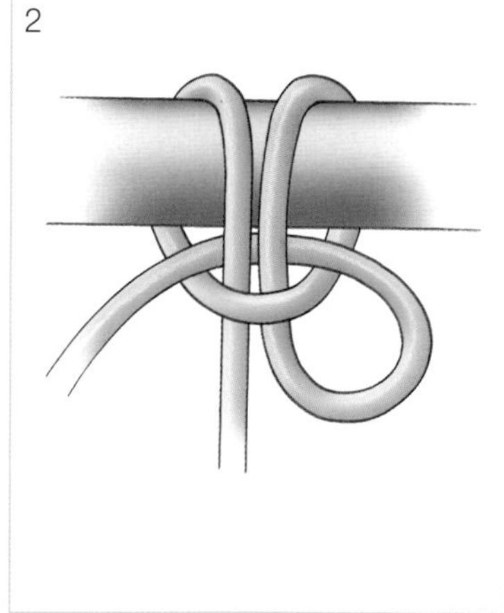

Midshipman's Hitch

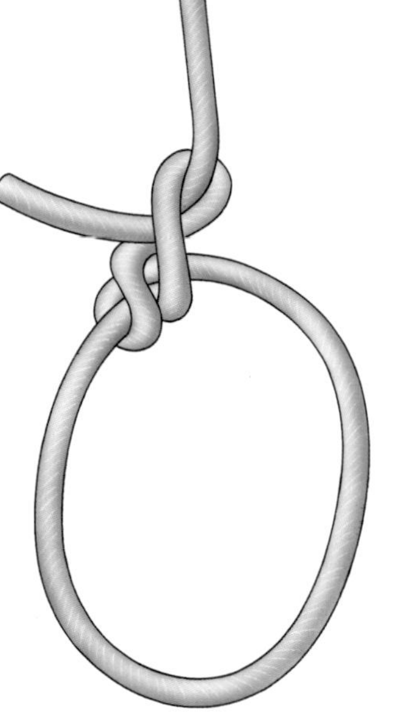

This knot is useful for guylines, as it can be adjusted by sliding into position, and will lock when a load is applied to it.

1 Make an overhand crossing loop and bring the end up into the loop.

2 & 3 Wrap the end around the rope, again coming up into the loop, trapping the first turn. Take the end out of the loop and form a half hitch above the loop. Work tight.

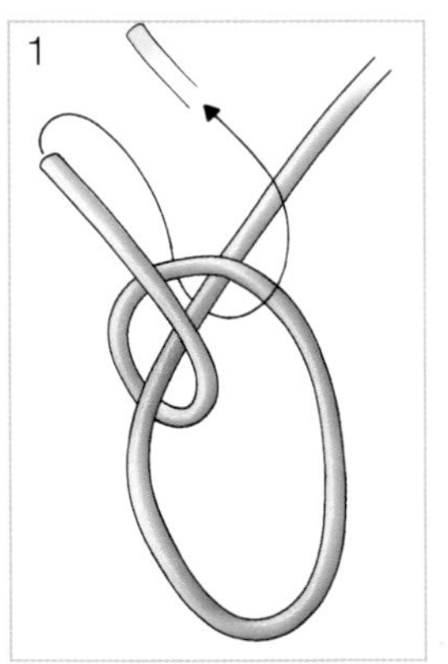

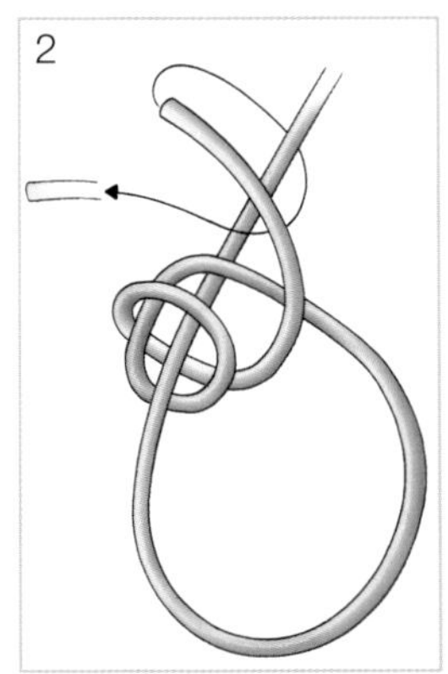

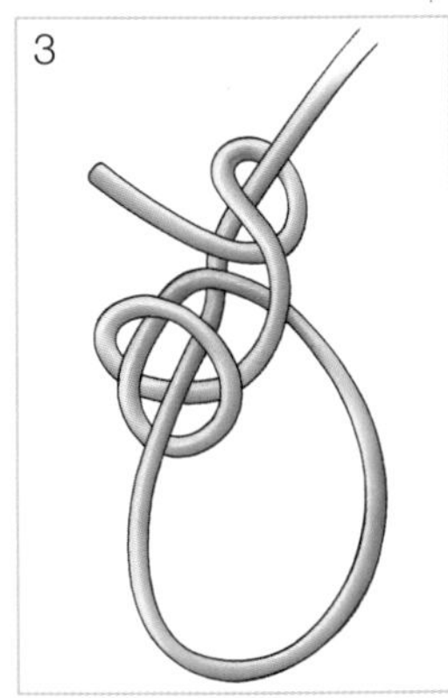

Miller's Bag Knot

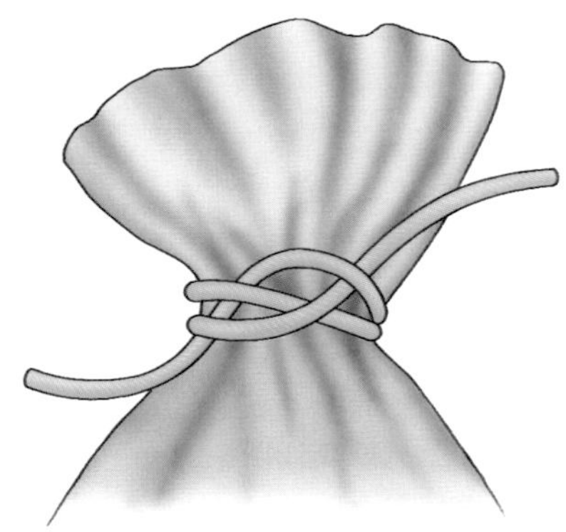

As the name suggests, millers used this knot to tie the necks of sacks of flour. It is quick to tie but does not grip as securely as the constrictor or boa. You can experiment with all of these knots and decide which one best suits your purpose on different occasions. It is very close to, but not quite the same as, the transom knot.

1 Take a turn around the neck of the sack, but do not pull tight.

2 Slide your hand, with forefinger outstretched, under the first turn and pass another turn below the first. Use the finger to hook the end up and out between the turns, over the second but under the first, and pull tight.

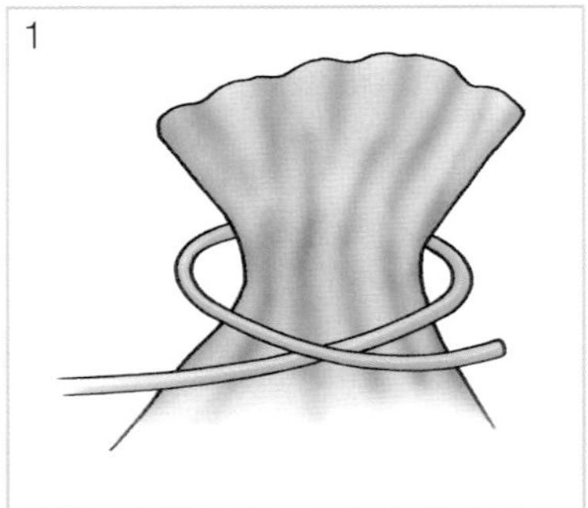

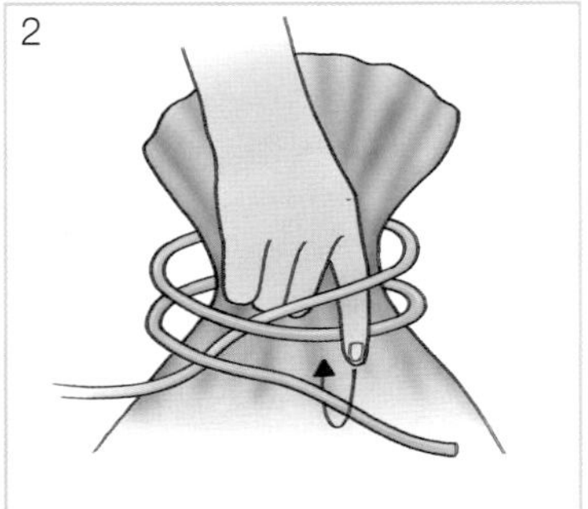

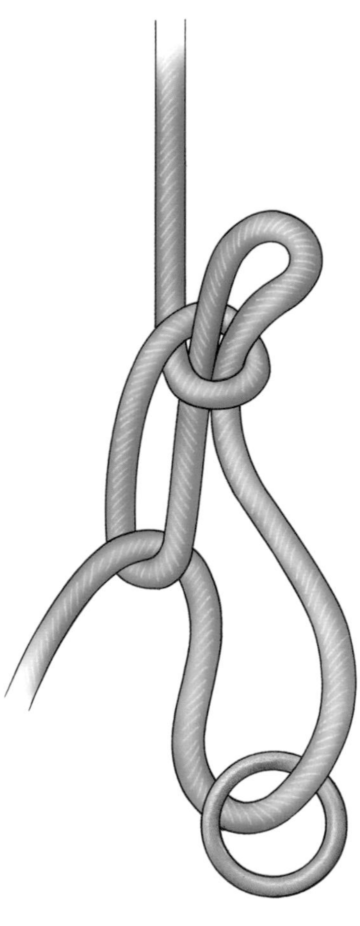

Waggoner's or Trucker's Dolly Knot

For centuries, loads have been tied down securely on the backs of wagons using knots. As its name suggests, this knot has been a favorite through the ages as it is quite secure, gives a mechanical advantage of two to one, and when unhooked the rope may be coiled without wasting time undoing tangles.

This is what you use to hold a canoe firmly on the roof rack or trailer. It is not the easiest knot to learn, and regular practice is required to become proficient, but it only takes a few seconds and has innumerable uses. Time will be saved in tying if you have hooks at the edge of your trailer bed rather than the ring shown in the illustration, but either way it is easy to tie.

There are several variations and improvements, though only the basic knot is shown here to avoid confusion.

Secure one end of the rope at a front corner of the trailer or roof rack. (This could be by a couple of half hitches or by passing a spliced eye over the hook.) Throw the rest of the line over the load and run around after it. You will tie the first dolly on the side opposite the start of the line. Take hold of the line and pull to remove slack and to ensure that the end is secure.

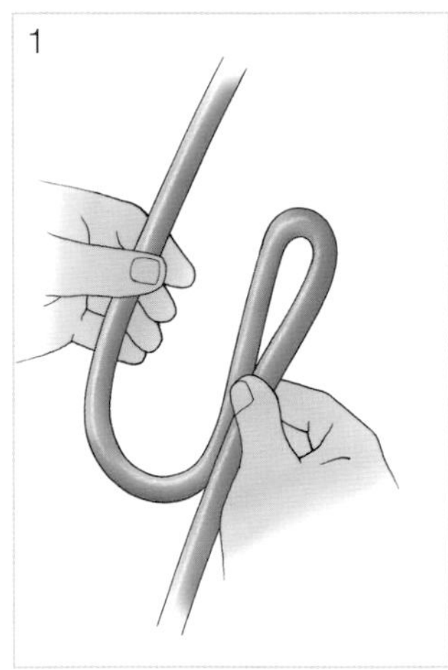

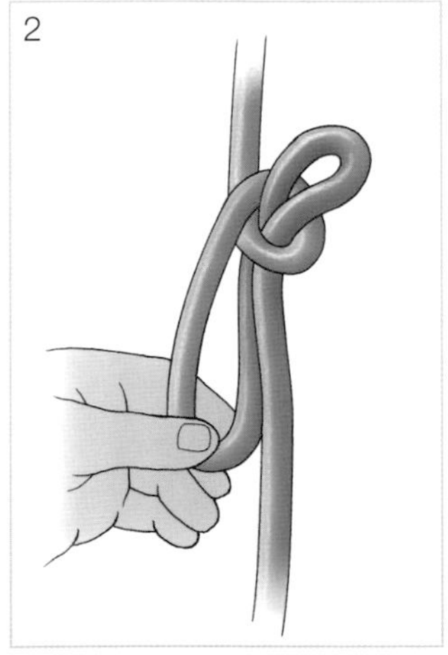

1 Holding the line with your left hand, take a bight in the right hand, bring it across the line above your left hand, and twist as for the bowline. This time you use your whole wrist rather than just your fingers, and a bight instead of the end. You are now at the stage of illustration 2, with a bight sticking up and a loop hanging down.

2 Make sure that the bight and loop are long enough and support the loop with the left hand. Reach through the loop with the right hand, grab the working part of the line, and pull a bight through the loop. This is passed over the hook at the edge of the load platform and the slack is pulled out by hauling on the working part. The slack slides around the hook and the base of the loop in the same way as in a tackle. When doing all this you must be careful not to spill the bowline twist part of the knot (your left hand will deal with this while the right passes the hook). If there are rings but no hooks, you will have to feed the complete length of the line through before hauling tight. Once the line is tight, a half hitch or two around the hook will hold it and the line is led to the next hook on this side. It is enough to pass the line around here in a half hitch before throwing the bulk of it back over the load and repeating the process on the other side. Continue until the load is secure, then make the line fast.

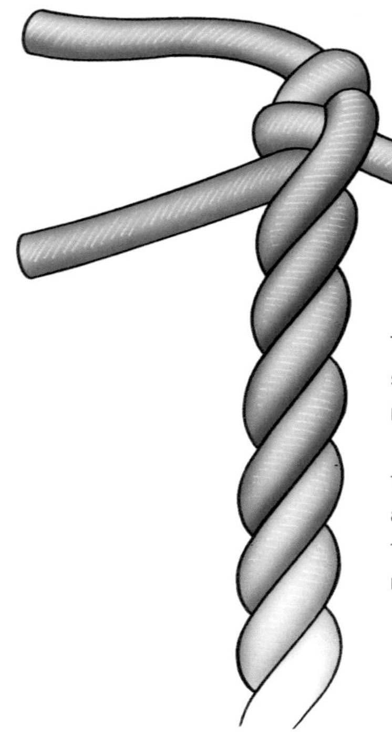

Crown Knot

This is hardly ever seen on its own, but it is shown here to demonstrate a principle before moving on to the back splice.

In addition, if you tie three (or more) cords together at their ends it is possible to produce an attractive sennit or braid by continually repeating the crown knot. In this application it is tied in laid rope as though you are starting the back splice.

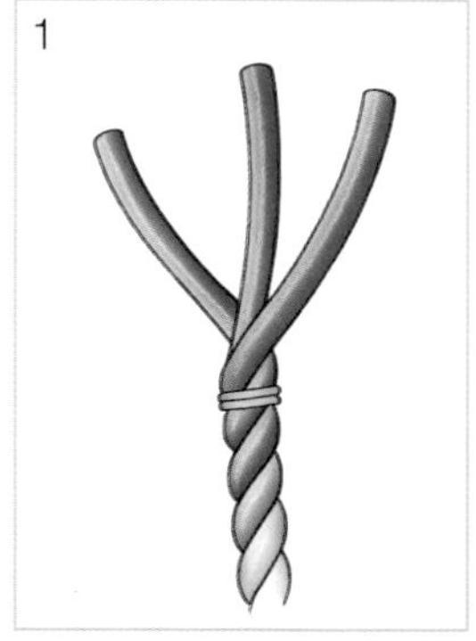

1 Place a constrictor knot on the rope a few inches from the end. Unravel the three strands down to the constrictor and put a whipping on their ends or just wrap a little masking tape around the ends. This keeps the strands from unraveling.

2 With the ends pointing up and separated, take one strand and fold it over between the other two strands. Allow it to stand up in a sort of loop.

3 Take the next strand and fold it over and to one side of this loop so that its end comes down between the other two strands. This strand can also stand up and if looked at from the side, vaguely resembles the outline of a crown.

4 The third strand is now folded over the second strand and through the sticking-up loop of the first strand. Carefully pull all the strands tight as far up as the constrictor. You should have each strand held down by another strand crossing it and they will point out and away from the main cord at 120 degrees to one another.

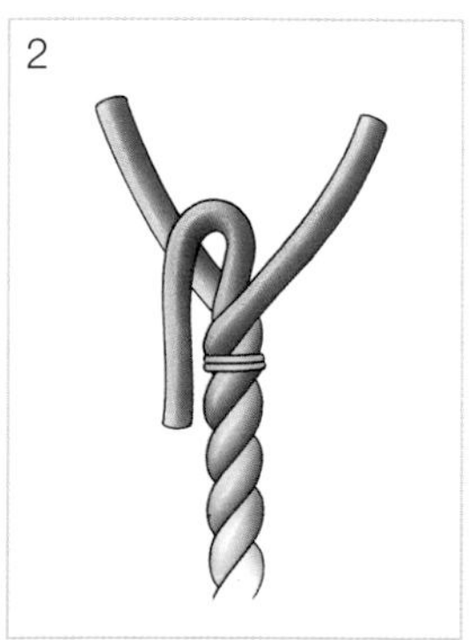

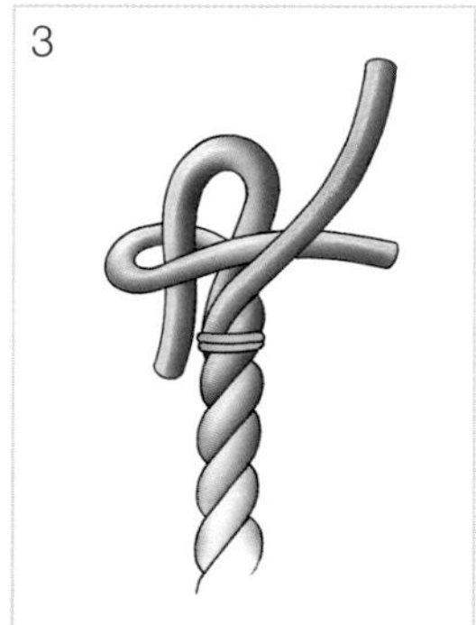

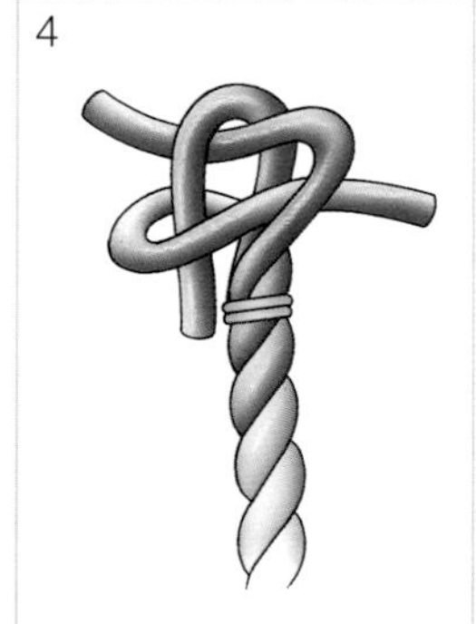

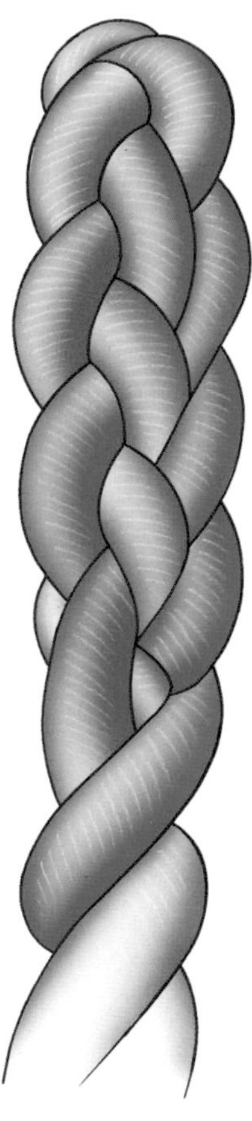

Back Splice

This splice is used to prevent the end of a rope from fraying. It gives a permanent thicker end to the rope, which may or may not be an advantage. It will not now pass through blocks or small holes so easily, but is more comfortable in the hand.

1 Put a constrictor at the point you wish the back splice to commence. Unravel to this point and make a crown knot, not forgetting to tape or whip the ends of the strands. It is not shown in the pictures, but I like to leave the constrictor in place until the first tucks have been made. I then cut it carefully with a scalpel and remove it before finishing the splice. The strands, A, B, and C, are sticking out across the main strands of the rope. Take one strand and ease up the main strand across which it lies. A Swedish fid is useful here.

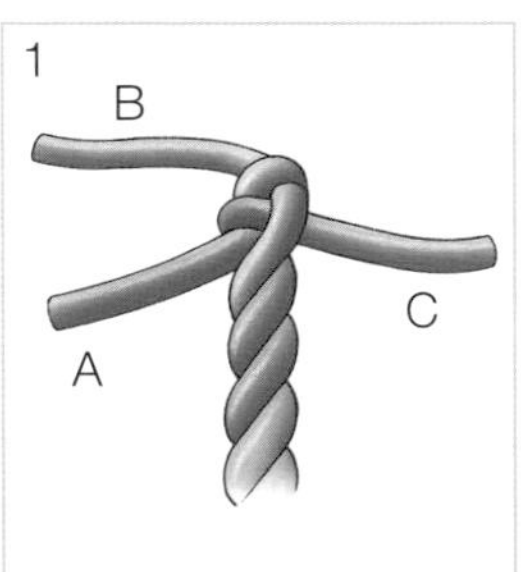

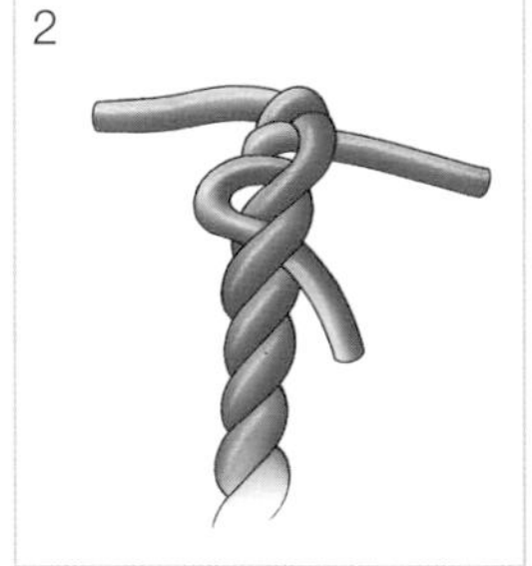

2 Pass the end of the back splice, strand A, through the gap and under the main strand, as in picture 2.

3 Turn the rope 120 degrees and repeat the process with the next back splice, strand B. Repeat for the third strand.

4 Continue to raise a strand and pass the ends through the gaps. Work systematically and go from one strand to the next in order. Do not try to tuck one strand all the way before tucking the next, as you will ruin the splice. Each time you tuck, pull the strand firmly so that there is no slack to confuse you.

5 When you have completed about five tucks for each strand, the splice is complete. Cut the ends off but leave them raised a little above of the surface. Place the splice on the floor and roll it with your foot. This crude technique is the quickest and most effective way to tidy up the strands in a splice.

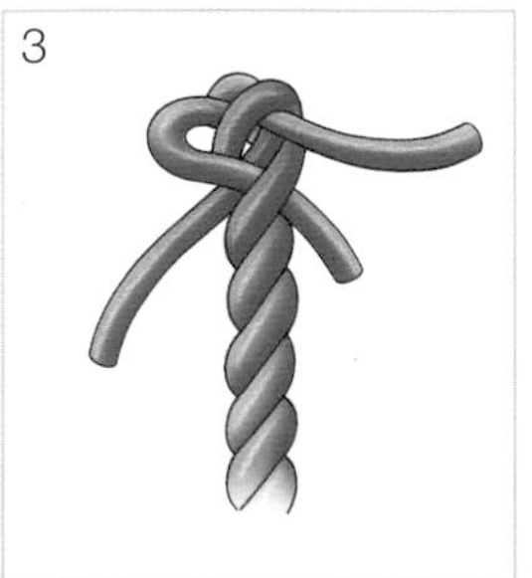
3

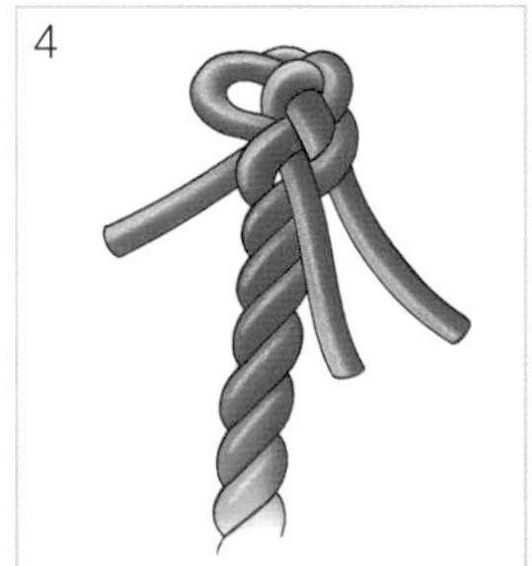
4

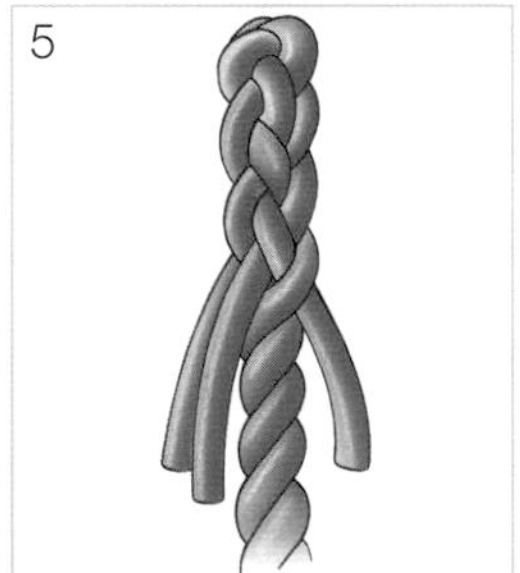
5

Eye Splice

This is a method for forming a strong permanent eye at the end of a rope.

This will be a "soft" eye. If a protective thimble were inserted into the eye, which takes a little practice, it would be a "hard" eye.

1 Prepare the rope. Put on a constrictor some distance from the end of the rope. Separate the strands and tape or whip their ends. Decide how large the eye will be and put a second constrictor at the point where the eye starts. Move the separated ends up to the starting constrictor. Let A and B sit on top of the rope while C goes to the rear.

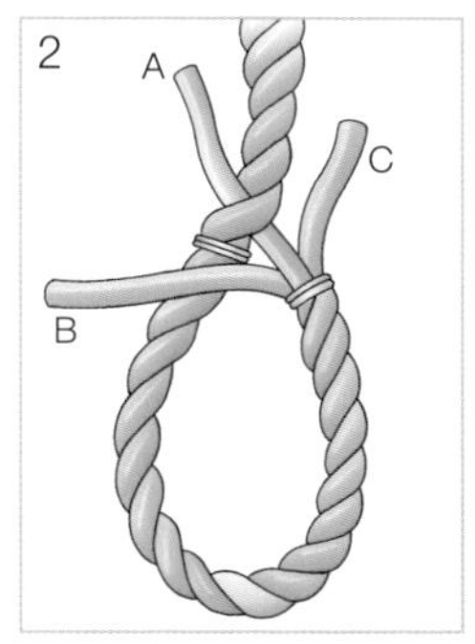

2 With a fid, raise the strand that is closest to A and pass A through the gap.

3 Take B and pass it through the gap formed by raising the next strand after that lifted for A. Now we have two strands coming out from under successive main rope strands.

4 Turn the eye over. Insert the fid at the point where B has emerged and raise the strand to its left. C is now led, apparently in the wrong direction, under this strand. We now have a strand from the end (A, B, C) going under and emerging from each of the gaps between strands on the main body of the rope. Now carry on as for the back splice. Bring the strands over and under the main strands in sequence (A, B, C) until there are five complete tucks (for synthetic rope), although it is considered that three is sufficient when splicing natural fiber rope.

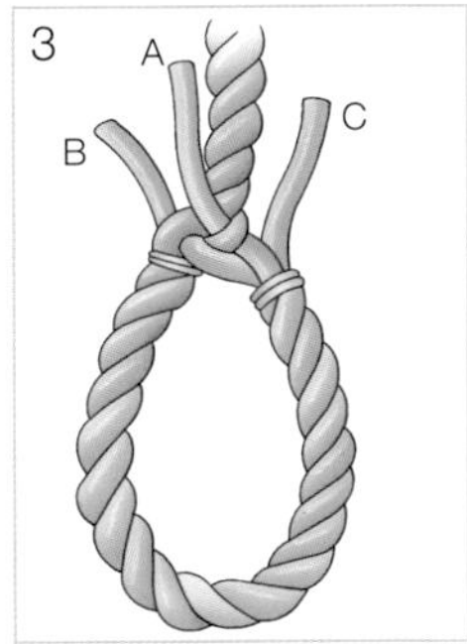

Finish off as for a back splice, but you may wish to taper the splice. To do this cut out about a third of the fibers in each strand and make another tuck. Do the same with what is left and make another tuck. Cut away half of the remainder, tuck again. After the next tuck, cut off any end and carefully roll underfoot. Your eye splice may twist and close up in use. To overcome this, give the rope between the constrictors a half twist, as though to unlay it, before commencing the tucks. You should now get a perfect flat eye splice.

Short Splice

Having mastered the previous splices, this technique for joining the ends of two ropes will present no problem. It does make a thick point on the rope, which will not pass easily through blocks, but otherwise is a strong join.

1 As before, prepare the two ends. Place a constrictor on each rope, unravel the strands, and tape or whip their ends. Offer the two ends up together by pushing the two forks close. Tie the strands of one to the body of the other to keep them out of the way. A constrictor will do this for you.

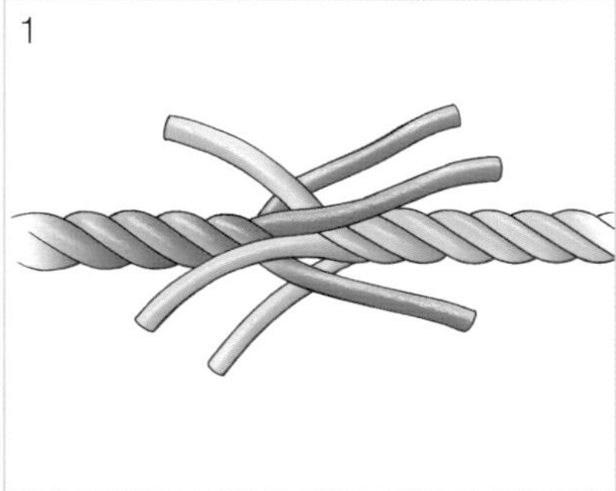

2 & 3 Starting with one strand, raise the strand of the other rope that it crosses and pass the end into the gap. Proceed to the next strand and do the same. The third strand is tucked in the same way. Continue to tuck the strands in sequence until you have completed five tucks.

To finish, turn the joint around or move to the other side of the rope. Remove the constrictor, being careful if you have to cut it. Then tuck the strands from the other rope in the same manner as for the first end. Finish off as before and roll the splice to firm it up.

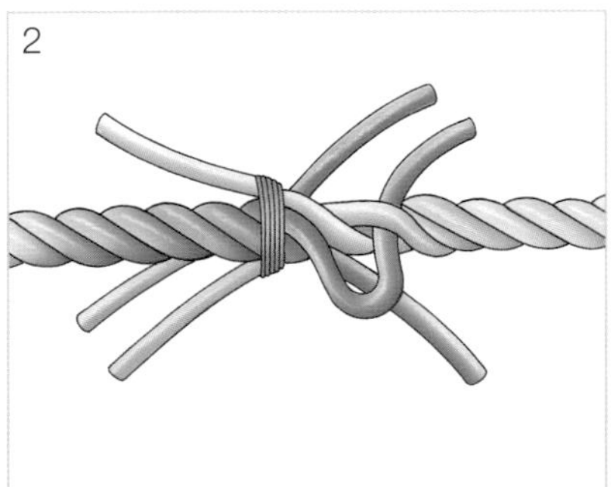

Square Lashing

The next few knots will enable you to successfully build almost any camp project that you may desire.

A certain mystique has developed about lashings, suggesting that they are more difficult than is really the case. In fact, as long as you approach them sensibly, they will not present a problem.

Square lashings are used to tie two poles together at rough right angles. As with all lashings, the cord used must be much thinner than the poles, and as much pressure as possible should be applied at each turn. A single square lashing does very little, so you will find that most projects require a whole series of them. Everything from ladders to scaffolding and bridges to ballistae can be made, and square lashing will be involved somewhere.

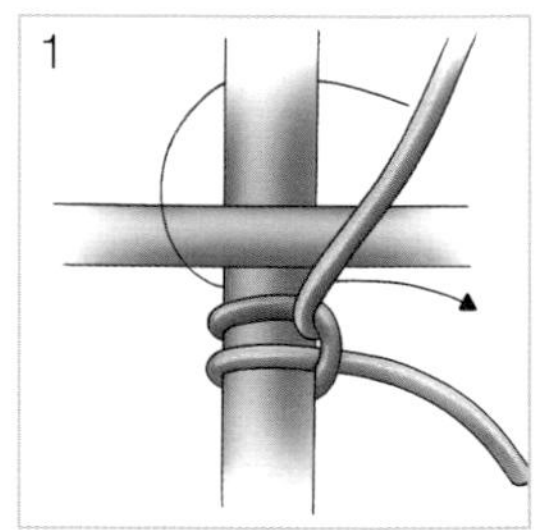

1 & 2 Form a clove hitch around the vertical spar. Pull it tight. Place the crossing spar in position just above the clove hitch and lead the rope up, over the spar, around the vertical pole, and back behind the horizontal spar. Pull tight again.

3 Repeat this until you have made at least three complete turns around both poles, pulling tight each time.

4 Now you start the frapping turns. These serve to pull everything even tighter together. Bring the rope up and over the turns just applied but go between the two poles. This compresses the first set of turns and locks everything rigid. Pull tight at every turn. Make three frapping turns. If you think you need more, then perhaps your first turns were not tight enough (it never hurts to start again if you are not sure). When you have reached the last frapping turn, secure the end with a clove hitch around the horizontal spar. By forming it as two half hitches, you will be able to make it tight, pulling on each half hitch as it is formed.

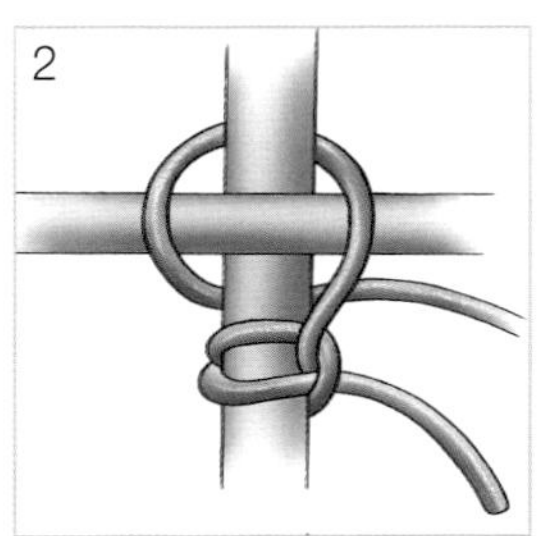

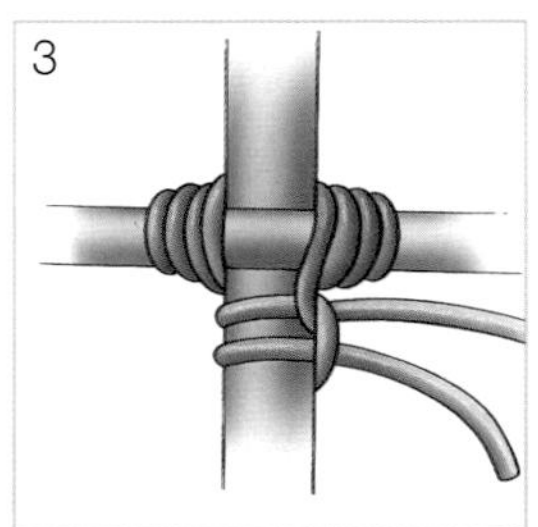

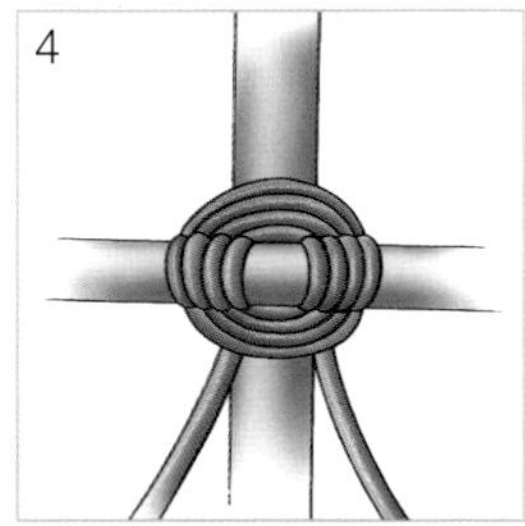

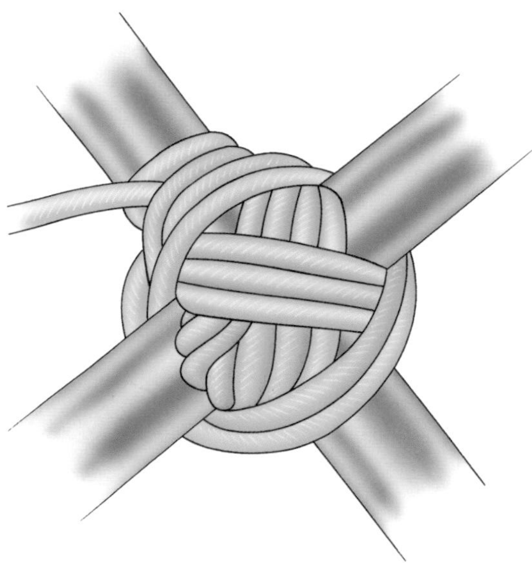

Diagonal Lashing

As the name suggests, this lashing secures poles or spars that cross diagonally. The poles may wish to spring apart, but tied correctly this knot will hold them securely in place. Pull tight every time and make sure it is safe before using it.

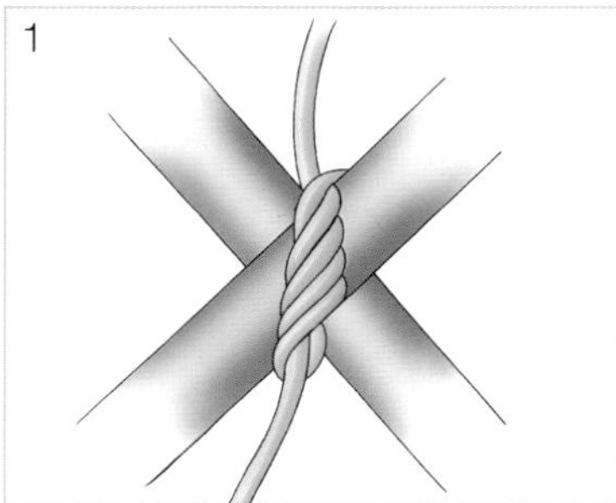

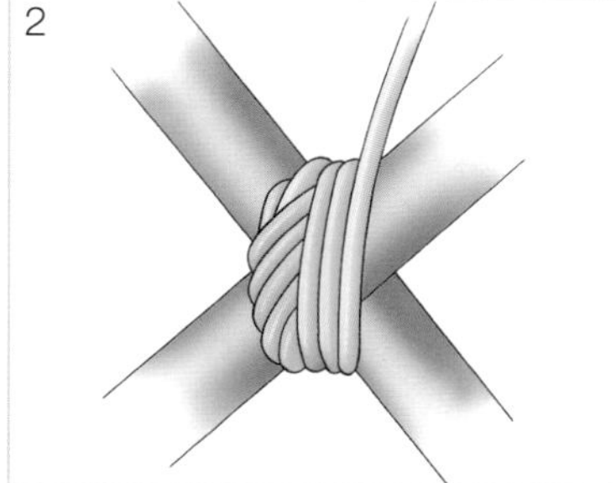

1 The spars will often already be in place as you start this knot, as a project is seldom started with a diagonal. Make a timber hitch around both spars and pull tight.

2 Take several turns, three or four, in a vertical direction around both spars, pulling tight each time.

3 Now take turns in a horizontal direction; three or four should be enough, and again pulling tight. The frapping turns are added next: Three or four turns that cross all the previous turns without going around the spars, but between them. Finish off with a clove hitch formed from two half hitches, as before.

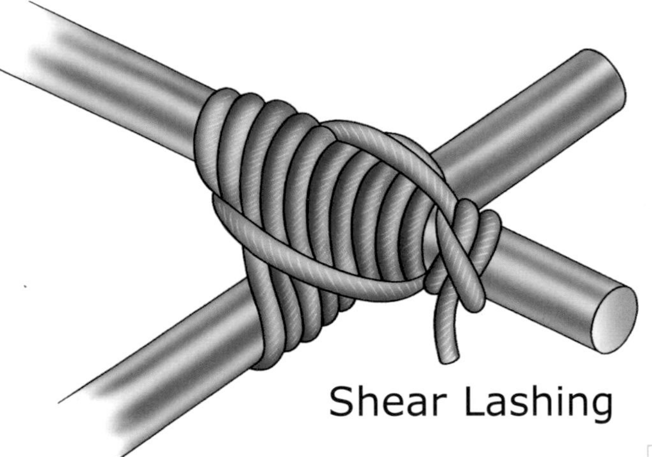

Shear Lashing

The name of this knot refers to shears or shear legs, which are used to raise heavy weights. Sometimes known as an A-frame, they are used all over the world when loads need to be lifted.

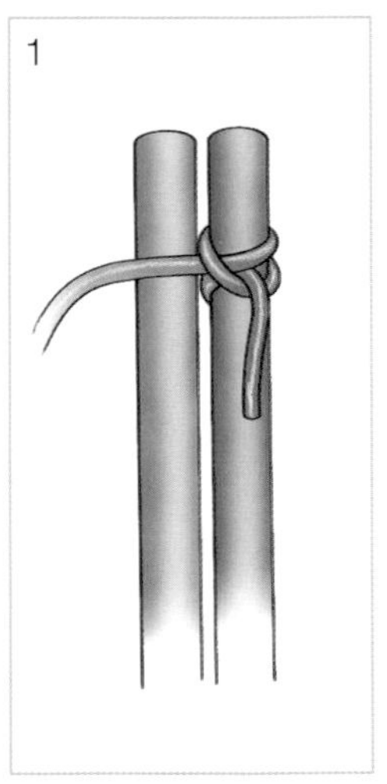

1 Place your two spars side by side, with a small gap between them. Supporting the ends on a brick or block makes it easier to pass the turns. Start with a clove hitch around one of them.

2 Take several turns, perhaps ten or twelve, around both poles, but, unlike with the other lashings, do not pull these tight.

3 From the last turn, bring the rope up in frapping turns, perhaps two or three; again, these need to be firm but not very tight. The feet of the shears are then drawn apart prior to raising the legs, and this action tightens the lashing. Usually a light spar is lashed across the base of the legs to keep them from opening too wide or closing up.

4 Shear lashings may also be used to join two poles to form a longer one. There are differing views on how to apply the lashing. One school of thought requires the poles to be very close together and does not use frapping turns. Every turn is pulled as tight as possible, starting and finishing with a clove hitch. The other method also pulls the turns tight, but does allow for frapping turns, which are also pulled tight. In both cases the poles are overlapped and two lashings a little distance apart are needed, as one on its own would not be safe.

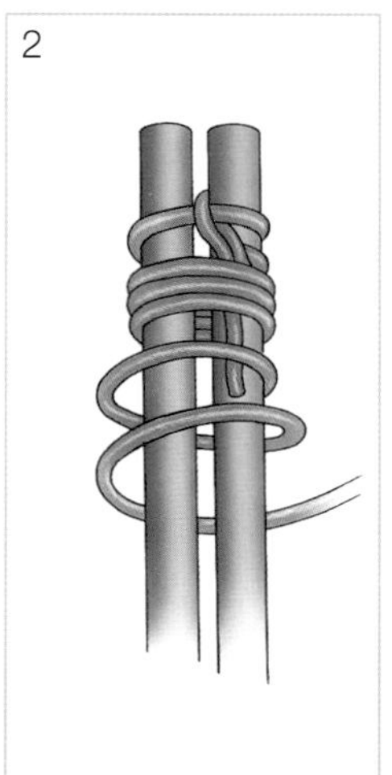

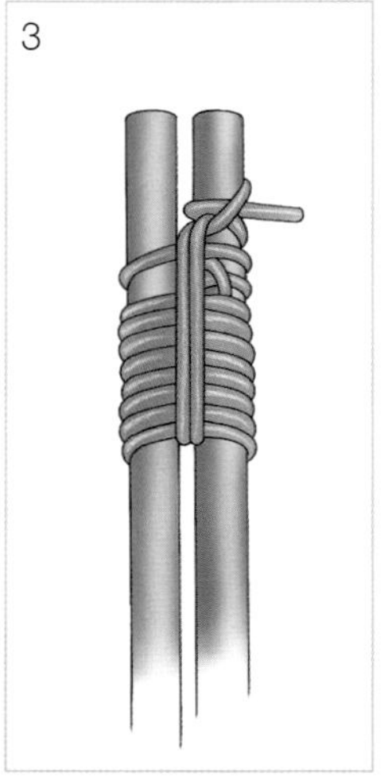

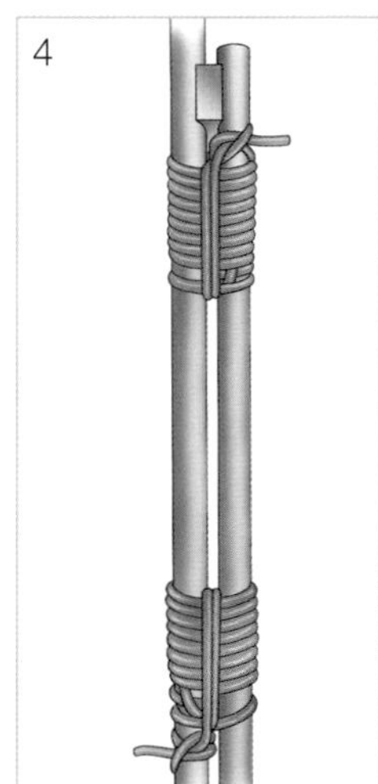

Climbing Knots

In addition to traditional rock climbing, these knots can be used for rappelling and industrial access techniques. Most people today use mechanical aids to make life simpler, but the final backup for the most sophisticated equipment is cord and knots.

In this section, more than in any of the others, thorough training and instruction in the techniques is essential before you put the theory into practice, as lives can often depend on the knots being tied and used correctly. No matter how proficient you become in tying them, always pay very close attention to what you are doing. The knots should be firmly implanted in your memory, together with the occasions for which each one is best suited, so that when you get vertical you will not fumble.

As with the other knots in this book, these have many other applications, and the only limit to their use is your imagination. I once saw the water knot tied in the silk cord of a monocle and have hung many pictures from an Alpine butterfly.

Keep your mind open but hold on tight.

Contents of Climbing Knots

Figure Eight with Two Loops	148
Figure Eight with Three Loops	150
Square Knot with Fisherman's Knot	151
Munter or Italian Hitch	152
Water Knot	154
Round Turn Bowline	156
Bowline with Yosemite Tie Off	157
French Bowline	158
Alpine Butterfly	160
Spanish Bowline	162
Prusik Knot (1)	164
Prusik Knot (2)	165
Prusik Handcuffs	166
Bachman Knot	167
Kreuzklem or Heddon Knot	168
Klemheist or Headon Knot	169
Mariner's Knot	170
French Prusik	171
Extended French Prusik	172
One-Handed Bowline	174
Tarbuck Knot	178

Figure Eight with Two Loops

When suspending a rope it is sensible to use more than one anchor point, but because of the anchor positions you may wish to connect two anchors separately onto a single rope. With this knot each anchor will have its own loop. It is also very secure and yet easy to undo, making it a very useful knot for climbers, though its applications are endless.

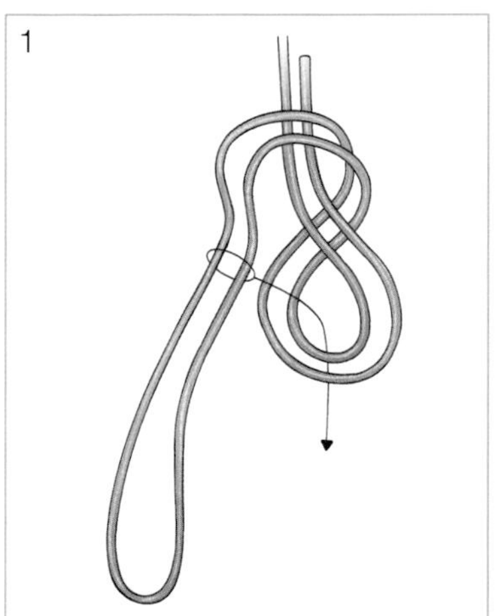

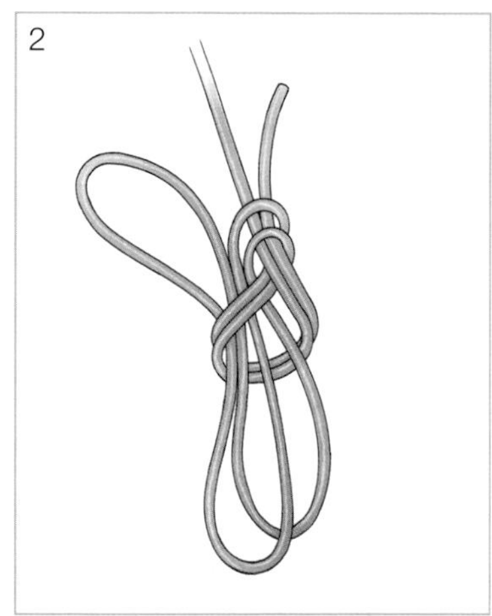

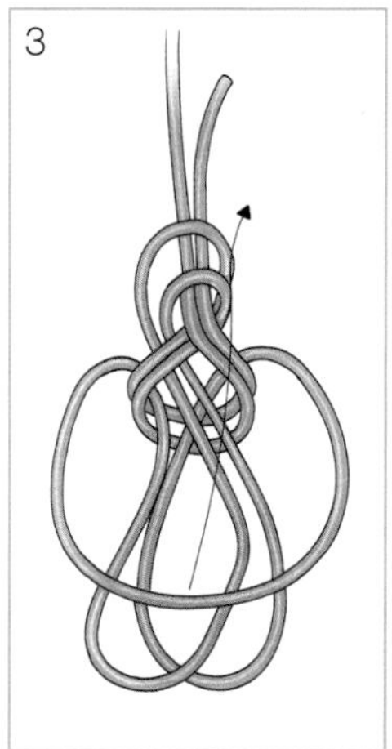

1 & 2 Double a suitable length of the rope and start to make a figure eight with the bight, but instead of passing all the doubled rope through the last loop, only pass a bight of the doubled rope. The knot will be like illustration 2, with one loop protruding from the top of the knot and two loops hanging down.

3 Allow the top loop to fall to the left (in this case) and come up around the hanging loops. You carried out a similar move when making a bowline on the bight. Lift this loop above the knot and then pull the hanging loops to tighten.

Figure Eight with Three Loops

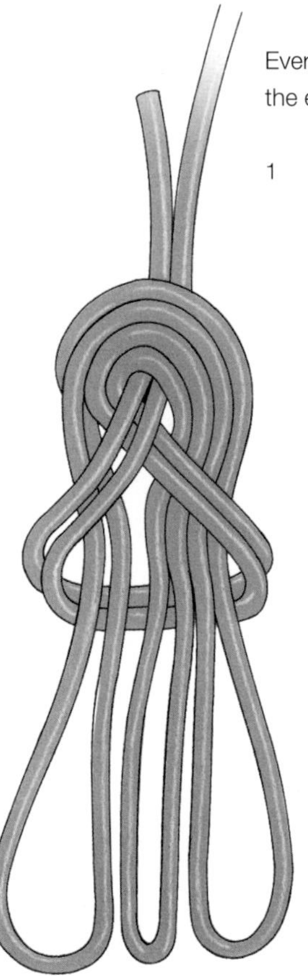

Every now and then, you might need three loops in the end of a rope and this is one way to tie them.

1 Proceed as for the previous knot but stop when the two bights are passed through the end loop. With the single loop continue to tie a conventional figure eight by bringing the bight in front of the standing part, leading it around behind the knot and up through the hole. Dress the knot tidily and pull tight.

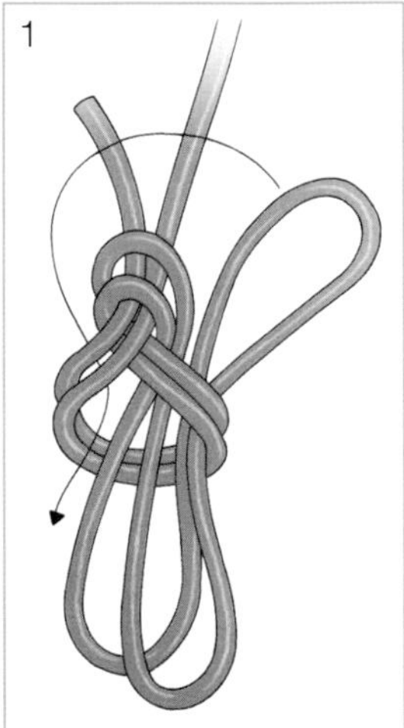

Square Knot with Fisherman's Knot

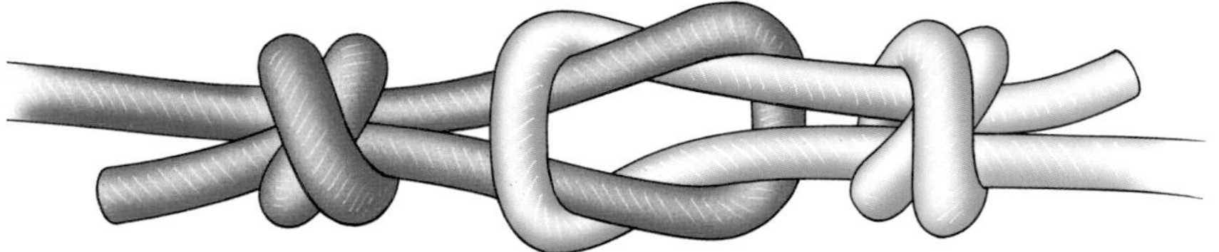

Earlier I told you not to join two ropes with a square knot if your life depended on it and recommended the fisherman's knot instead. However, if there has been a hefty load on the fisherman's knot, it may be hard to separate the coils, so if you anticipate a heavy load this variation might be useful. It is also known as the square fisherman's knot.

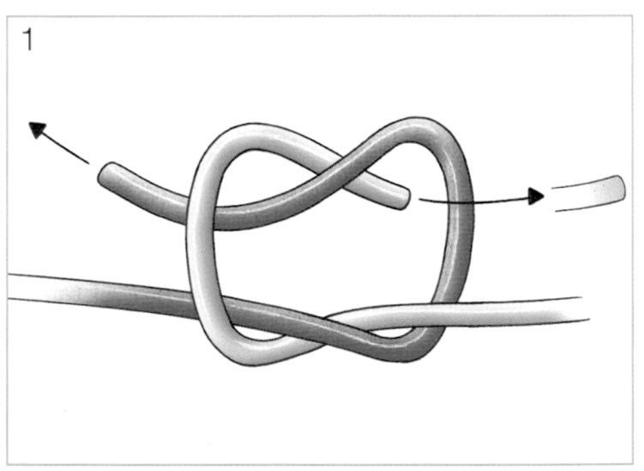

1 First tie a square knot as usual, then make the coils for the fisherman's knot on either side of it. Work the coils up to the reef and use as normal. The square knot will allow enough slack for the coils to be untied when unrigging.

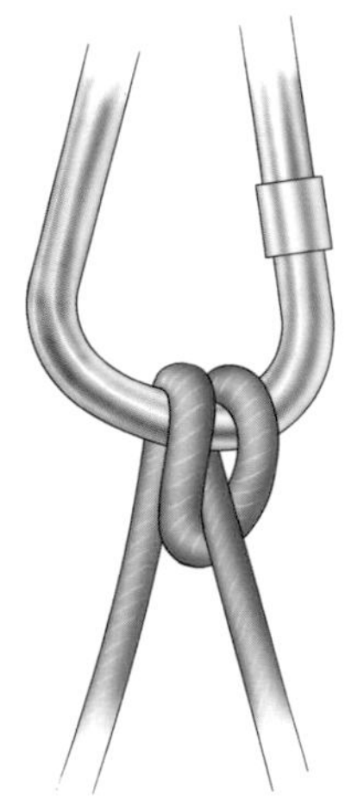

Munter or Italian Hitch

This friction hitch is used by belayers to absorb the energy of a fall and to lock up. It will reverse itself, allowing rope to be paid out when needed. It must always have an attendant, as it is no use without proper control of the rope passing through it. Two methods of tying the knot are shown here; you can choose which one best suits you and the circumstances.

Method One

1 Pass the rope through the screw gate of the carabiner, which should be attached to the anchor point.

2 & 3 Make an overhand loop in the rope and pass the carabiner through it, closing the gate and screwing it shut.

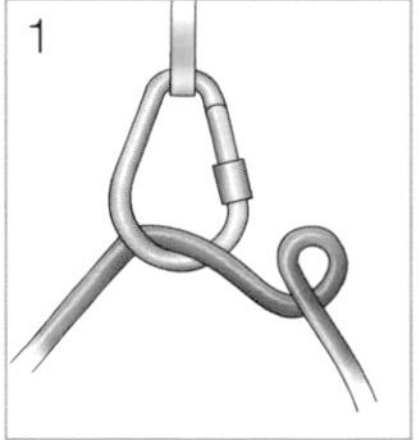

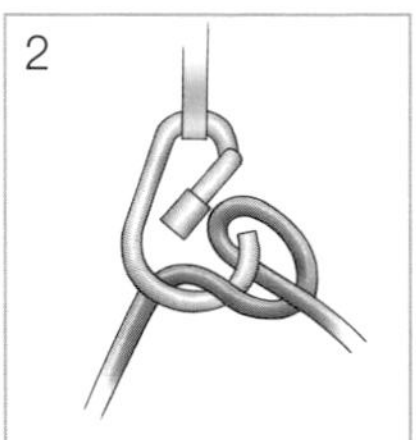

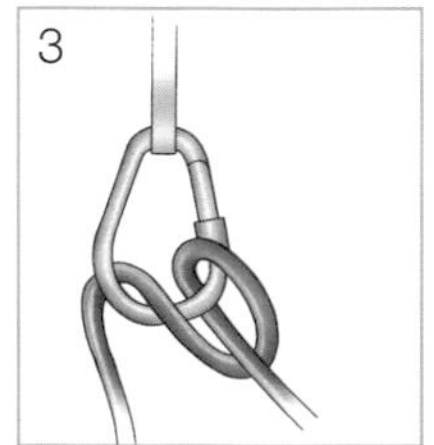

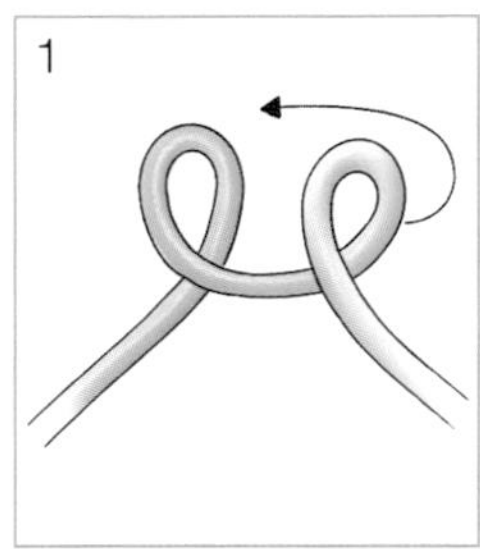

Method Two

1 & 2 Make two overhand loops and give the second loop another clockwise twist. Feed the carabiner through the two loops to form the hitch.

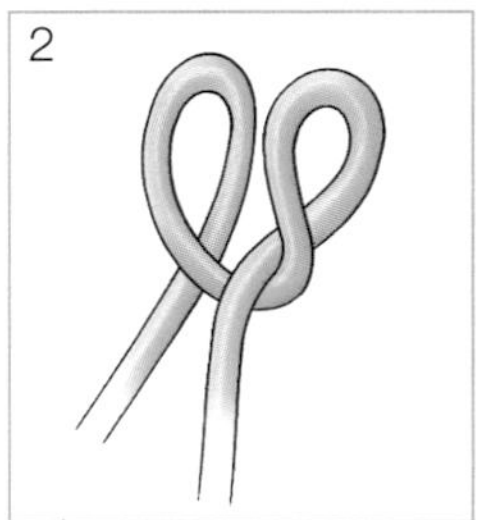

Sometimes a Munter hitch must be left with a load, such as during a rescue. A finishing variation is seen below.

1 & 2 Pass the control side loosely around the load line to form a loop. Form a bight in the standing end of the control side and pass this through to make a slipped thumb knot. Work this up toward the carabiner to lock the Munter hitch and if the bight is long enough, form a half hitch with the bight to lock it.

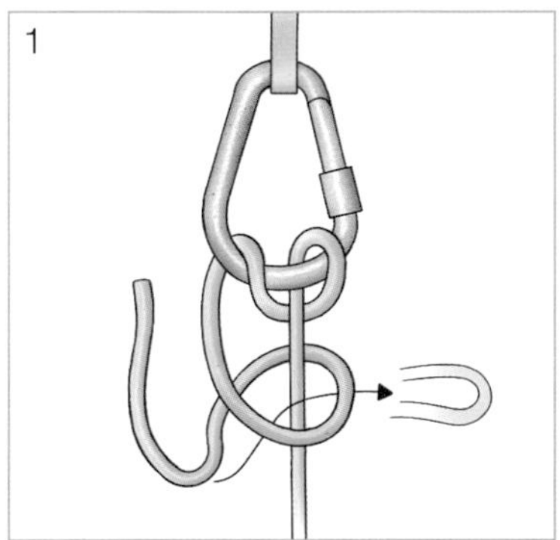

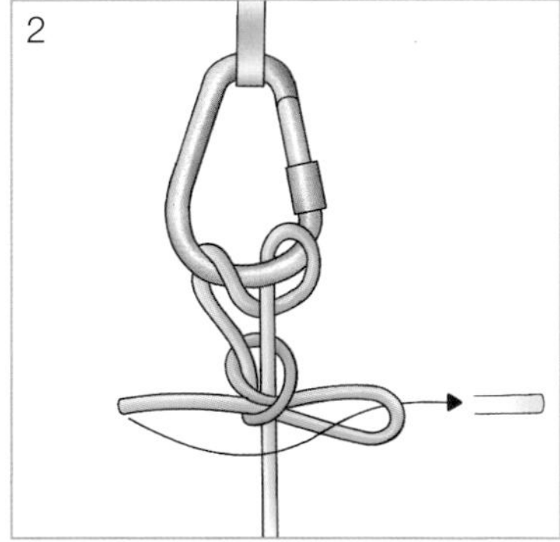

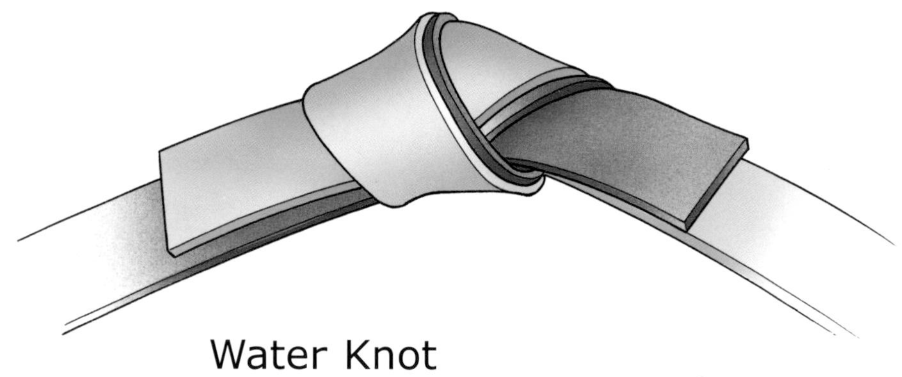

Water Knot

This knot is also known as the tape knot because it is used to join webbing tape to form slings, which are loops of webbing used by climbers to loop into a carabiner or to form "slip-and-grip" knots, and as an improvised harness. It is extremely strong, versatile, and flexible, and is essential for vertical travel. Sewn-joint commercial slings are excellent, but tied slings are just as effective, can be made the size you want, and are, of course, much less expensive.

This knot may also be used to join strips of ribbon or to mend belts.

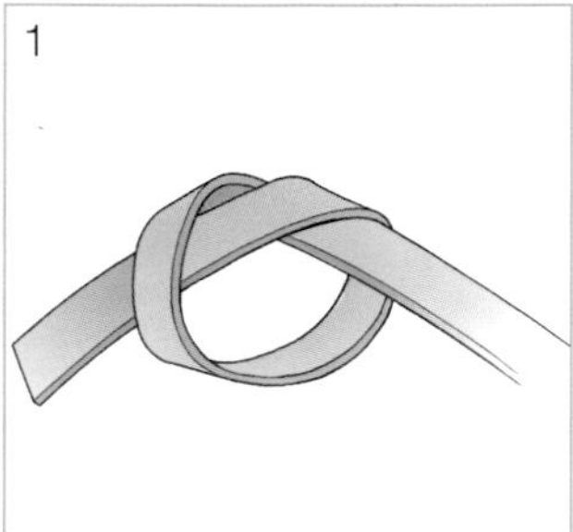

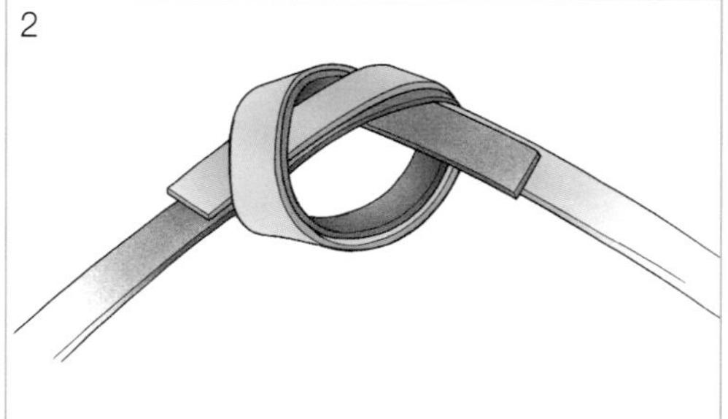

1 Make sure that your length of webbing tape is long enough for your sling with enough left to build the knot and the two tails. Form a thumb knot in one end of the tape, allowing at least six inches as a tail. Ensure that the tape lies flat throughout the knot.

2 Feed the other end of the tape into the knot from the outside working inward. You are making a second thumb knot, which lies directly on the first, but traveling in the opposite direction. Again ensure that you have a six-inch tail. Work the knot closed to give the size of sling you need and pull tight.

Secure the tails firmly to the main tape by means of heavy tape. This locks the ends and will give a visual indication should any dangerous creep occur in the knot during use. If a long tail is used it may be fed back from the "wrong" side to make a loop at the end of a length of webbing. Tape the end as before.

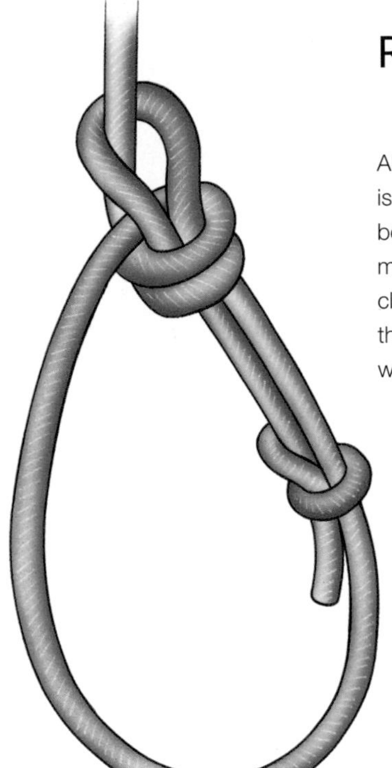

Round Turn Bowline

Also known as the double bowline, this knot is more secure than the single bowline, so its benefits for climbers are obvious. At first you might mistake it for the water bowline, but on closer examination, the difference is clear, though they both fulfill the same function. Use whichever one you find easiest to tie.

1 After taking the first twist to make the bowline, a second turn is made around the working end, which is then lead in the same way as the ordinary bowline.

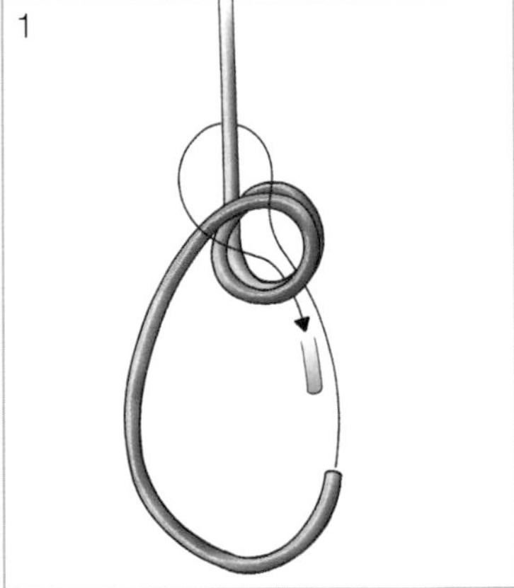

Bowline with Yosemite Tie Off

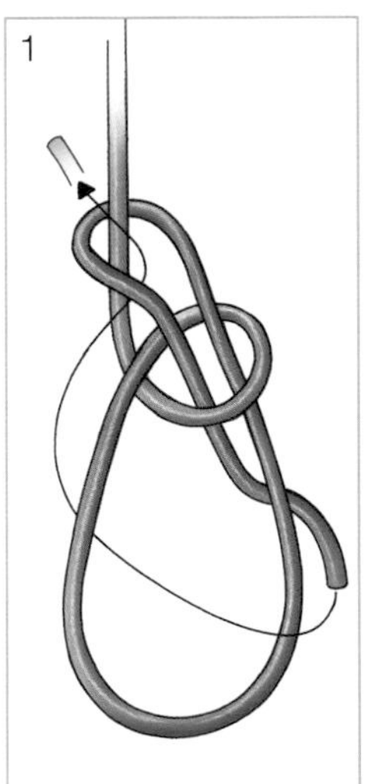

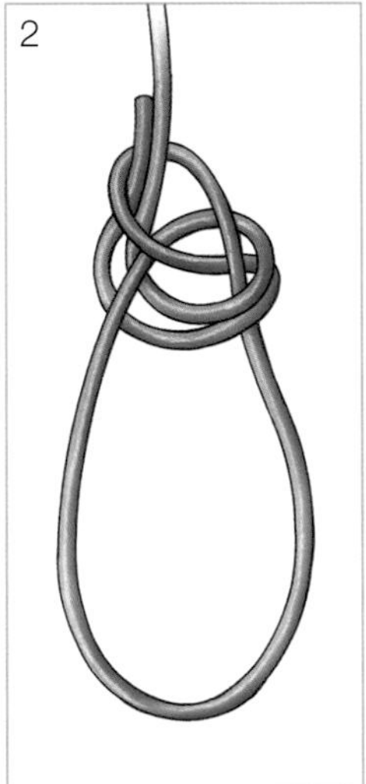

The main illustration on page 156 shows the tail tied in a thumb knot for security, but perhaps a more comfortable way to finish off this knot is the Yosemite tie off.

1, 2, & 3 For this you lead the tail of the rope around the outside of the knot, bring it back into the loop, and pass it up to emerge alongside the standing part. The first two illustrations show this on an ordinary bowline, while the third picture depicts it applied to the round turn bowline.

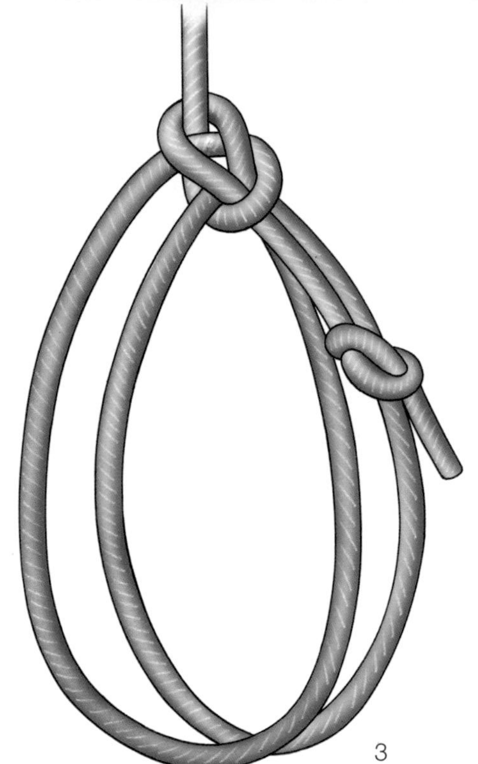

French Bowline

Also known as the Portuguese bowline, this will allow adjustment of the loops after tying. It may be used in a rescue; the victim sits in one loop while the other loop is adjusted around the body. However, it is not comfortable and it also helps if the victim can hold on.

The knot is a self-equalizing anchor and is used where the direction of pull may change, for example, when descending a cliff you may wish to change the point of departure to avoid an unexpected obstacle on your next descent. This knot will allow you to do this without having to rerig at the top of the cliff.

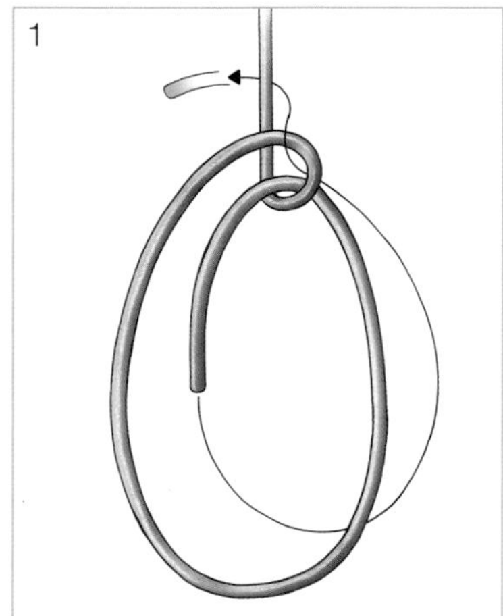

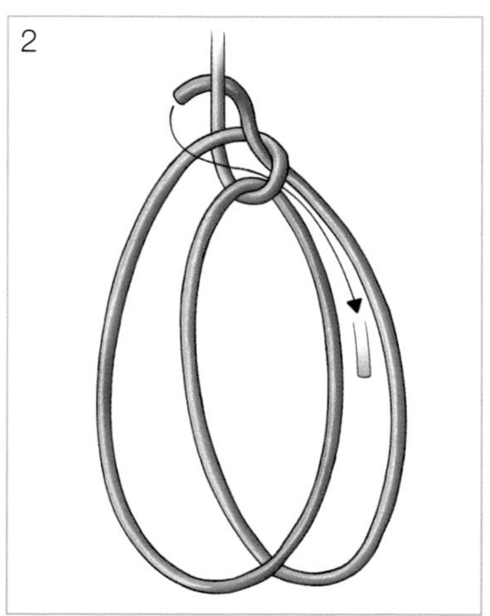

1 Make the twist as for an ordinary bowline with a long working part. Instead of going behind the standing part, bring the working part down to form a second loop.

2 The end is then brought up into the eye formed by the twist and is taken around like a normal bowline.

3 The third and final illustration (opposite) shows the end tied off with a thumb knot.

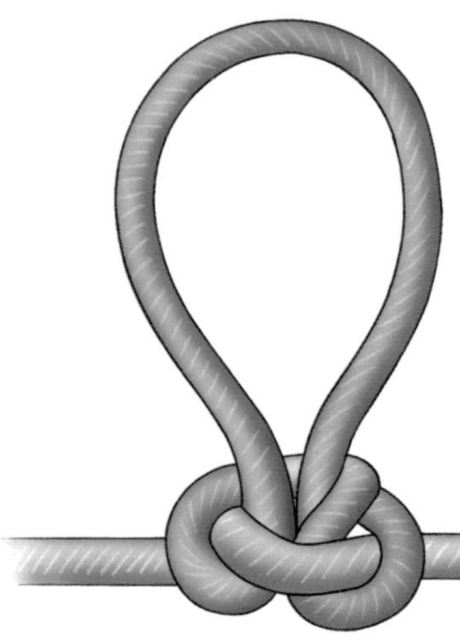

Alpine Butterfly

Tied in the middle of a cord or rope, this knot allows it to be attatched to a hook or carabiner. It will accept load on any of its three arms without failing and makes a good handle in a hauling rope. There are many other uses—time spent learning this knot will not be wasted.

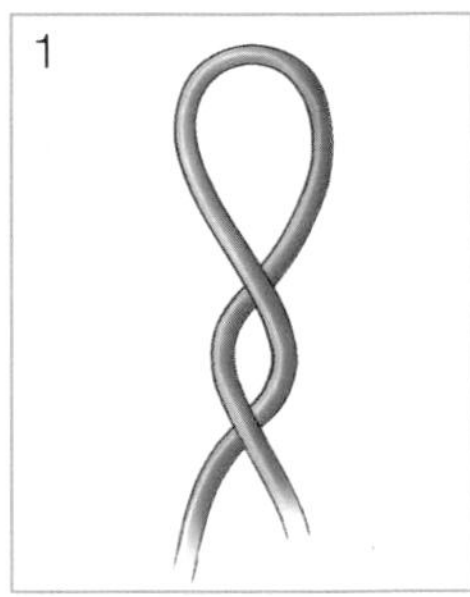

Method One

1 Hold the rope where you want the center of the loop and let it hang down. Turn your wrist clockwise twice to give two crossings in the rope.

2 Holding the rope at the top crossing, let the loop fall down behind the crossings. Bring it up in front of the lower crossing and through the gap between the crossings. Pull all three ends to tighten. The loop counts as one end.

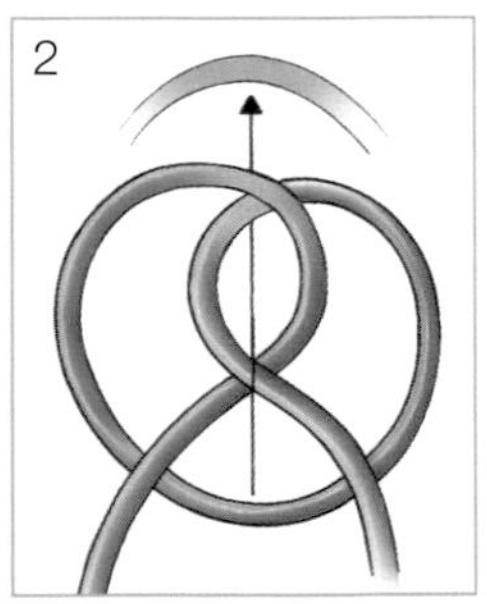

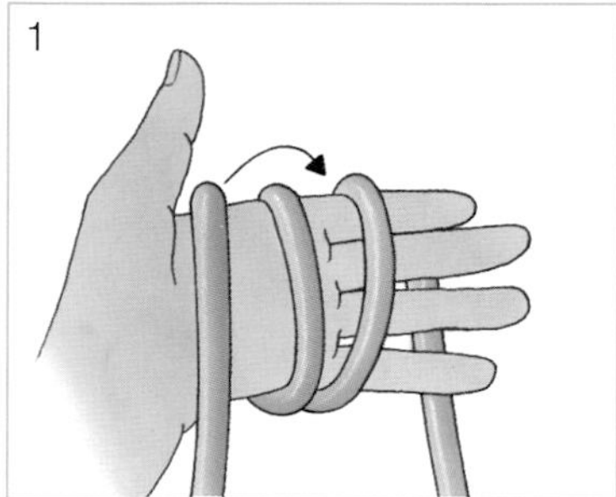

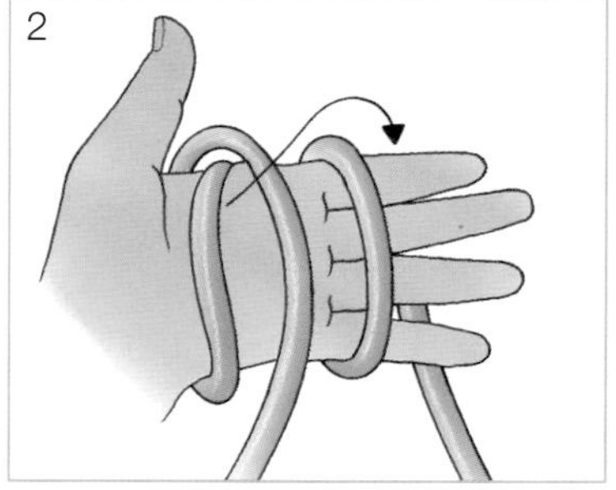

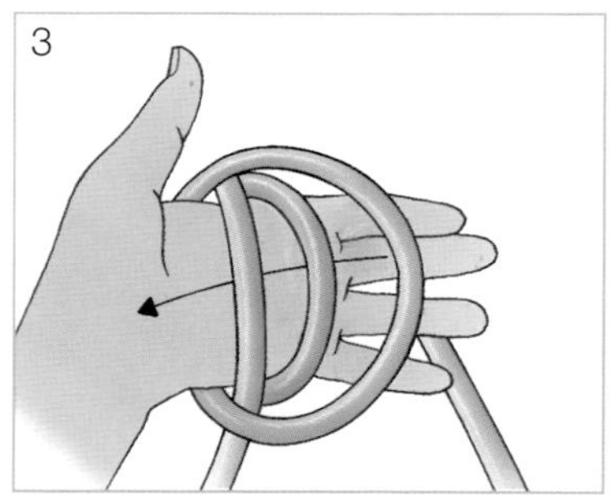

Method Two

1 Rest the rope over the open fingers of your left hand and wrap it around them twice. Lift the turn nearest your thumb over the middle coil to become the new middle coil.

2 Take the turn now nearest to your thumb and lift it over the other two coils. This is going to be the loop, so you can pull out as much line as you require for the finished loop.

3 Pass the loop under the two coils on your hand. Remove your hand and work the knot into shape. Pull tight.

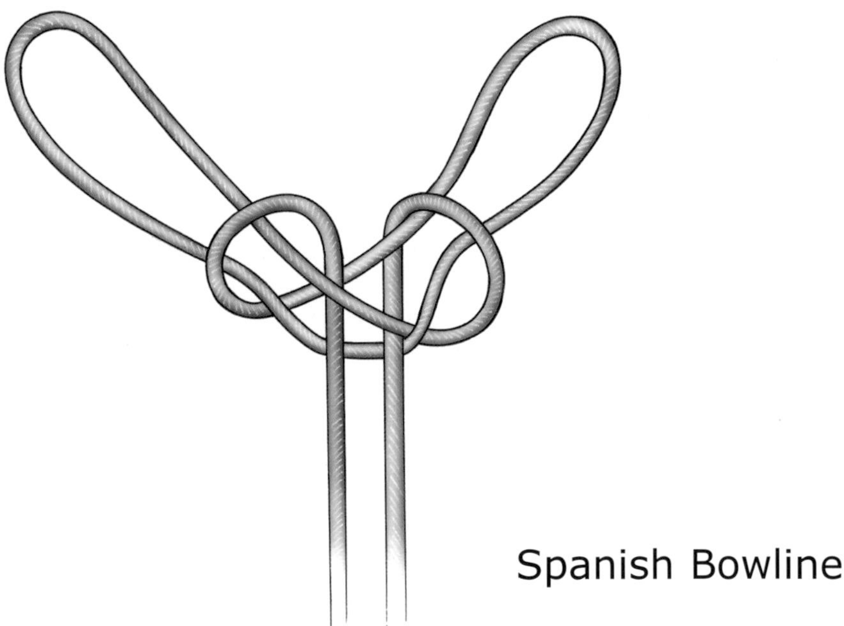

Spanish Bowline

It is claimed that this knot was once widely used for rescue work, the victim having a leg in each loop, with a further hitch around the chest. However, this would not be very comfortable.

A more useful application today is when slinging two poles or a ladder for use as a scaffolding. One pole can go through each loop and the position can be adjusted by moving the loops. It would, of course, need a Spanish bowline at each end of the ladder if the ladder were to be fully suspended.

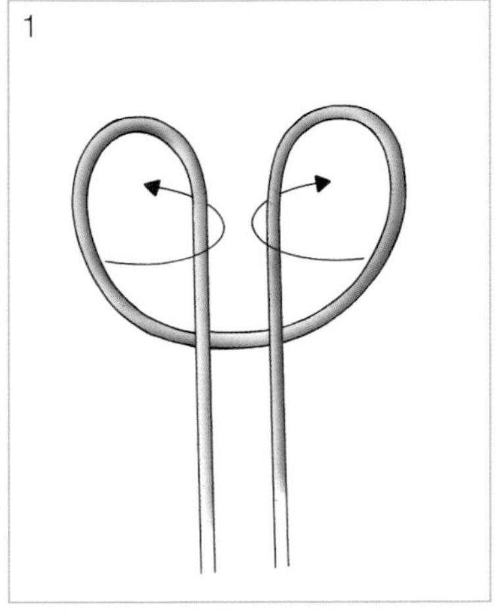

1 Middle the rope, or take a large bight, then allow the top of the bight to fall down and away from you. Holding the tops of the two bights just formed, give each a twist toward the center.

2 Pass the left loop through the right loop.

3 If the ropes are crossed, let them hang and they will move into the correct position. Bring the sides of the large loop up through the loops immediately above them. Work into shape and pull tight.

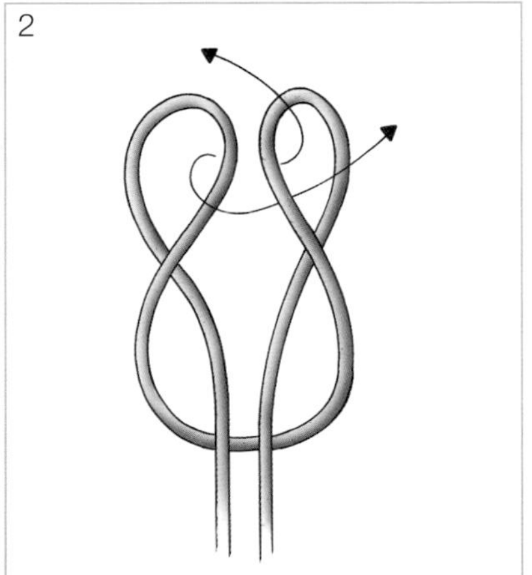

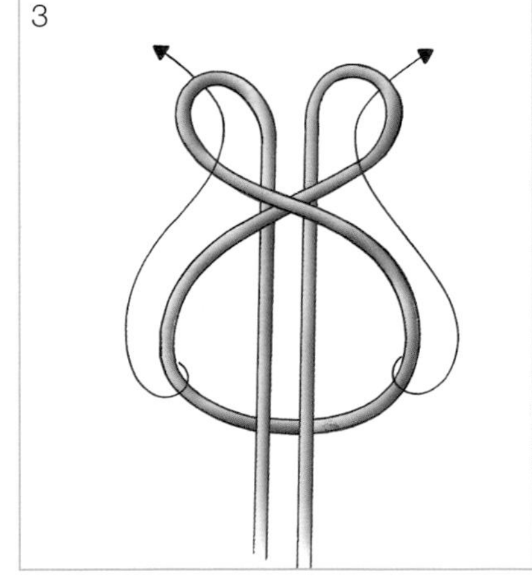

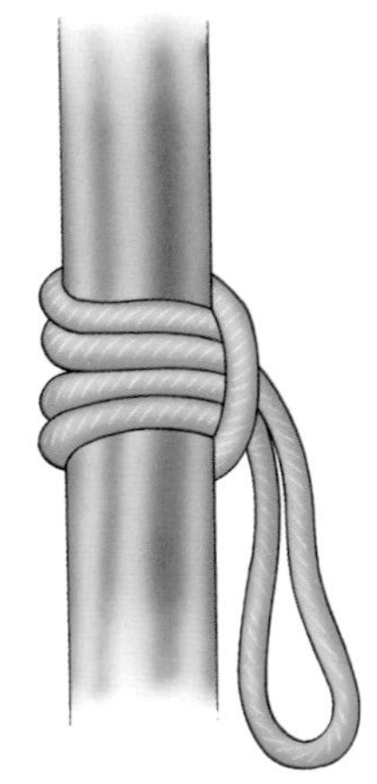

Prusik Knot (1)

Originally devised for the repair of broken violin strings, this knot has been adopted as a slip-and-grip knot for ascending or descending a rope in the absence of modern mechanical aids. James Bond, played by Roger Moore, tied it with his shoelaces to move along a rope in one film. All of the knots in the next section (except the mariner's knot) fulfill a vital function in protecting life when ascending or descending a vertical face, as they will lock when load is applied but slide when not under load.

It must be formed in cord that is much thinner than the rope around which it is tied, but the cord must be strong enough to support the climber safely. Usually tied with a loop of accessory cord, the illustrations show an endless loop.

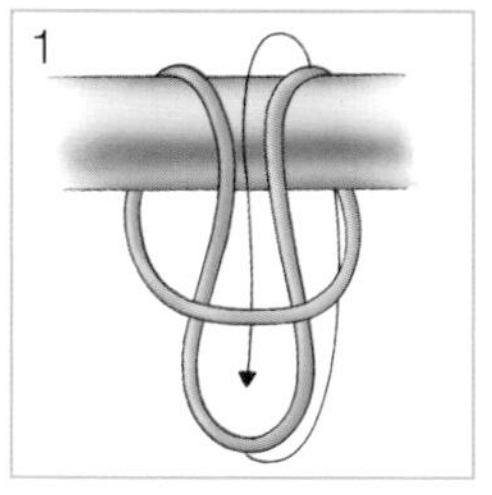

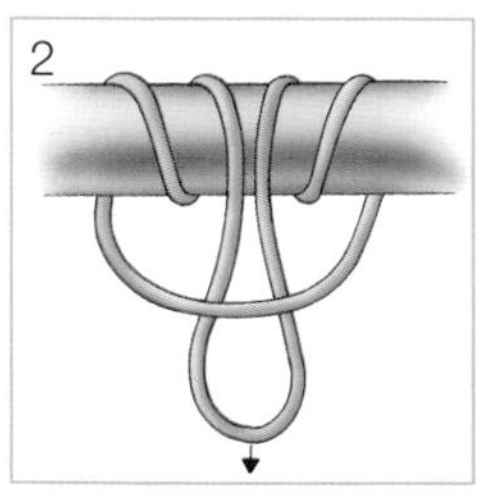

1 & 2 Place the loop across the main rope. Feed the front loop into the back loop and take the first loop up behind the rope and over the top again. Bring it down once more into the back loop and feed over the main rope.

With some rope, this will be sufficient, but usually at least three passes are needed. If not loaded, the knot can slide without difficulty along the rope, but when load is applied it will lock into place. It is possible to complete these moves with one hand, but care is required.

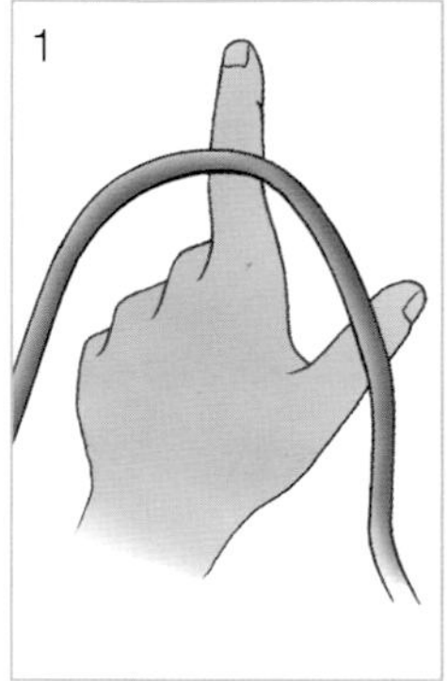

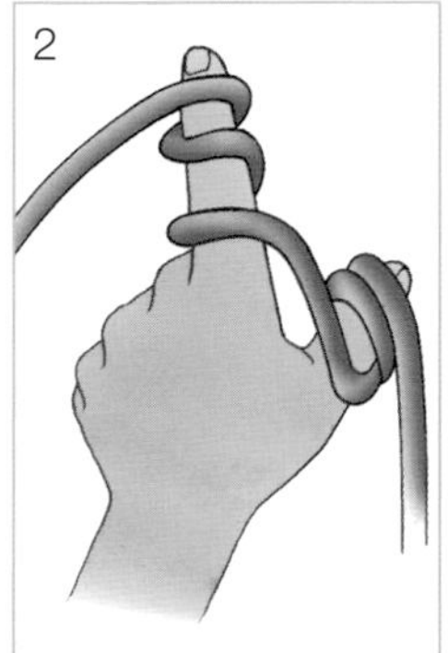

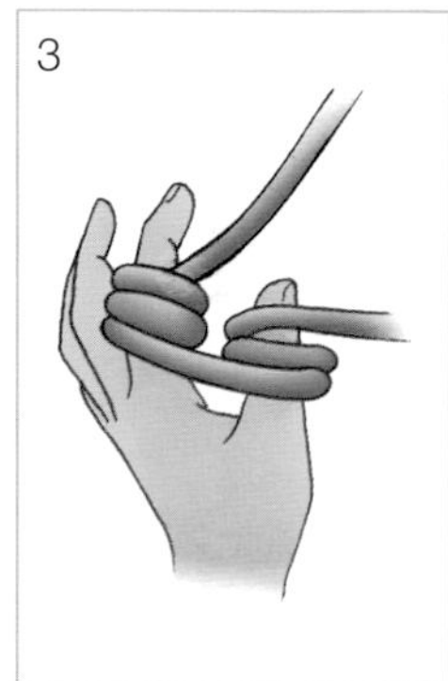

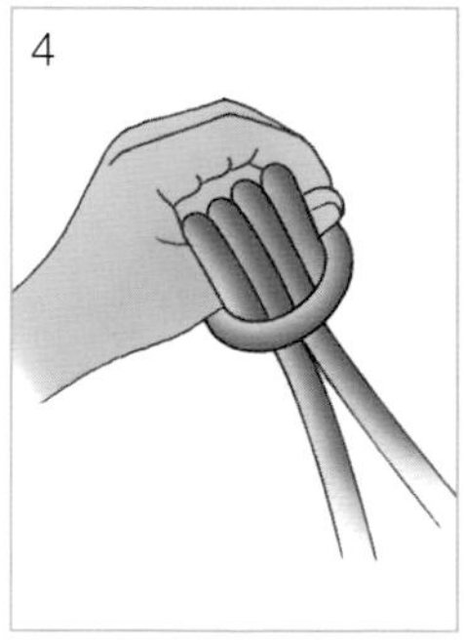

Prusik Knot (2)

1 Rest the cord over the back of the forefinger and thumb.

2 Take three turns around the forefinger and the same number of turns around the thumb.

3 & 4 Touch finger and thumb together and slide all the coils onto the thumb.

The knot is now formed and may be slid onto the end of the main rope for final positioning before use.

Prusik Handcuffs

Included here because of its close relation to the previous two knots, this knot can be tied with a thin, but strong, piece of cord or even improvised with a bootlace to form a pair of handcuffs. This is only a temporary measure and, should you be taking a prisoner in any games or exercises that you are taking part in, they should be guarded at all times if you wish to keep them.

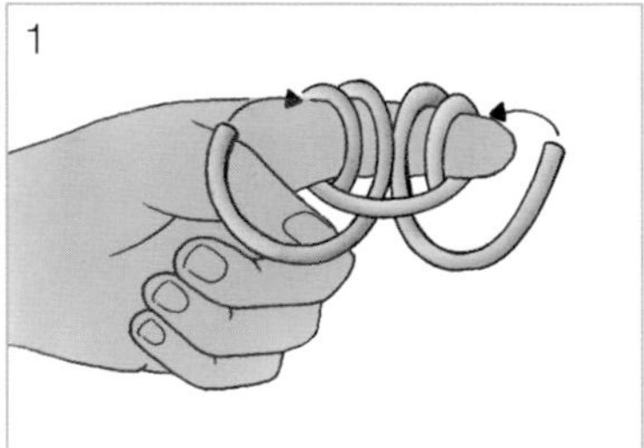

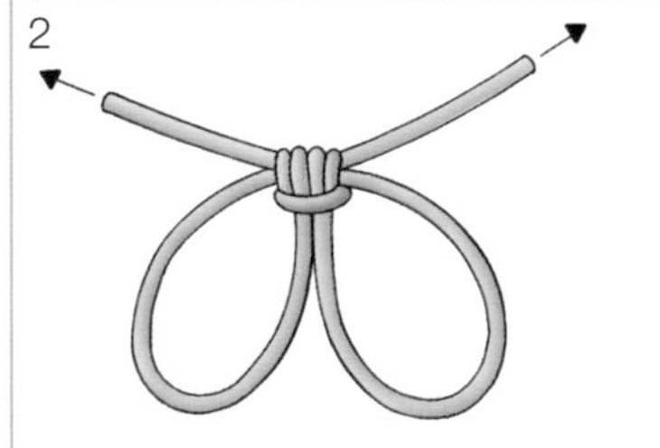

1 Tie the knot on the fingers using the same method as in Prusik knot 1, but with two ends of the line at the front rather than a loop.

2 The ends of the bootlace are passed along the finger from opposite sides. Slack must be worked out of the coils before they can be used, when the ends are knotted to secure the prisoner.

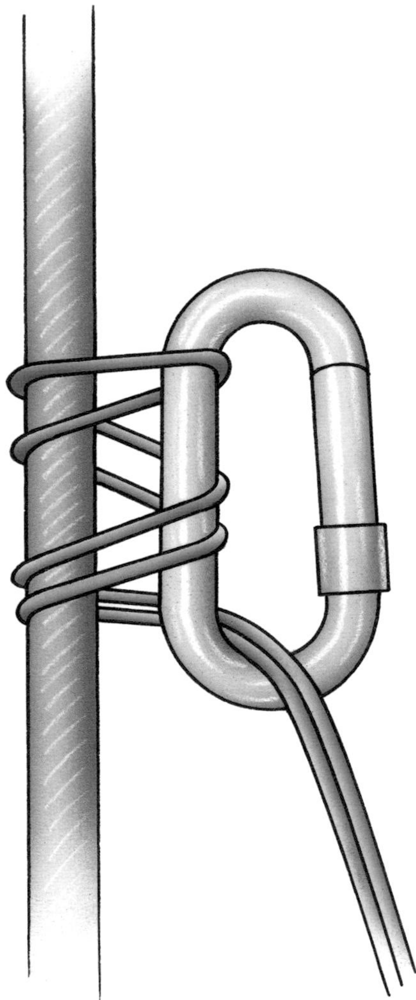

Bachman Knot

Sometimes the Prusik knot becomes stiff and hard to move along the rope. Many other knots and variations have been devised to solve this problem, and often include the word Prusik as a generic term for slip-and-grip knots used in this way.

The first variation devised was to tie the Prusik around a carabiner, which acted as a handle when sliding and gave a smoother surface in contact with the main rope.

As can be seen in the illustration, the Bachman knot is tied by hooking the Prusik loop through a carabiner and then going around the rope and through the carabiner several times, finally leaving the rope through the carabiner.

Kreuzklem or Heddon Knot

This is another application that attatches a loop to another rope. A simple knot to tie, it is suitable if you need a loop to suspend something from in a hurry. It can, of course, be adapted for many other purposes.

1 The loop is passed up and around the rope once and the end is brought back down to trap the upward turn. The upper end is fed through the bight at the lower end and the knot is pulled firm.

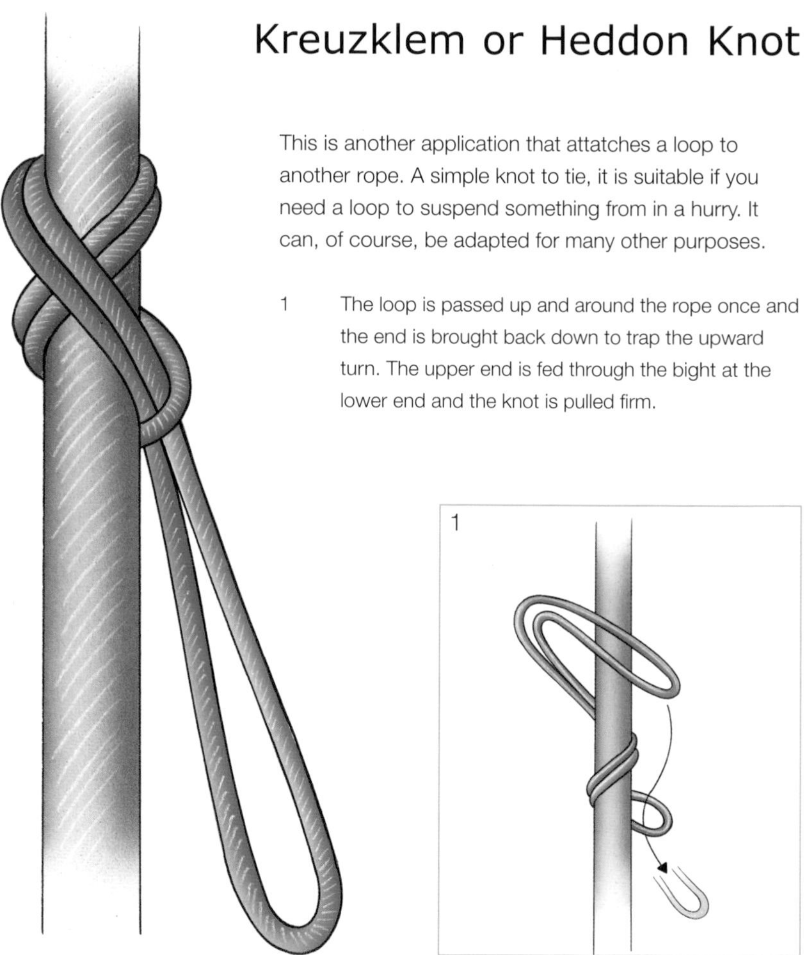

Klemheist or Headon Knot

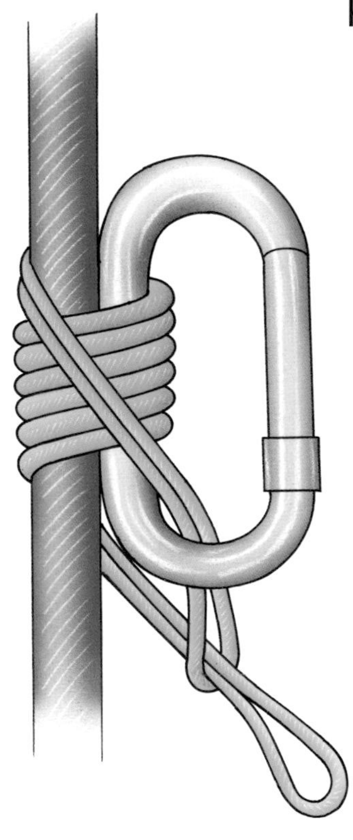

Yet another variation on the theme is the Klemheist knot, also known as the Headon knot. This will work with or without a carabiner.

1. Wrap the Prusik loop several times around the rope in a downward spiral, ensuring that the turns lie flat and do not cross.

2. Take the lower end up and pass it through the bight at the top end. This, too, may be formed around a carabiner. Pull tight across the loops.

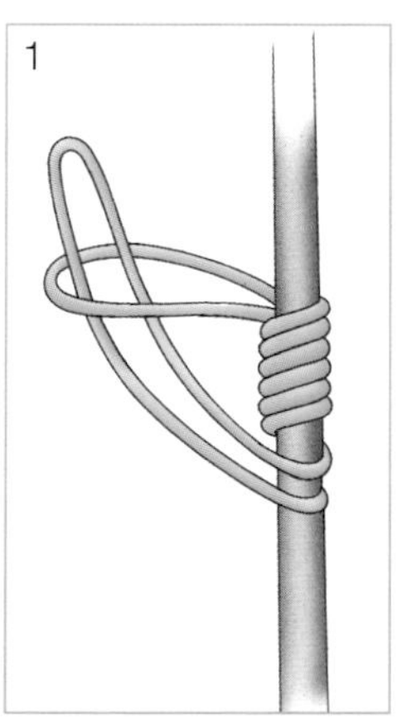

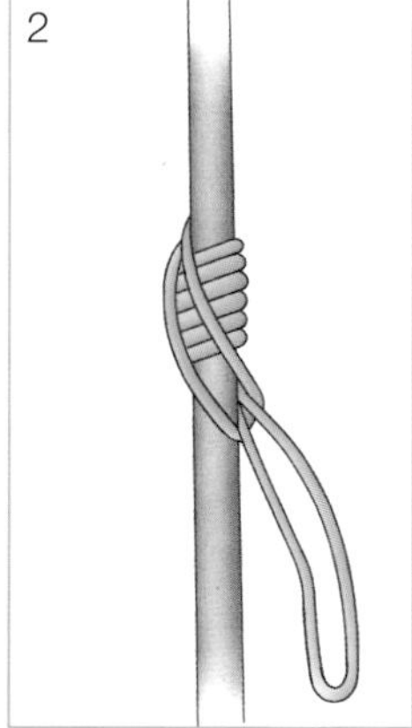

Mariner's Knot

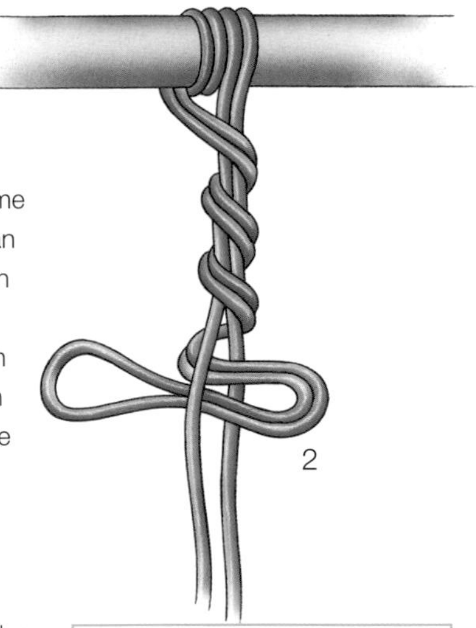

As this is never used by sailors, the origin of its name is a mystery. It is especially useful as a sling that can be undone easily while under load, say from a fallen climber, but it allows control at all stages.

It is best tied with webbing and works well with tape up to about half an inch wide. However, it can also be tied with rope, as shown here. Consider the bar in the illustration to be the lower end of an anchored carabiner.

1 The lower end of the sling is attached to the fallen person and the loop is taken twice around the carabiner.

2 The tail of the sling is then wrapped four or five times around the standing part of the sling. A bight is passed between the two legs of the standing part and tension and friction will hold everything in place.

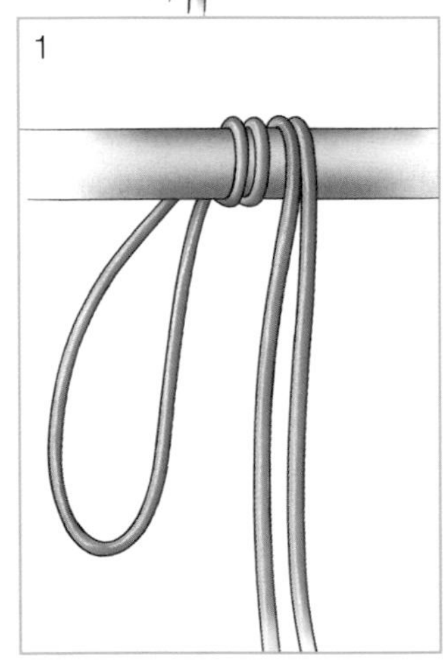

To undo, ease the end out from between the legs and gradually remove the turns until all is as you intend. In the event of slippage, the turns can easily be replaced.

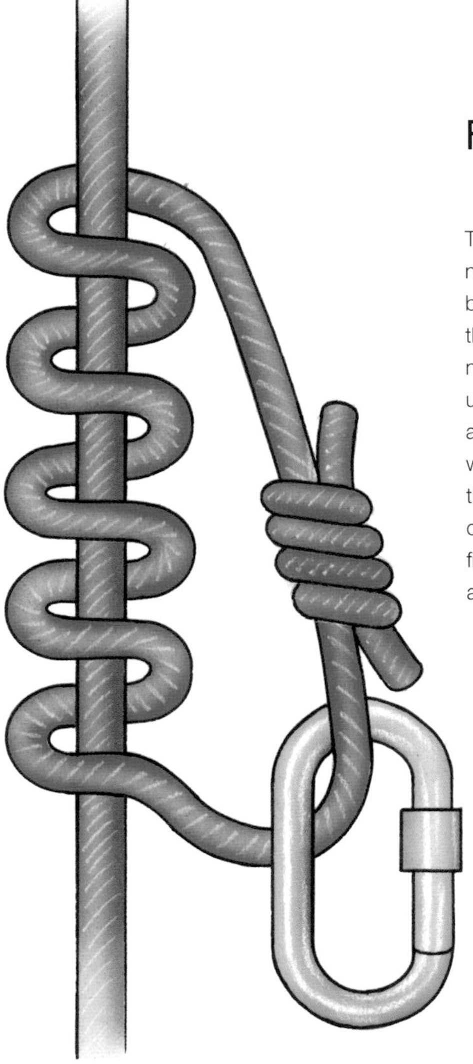

French Prusik

This Prusik variation is very simple and needs no step-by-step guide. It is tied by wrapping a length of cord around the rope several times. The exact number depends on the materials used and it is best to practice in advance if you know that you might wish to use this knot, to ascertain the optimum number. Tie the ends of the cord together with a double fisherman's knot. Clip in the carabiner and it is ready for use.

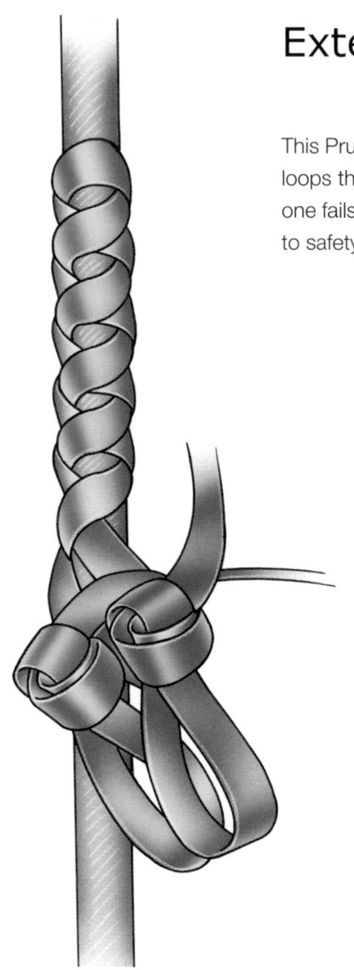

Extended French Prusik

This Prusik knot is tied with webbing tape. The two loops that you are left with provide extra security—if one fails the other should hold long enough to return to safety.

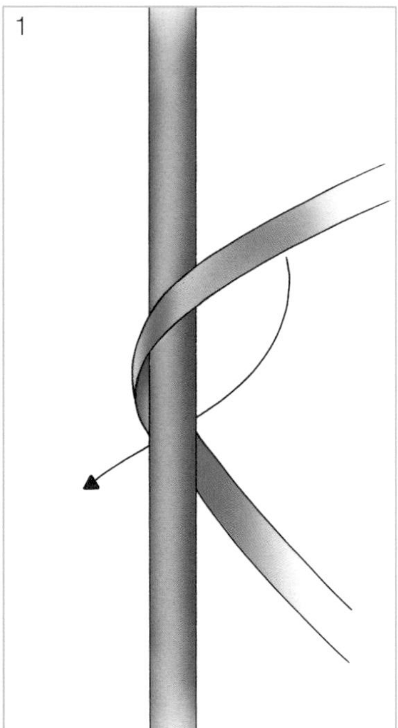

1 The tape is centered and laid across the main rope.

2 & 3 The sides are wrapped down simultaneously in opposite directions, keeping the tape flat and smooth and the wrappings as close together as possible.

At each end of the tape, tie a loop using a water knot. The carabiner fits into the two loops.

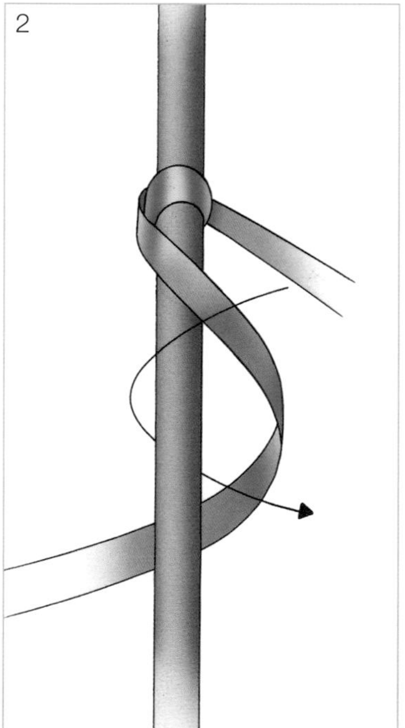

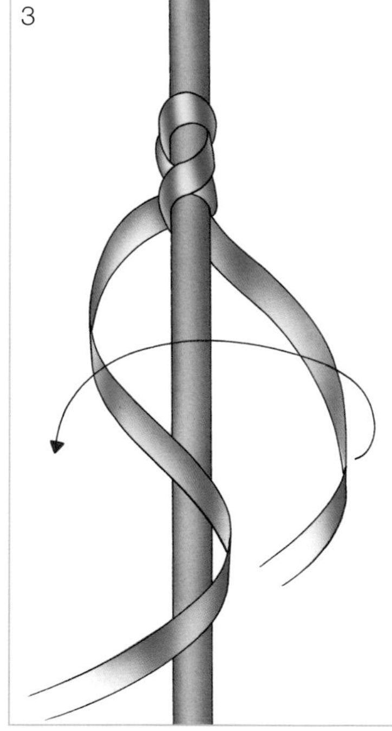

One-Handed Bowline

Hopefully, you will never need to use this technique in a serious situation, but there are many occasions when the technique shown on the next few pages will be of benefit. It is used if you are holding onto a cliff or have fallen overboard and another passenger has given you a rope without a loop in the end.

In some ways the title is a misnomer, as the other hand is holding onto the rope to produce a little slack and enable you to tie the knot, but in a pinch it can be tied with a single hand.

You can tie with either a bight or just an end. I prefer the bight for reasons that will be explained later, but as long as you are successful it doesn't matter.

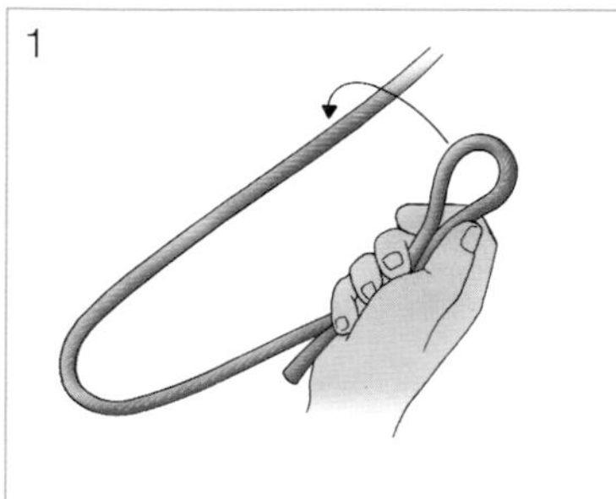

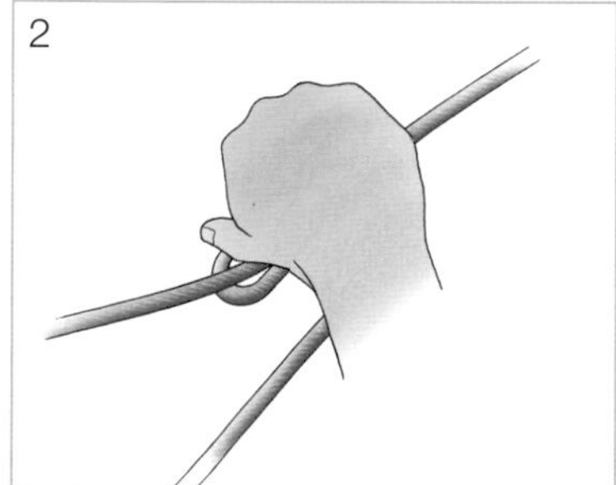

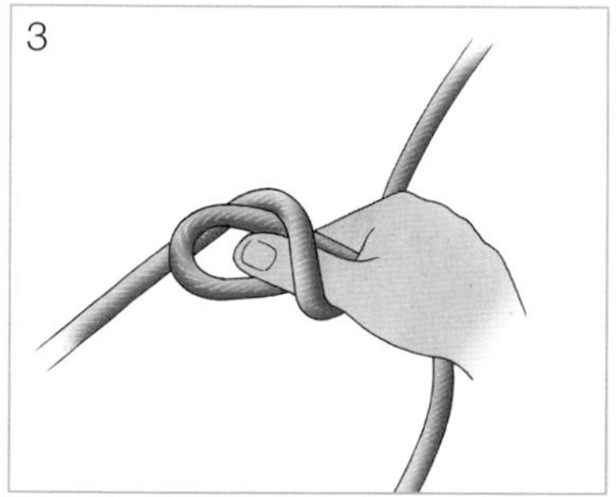

1 Reach forward with the hand that is not tying (the left for right-handed people) and grasp the rope almost at an arm's length in front of you. Pass the rope around under your arms so it emerges on the side of your tying hand. Take a small bight in the clenched fist of your tying hand with a small part projecting in front of your hand.

2 & 3 Place it across the rope with the back of your hand upward, and perform the twist down and in toward your stomach, then away.

4 At the end of the twist, the loop in the main rope should be across your knuckles. This will allow the rope to pull clear without trapping your wrist should anything go wrong. Another illustration I found of this method shows the whole wrist encircled by the rope. It must be stressed that this is wrong; if your other hand lets go of the main rope you would be trapped and even possibly lose your hand. This way, at the very worst, you would only lose a finger.

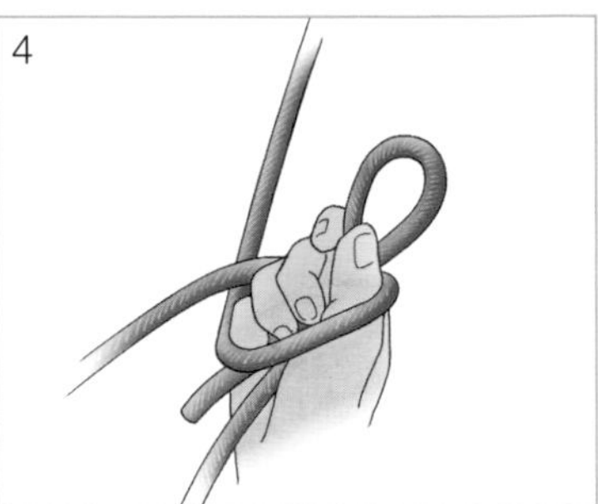

5 Extend your forefinger behind the bight and poke the bight around the main rope.

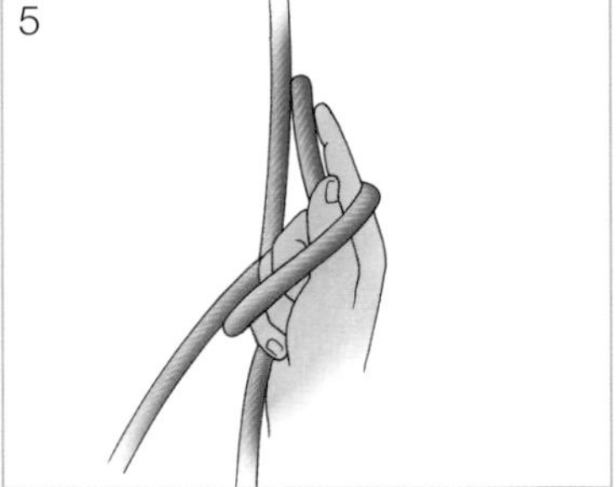

6 Trap the bight with your thumb and loop the forefinger back into the bight again.

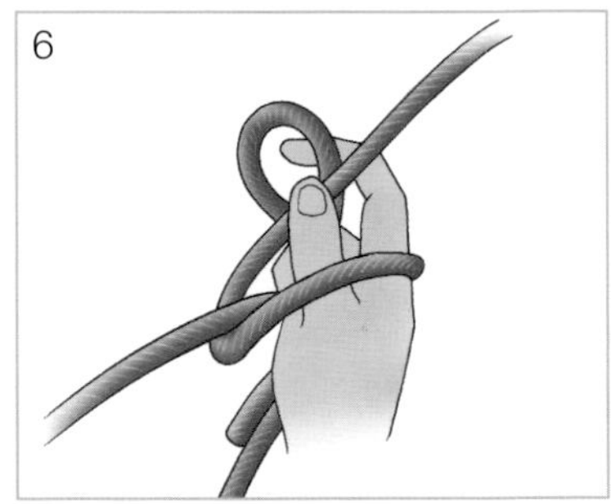

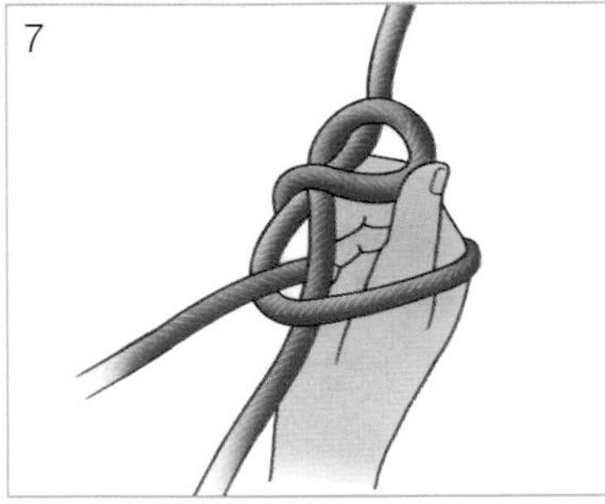

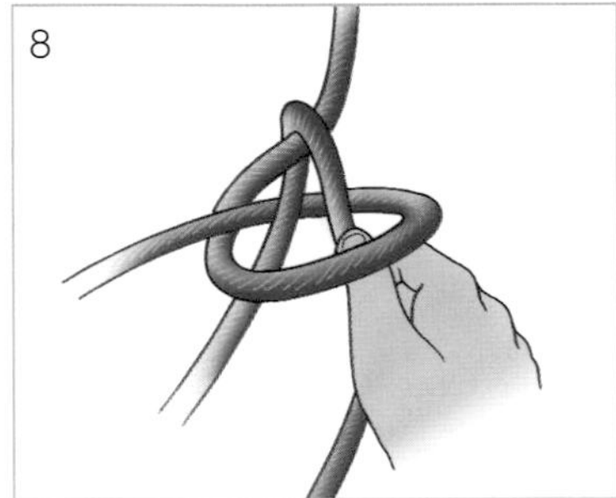

7 You could now allow the bight to spring open so you are holding the end, or you can keep firm hold of the bight.

8 & 9 Sharply remove your hand from the loop and pull through as much slack as you can manage. Haul taut.

If you have enough tail to tie a thumb knot to lock the bowline, then do so, but if not, hold tight to the end and to the knot so it does not come undone during the rest of the rescue. Using a bight will give you a safety tail.

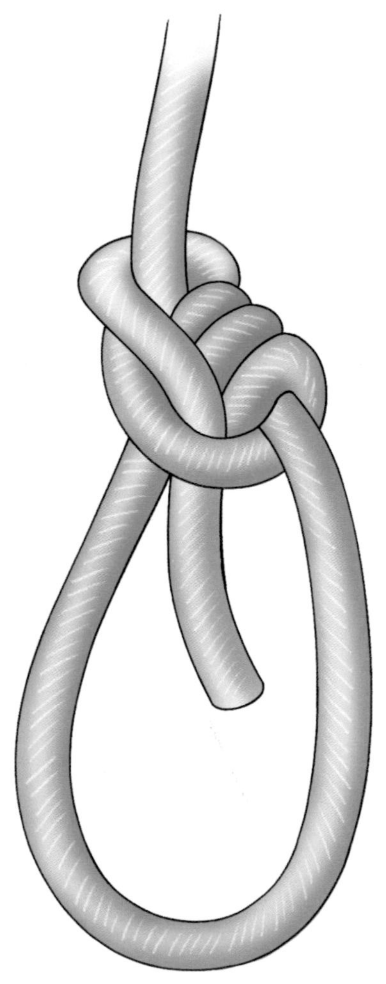

Tarbuck Knot

This knot was already known when it was promoted for use with early nylon climbing ropes. It is not now advised for kernmantel ropes because it can damage the sheath.

As a loop knot, it will lock under load but allow movement. Otherwise it is still very useful for climbers and also makes a good adjusting knot for guylines.

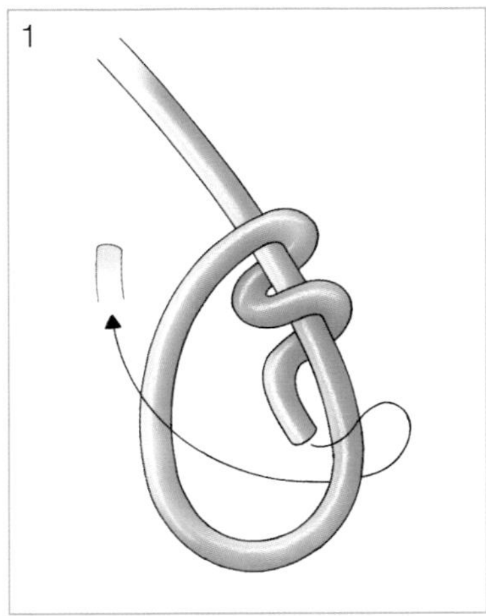

1 Make a loop and form two round turns about the standing part, working into the loop.

2 Lead the end outside the loop crossing in front of the turns just applied.

3 Pass over the standing part away from the knot and bring the end back. Feed the end down into the last loop formed so it is trapped against the round turns. Dress the knot and pull tight.

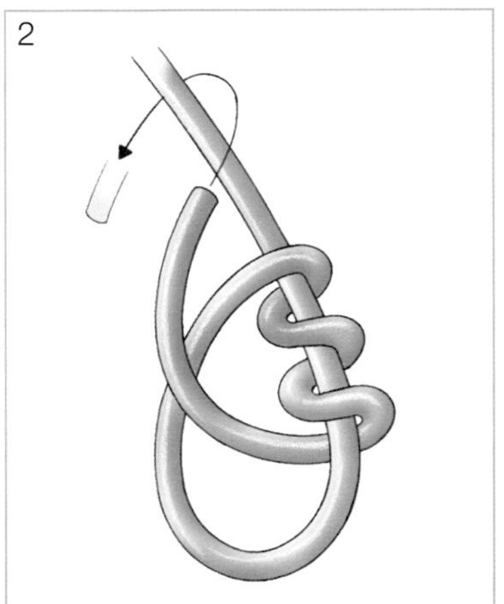

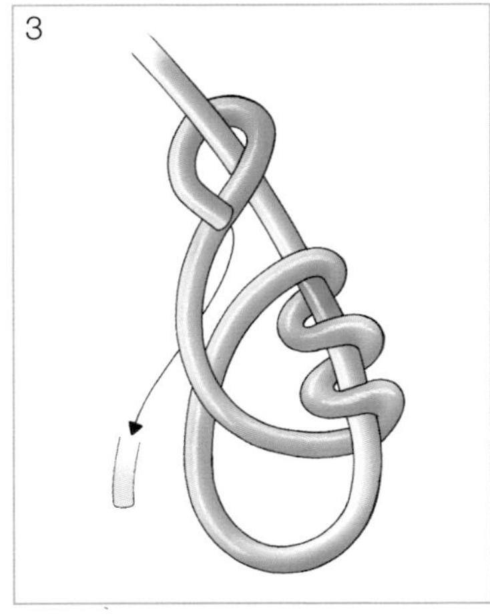

Boating Knots

Knowing the ropes was an important part of life and a matter of great pride to the old sailor. A huge variety of knots could be found on old ships, performing a number of functions. If, when you look at the rigging of an old ship, you can understand what the various bits of rope are supposed to do, it adds an extra dimension to the history, and a new respect for the sailors who worked onboard in the days before radios and other technology became common, when tying the right knot could mean the difference between life and death.

Although the ships have changed beyond all recognition since then, and the huge majority of sailboats are now used recreationally, a modern crew will utilize many of the same knots for surprisingly similar purposes. Simple mooring hitches and anchor bends still serve the same purpose, while traditional maritime knots such as the Turk's head are still practiced by many committed sailors and can take you into a special area of ornamental knot tying where the almost infinite variety is amazing. While they have less practical function than in the past, they will still impress the uninitiated and are fun to tie.

Once again, I know you will find uses, which are not boating-related, for these knots.

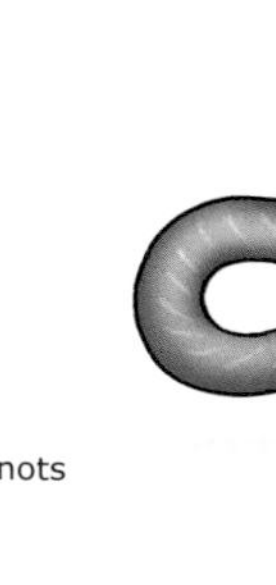

Contents of Boating Knots

Anchor Bend 182
Water Bowline 184
Interlocked Bowlines 185
Sliding Figure Eight Bend 186
Zeppelin or Rosendahl Bend 188
Bowline on the Bight 190
Triple Bowline 194
Buntline Hitch 195
Boom Hitch 196
Mooring Hitch 197
Lighterman's Hitch 198
Stitch and Whip Eye 200
Seizing Bend 202
Ground Line Hitch 204
Carrick Bend 206
Net Line Knot 208
Turk's Head Knot
Three Lead, Four Bight 210
Turk's Head Knot
Three Lead, Five Bight 212

Anchor Bend

This hitch is a close relation to the round turn and two half hitches, but is even more secure, especially when the rope gets wet and slippery. It is perfect for tying on to a small boat anchor, hence its name, though it is a good all-around securing knot and can also be used for mooring and a host of other chores. As such, it is a good knot to have in your basic repertoire.

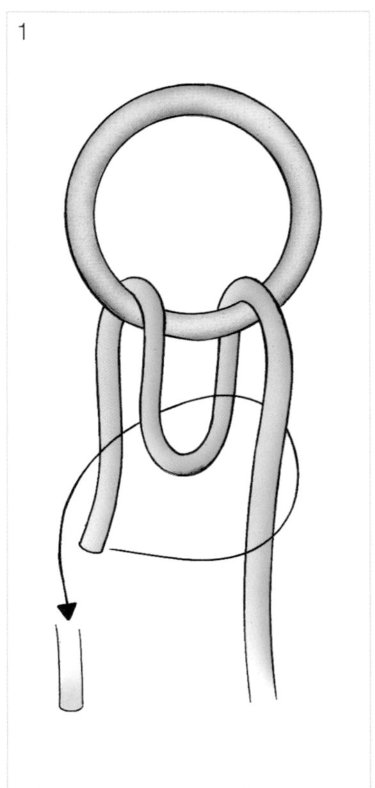

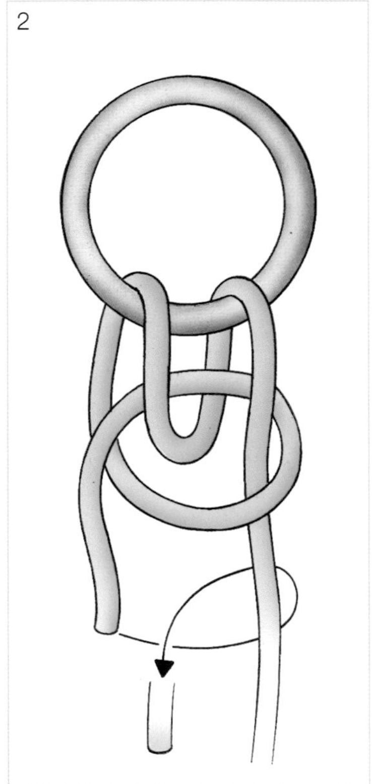

1 Take a round turn through the ring, leaving the turns loose. Make the first half hitch but feed the line through the round turn. Pull up.

2 Form the second round turn in the conventional way and tighten.

Water Bowline

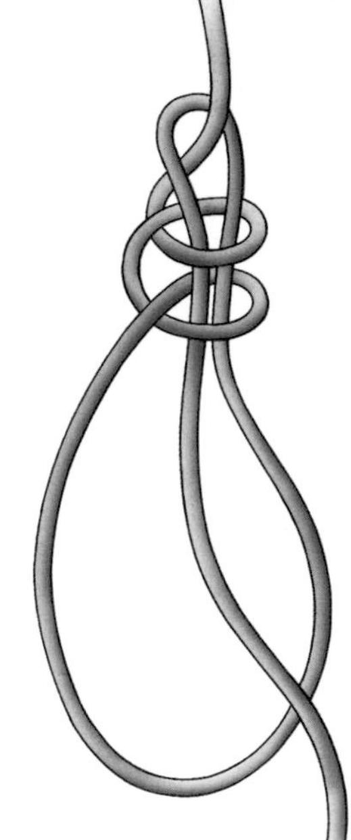

When a loop must be dragged through water, the buffeting it receives can loosen the knot and unravel the rope. This knot, with its extra loop, overcomes this problem.

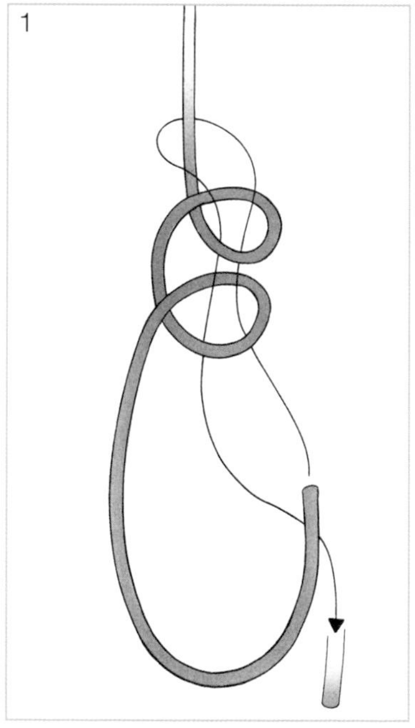

1 Make two overhand loops, one on top of the other, as for a clove hitch, and pass the end through both loops. Then come around the back of the standing part, as with a conventional bowline, and return through both loops. Haul tight.

You can form the loops with the twist used on the basic bowline, just carrying out the move twice, before finishing off as above.

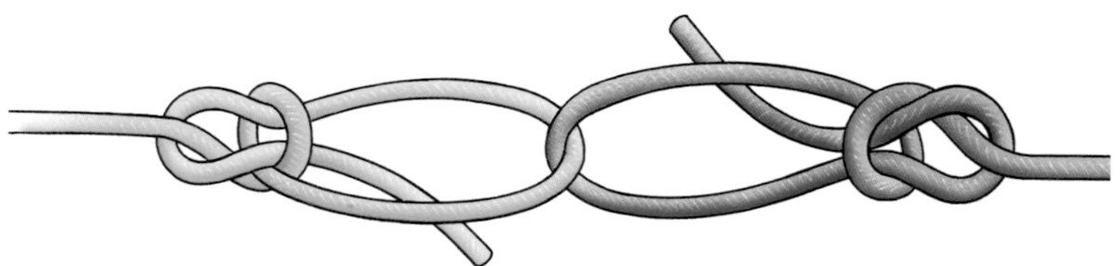

Interlocked Bowlines

This is a quick and secure way to join two lines when you have to haul a line through the water or over obstacles. If the lines need to be separated again, it is easy to undo. You could use the water bowline for each knot if anticipating a lot of rough handling.

1 Form a bowline at the end of one line. Pass the end of the other line through the loop of the first bowline and cast your second bowline in the end of the second line, ensuring that they are interlocked.

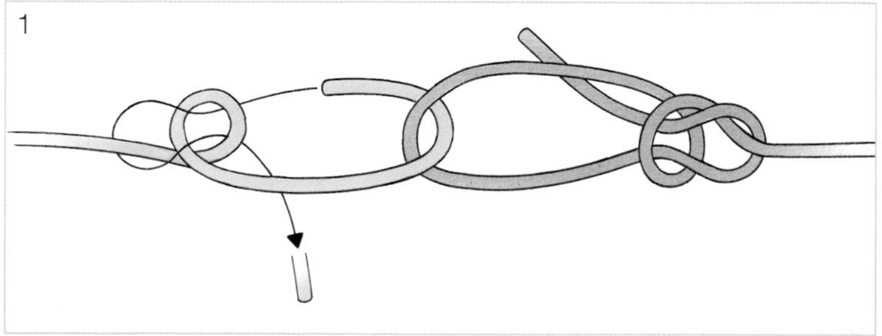

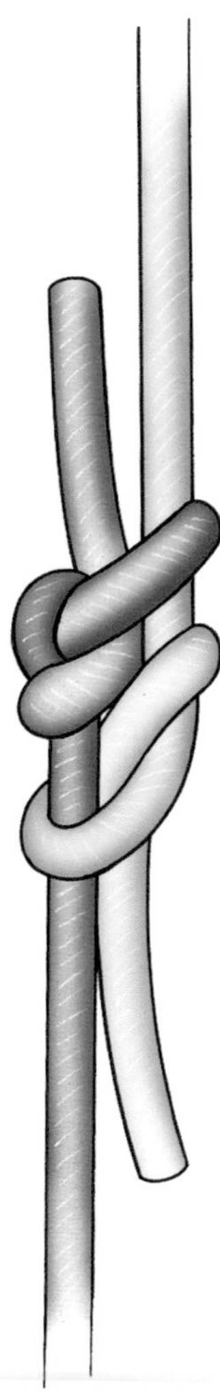

Sliding Figure Eight Bend

This is another way to join two ropes, which gives a tidier but lumpier knot than the interlocked bowlines but is not quite so easy to untie after tension has been applied.

1 Make a figure eight knot near the end of one line. Feed the second line through the end loop of the first knot alongside the tail end.

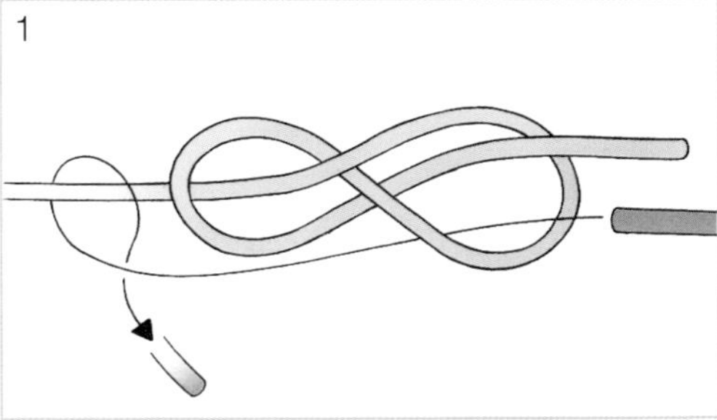

2 Take the second line a little way up the first and form another figure eight, trapping the standing part of the first in the end loop.

3 Pull both figure eight knots tight. Leave a gap between them if you wish to incorporate a shock absorber in the system. When a sudden load is applied, the friction of each knot gripping the standing part of the other will slow down the shock transmission as the two figure eights slide to jam up against one another.

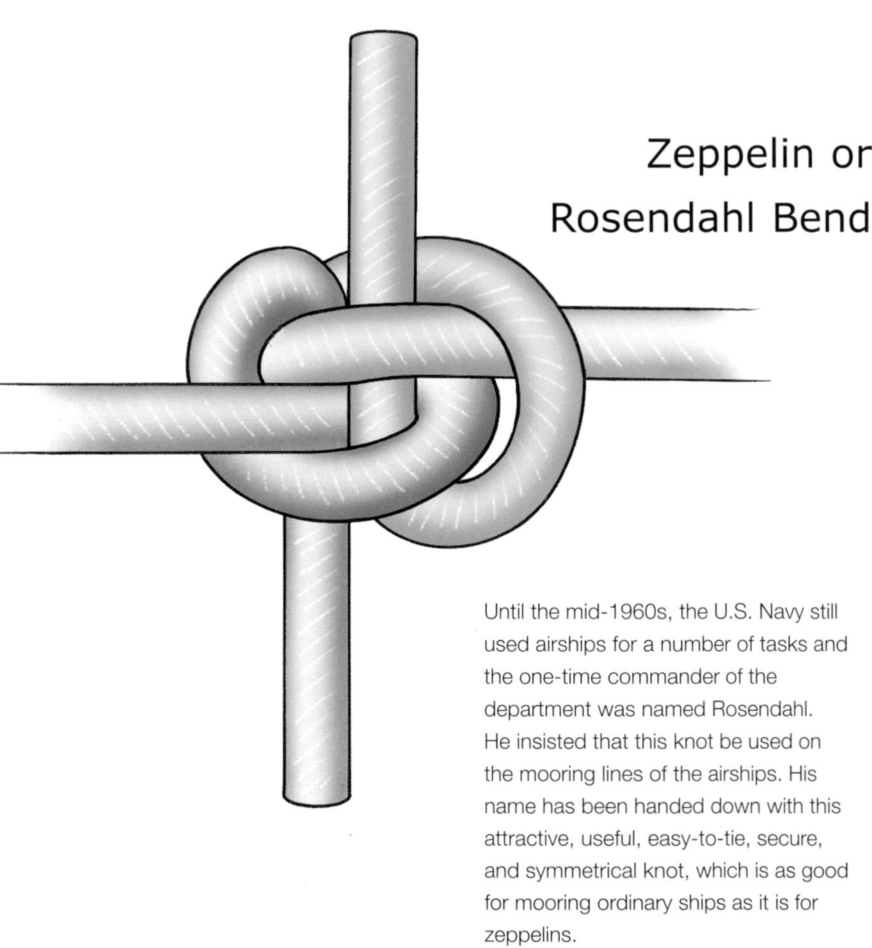

Zeppelin or Rosendahl Bend

Until the mid-1960s, the U.S. Navy still used airships for a number of tasks and the one-time commander of the department was named Rosendahl. He insisted that this knot be used on the mooring lines of the airships. His name has been handed down with this attractive, useful, easy-to-tie, secure, and symmetrical knot, which is as good for mooring ordinary ships as it is for zeppelins.

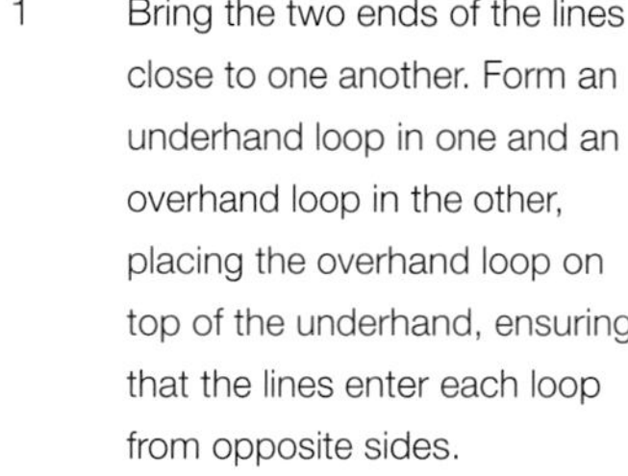

1 Bring the two ends of the lines close to one another. Form an underhand loop in one and an overhand loop in the other, placing the overhand loop on top of the underhand, ensuring that the lines enter each loop from opposite sides.

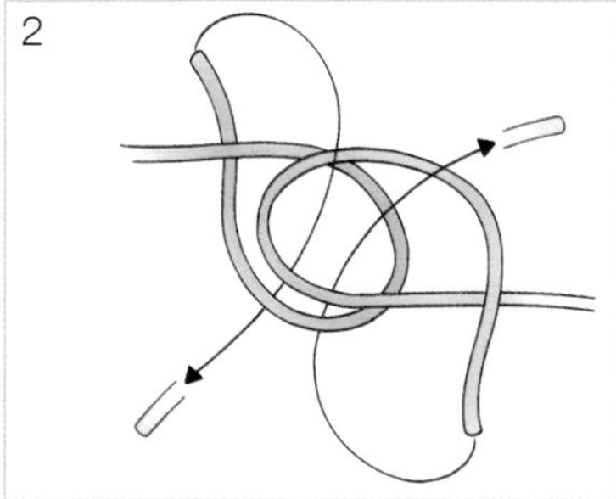

2 Bring the end of the underhand loop up, over both lines, into the overlapping loops, pass it down, and pull it under both loops. Take the end of the overhand loop down, bring it under the two overlapping loops, and pull it up out of both loops.

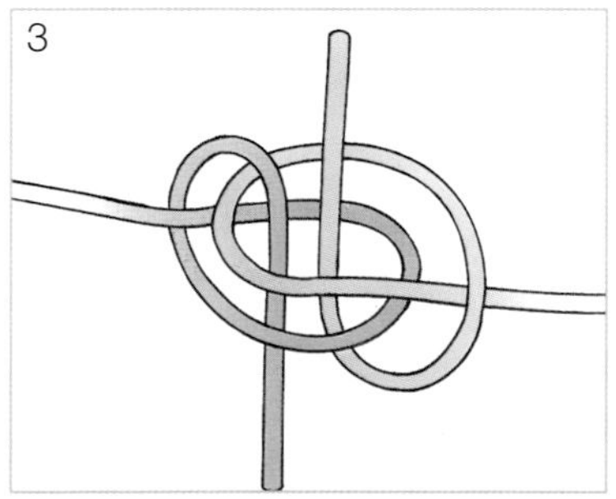

3 Heave on all four lines to tighten. It should look symmetrical, but the knot may require a little dressing to match the illustration.

To untie, force the crossing loops in opposite directions until enough slack is obtained to free the ends. The knot will then fall apart.

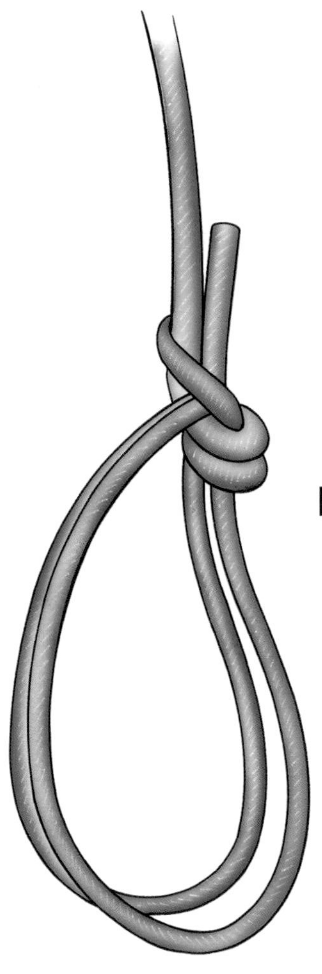

Bowline on the Bight

Sometimes you will need to have two loops in the end of a line for a number of reasons, and the bowline on the bight will usually provide a simple solution. Should the load be spread unevenly between the two loops, then it is sensible to tie off the loose end with a thumb knot to avoid the slight risk of spillage.

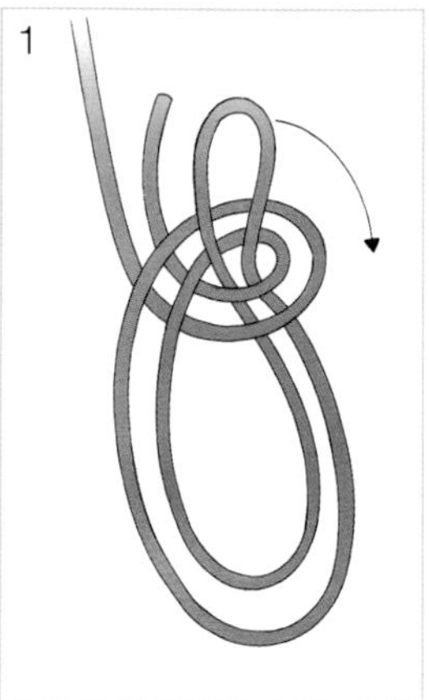

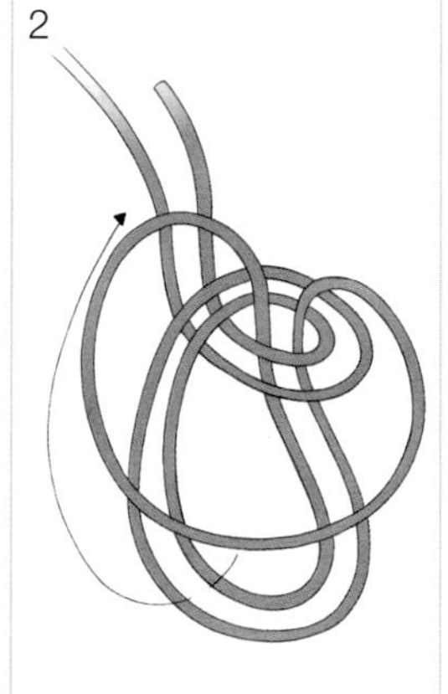

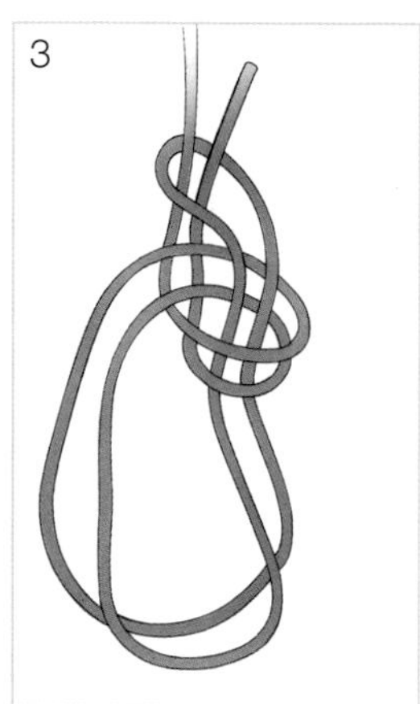

Method One

1. Double a section long enough for your needs at the end of the rope. Holding the end of the bight, make the twist, which you use for a normal bowline, and pull the bight up a little way through the crossing loop.

2. Allow the projecting bight to fall forward so that the two large loops may be passed through it.

3. Bring the bight up behind the knot and tighten by pulling the large loops while supporting the crossing loop. The size of the loops may be adjusted to suit the task before finally tightening the knot.

1

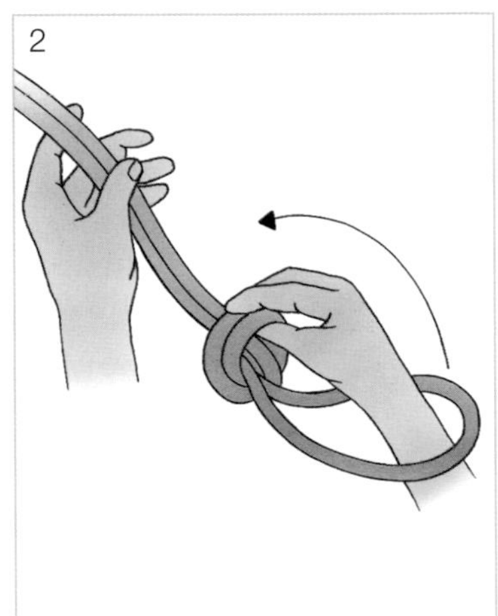
2

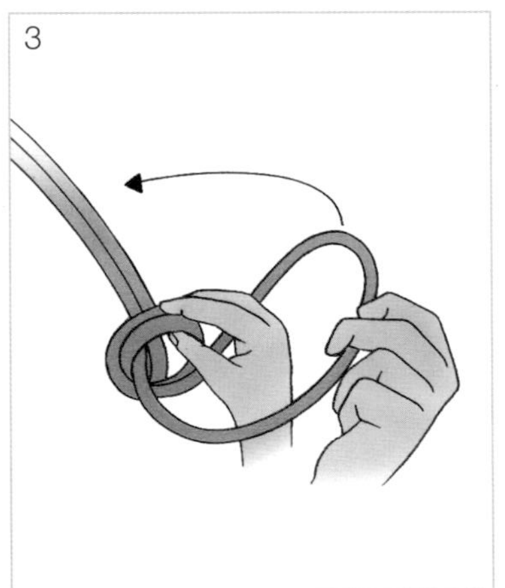
3

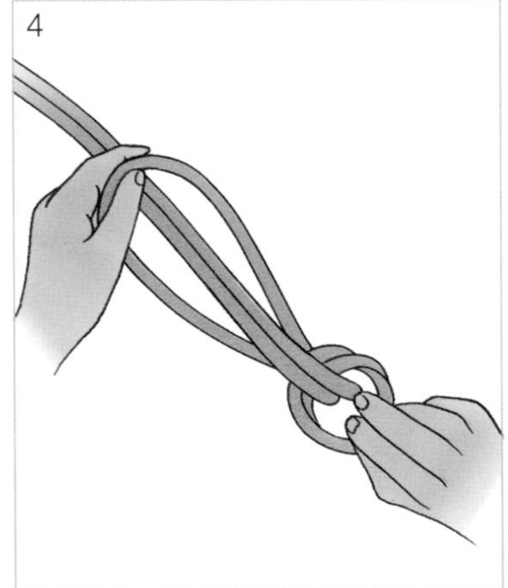
4

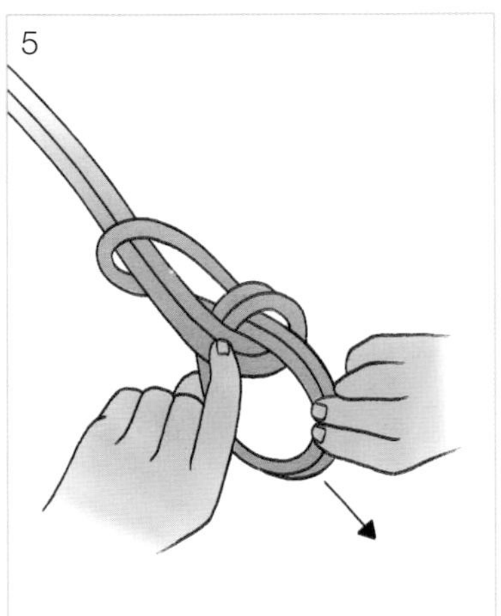

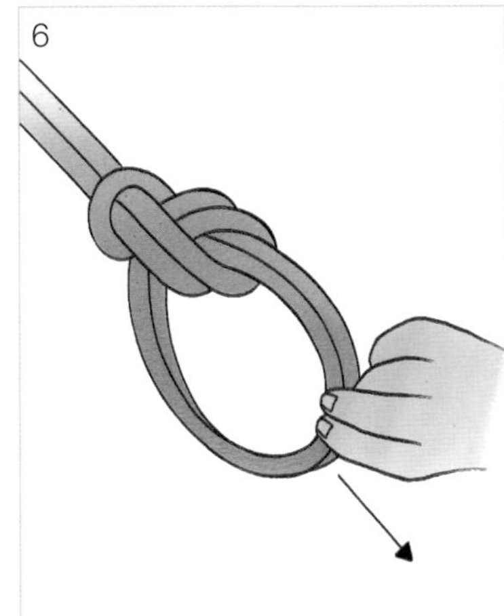

Method Two

1 A second method, probably of more use if the loops are not too big, starts by doubling the line and forming a loose thumb knot with the double cord.

2 The right hand, in this illustration, is passed inside the bight and grasps the far side of the thumb knot.

3 & 4 The other hand takes the bight, which is now around the right wrist, and flips it over the right hand.

5 & 6 The left hand then returns to the crossing, which it supports while the right hand pulls the double line down through the thumb knot to form the bowline on the bight.

Triple Bowline

Occasionally you might want three loops at the end of your line. This knot provides them. It has been used to rescue a person overboard, with a leg in two of the loops with the body being supported by the third loop. For whatever purpose you wish to use it, make sure that all loops are adjusted to the optimum size.

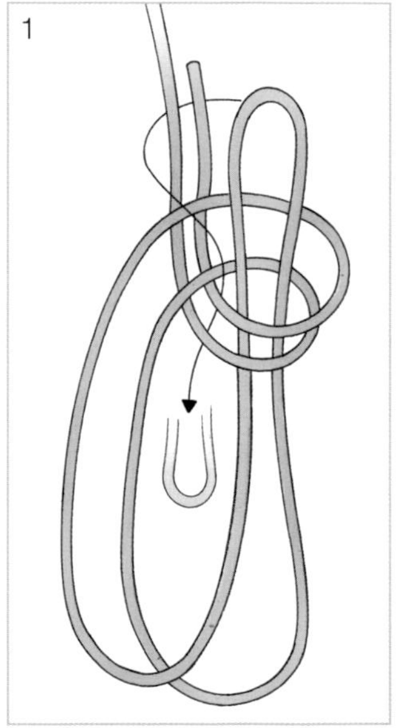

1 Start as for the bowline on the bight. Double enough cord near the end and make the twist. Pull the bight up through the crossing and continue as for an ordinary bowline, but using the bight. When the bight comes down through the crossing loop, you will find that you now have three loops. Adjust the loops to suit the task before pulling tight.

Buntline Hitch

This knot is used when the line is flapping about and other knots might be shaken loose. It pulls up to the object around which it is tied and holds fast.

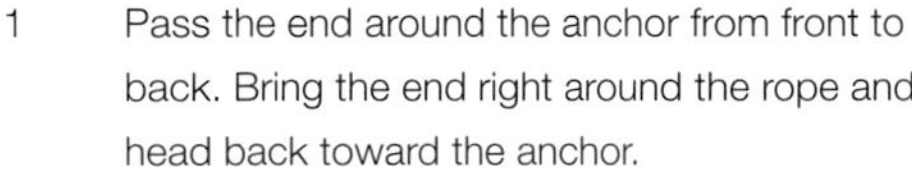

1 Pass the end around the anchor from front to back. Bring the end right around the rope and head back toward the anchor.

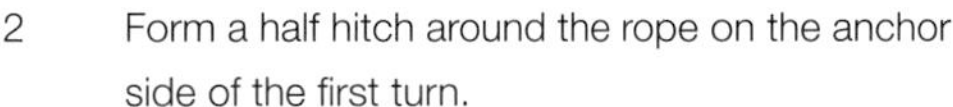

2 Form a half hitch around the rope on the anchor side of the first turn.

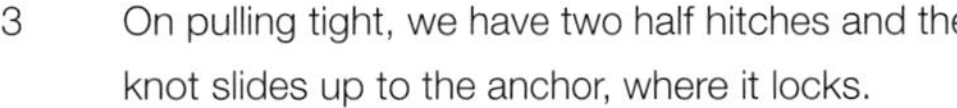

3 On pulling tight, we have two half hitches and the knot slides up to the anchor, where it locks.

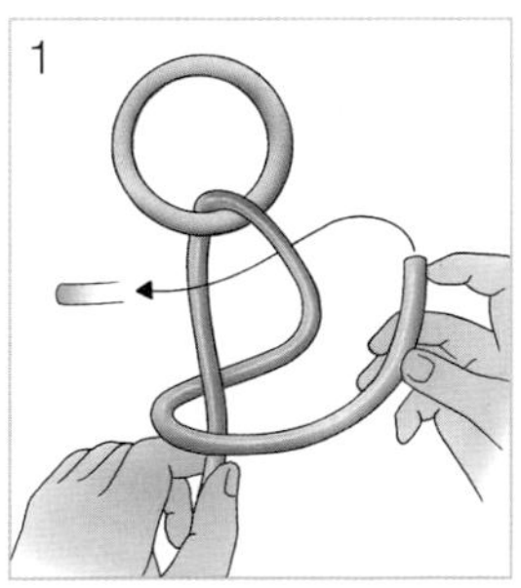

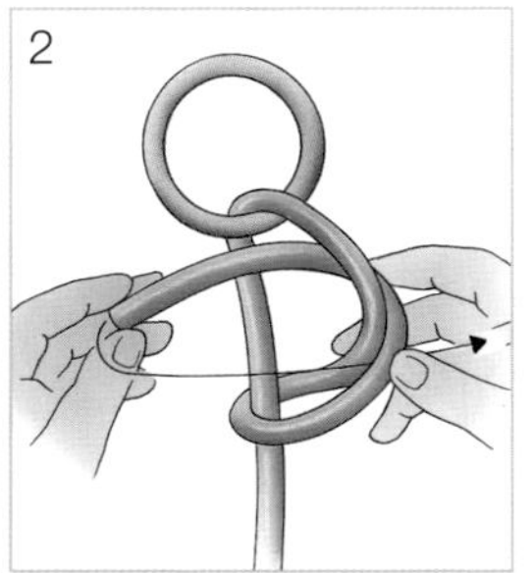

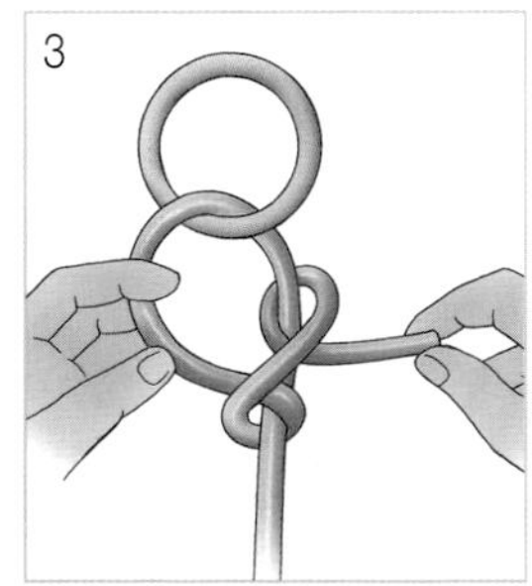

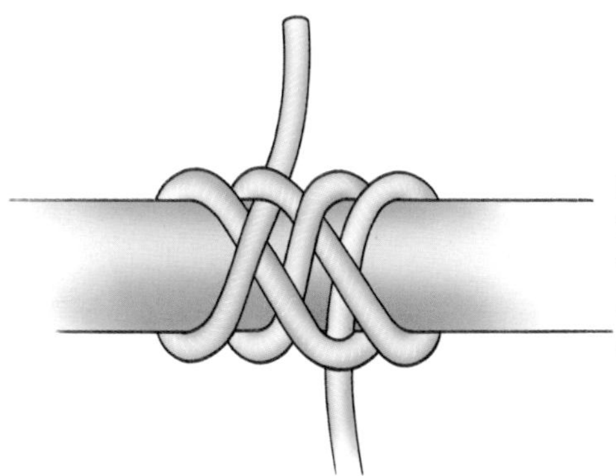

Boom Hitch

Here we have another knot that will take changes of direction and pull without spilling. Although it looks complicated, it only requires the end to be tucked once.

1 Take a round turn and continue as if for a clove hitch, but stay outside the crossing and go around again.

2 Bring the end up inside the first turn, that is to say next to the standing part, and take another turn, crossing over the first two turns. Bring the end up so that it crosses over itself and tuck the end under the next turn. Work tight.

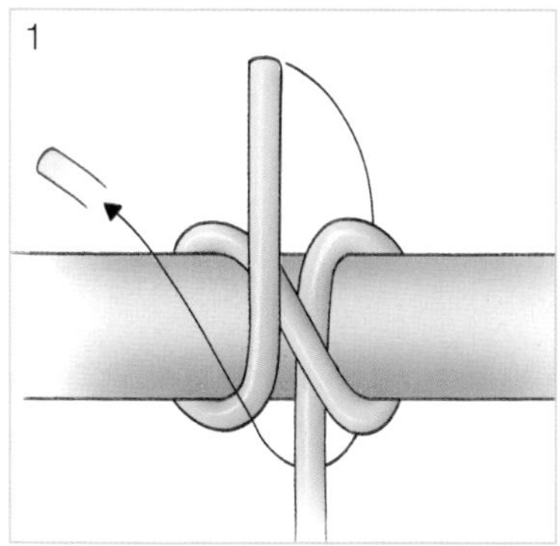

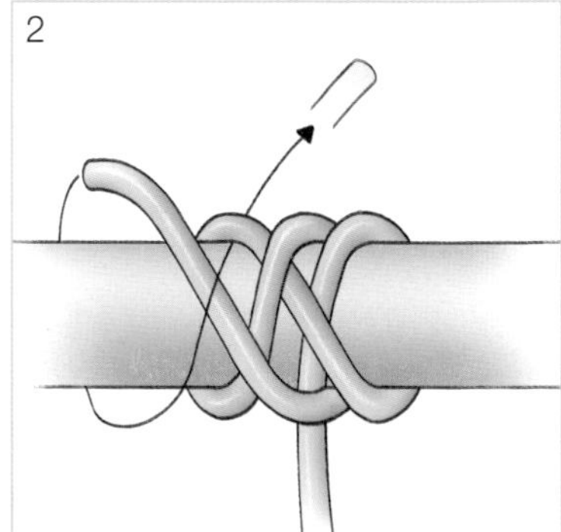

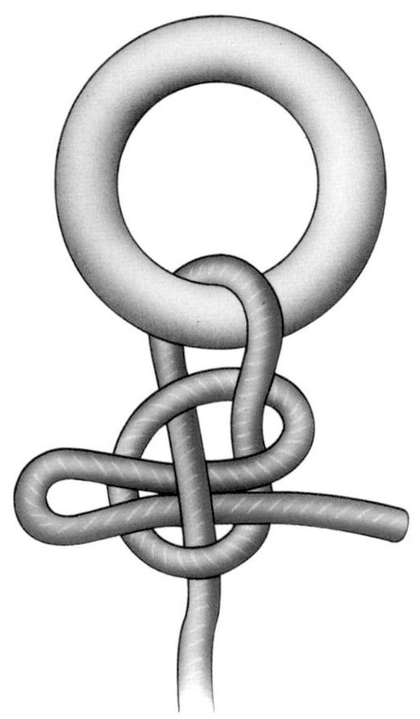

Mooring Hitch

This is another slide-and-lock knot that is quickly released. It is easily adjustable, so is often used when mooring.

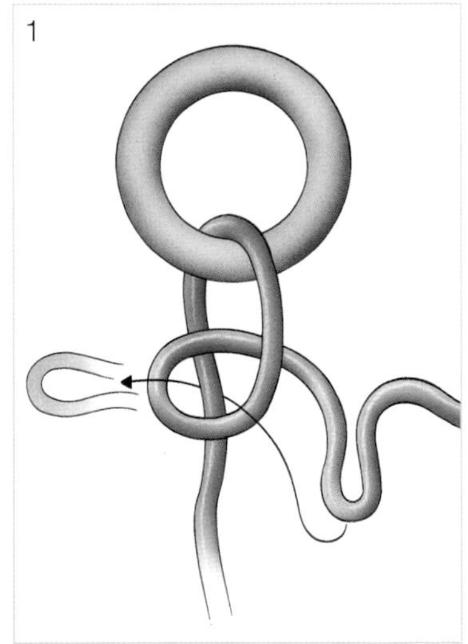

1 Pass the line through the ring and form a crossing loop on top of the standing part.Take a bight of the working part and weave it through the crossing loop and under the standing part so that it locks the loop in place.

The knot will slide up to the ring but can be released by giving the working end a sharp tug. If the working end is left long, the knot may be untied by pulling it from a distance.

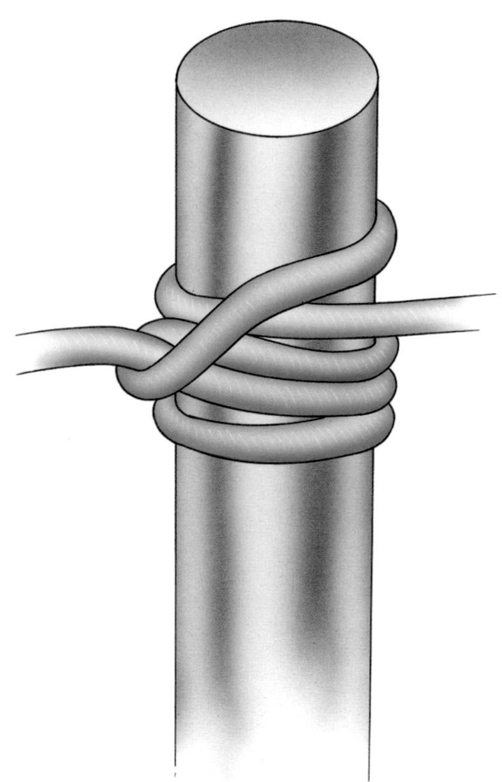

Lighterman's Hitch

This simple knot can hold a great load and yet can be released quickly, even when under strain. This could be important if a tow should founder and have to be cast off in a hurry. If it should freeze when tied around the picket pin mooring a boat in the winter, the pin can be pulled out of the center of the knot, which will undo itself when thawed or dragged in the water for a few yards.

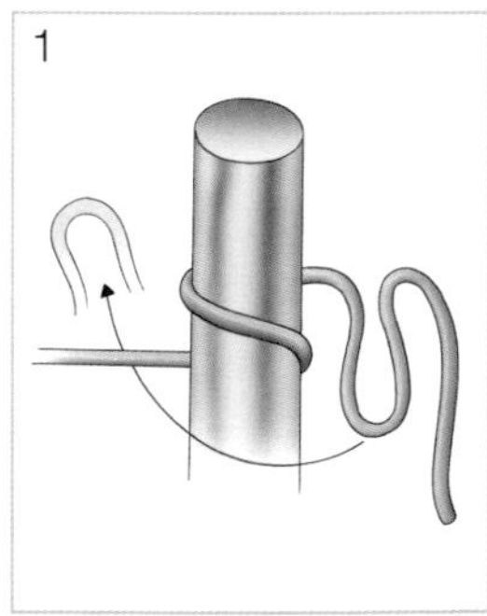

1 Take a round turn about the pin or bollard. This will hold the load while you carry on with the mooring. Leave a long working end.

2 Pass a bight of the working end under the loaded standing part and up over the pin, taking care not to twist the bight. This bight comes up from the far side of the standing part.

3 Take a bight of the working part and place it over the pin from the other side of the pin. Repeat the last two stages alternately until there is no chance of the load pulling free.

4 Finish off with a slipped half hitch around the standing part. To undo, slip the half hitch and just lift off the loops in turn from the pin until the round turn is reached. Don't forget to remove the pin and take it with you.

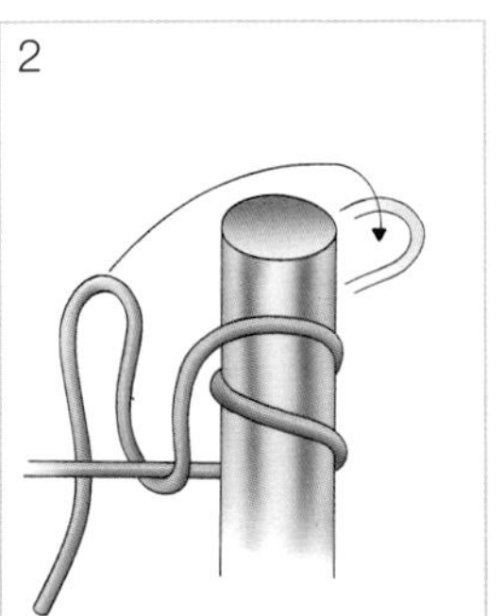

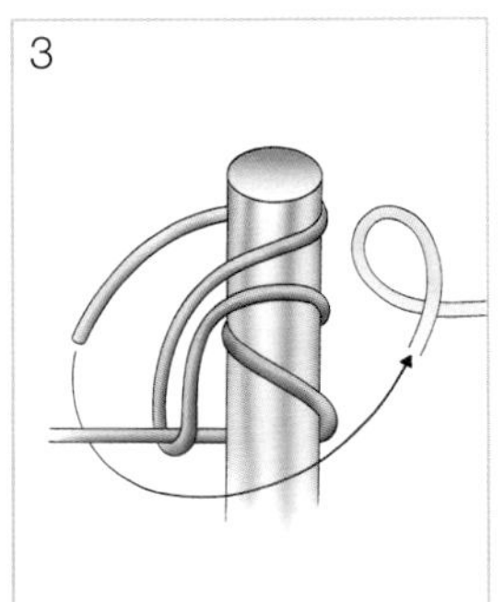

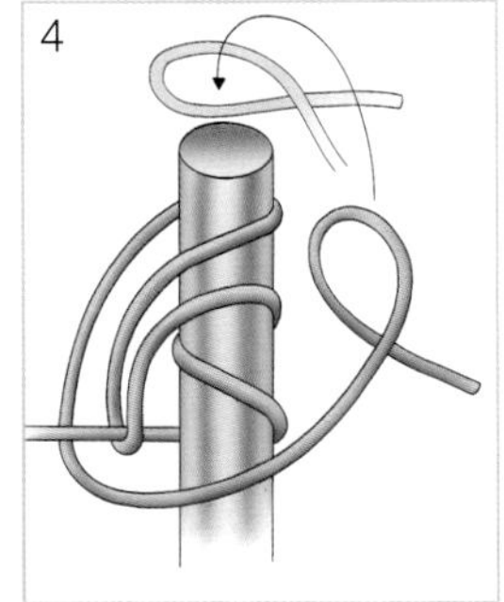

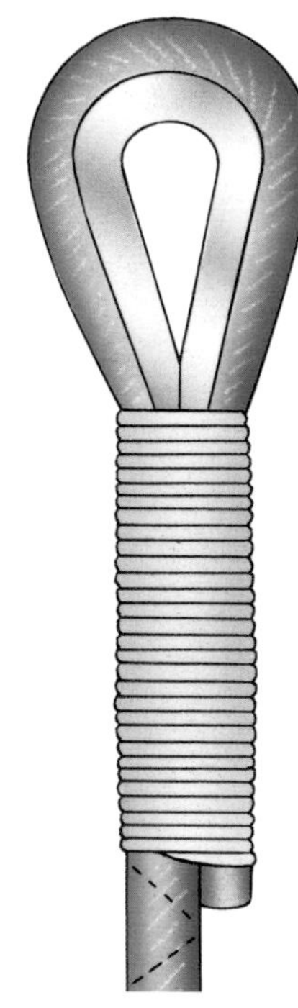

Stitch and Whip Eye

Splicing, as carried out with laid rope, is not possible in tightly braided rope with a core. To form a hard eye at the end of the rope (an eye with a thimble inserted to save wear on the rope), a stitched and whipped eye must be made. A soft eye (without the protective thimble) can also be made in this way, but if this is suitable for your needs then a loop knot will often do the job instead.

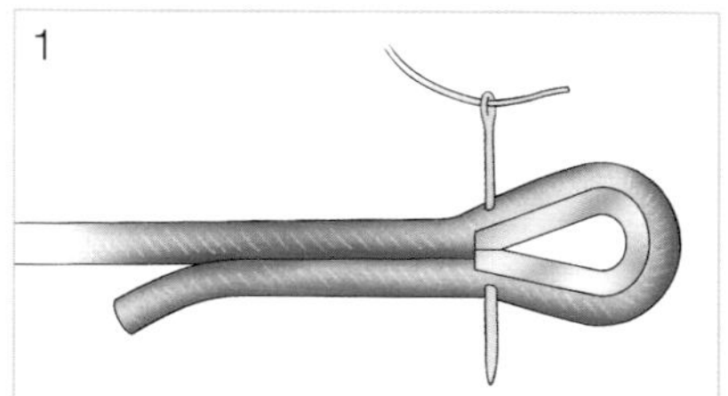

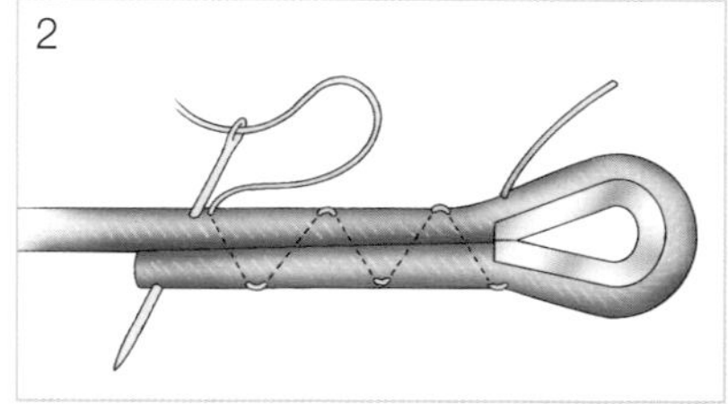

1 Make the loop of the eye and fit the thimble, leaving at least three inches of tail. Holding the rope in place, pass the needle threaded with waxed whipping twine through the two parts of the eye tight up to the thimble.

2 Sew through the rope to secure the tail to the main part of the rope. Go to the end of the tail and back again to the thimble.

3 Put on a tight whipping from the eye down. At about halfway, sew through the ropes again to lock the whipping.

4 Continue to the end of the tail and then sew through the standing part of the rope a few times to secure the end of the whipping. You could ensure the whipping is tight by hammering the two parts of the rope into close contact as you proceed. As the ends of the whipping are sewn in, there is no need to worry about doubling back to hide the end.

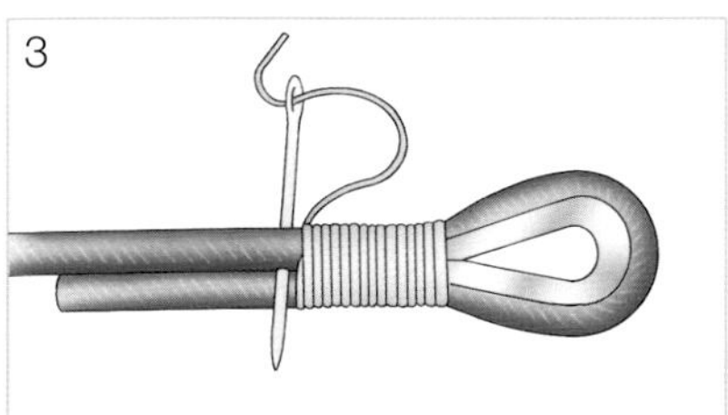

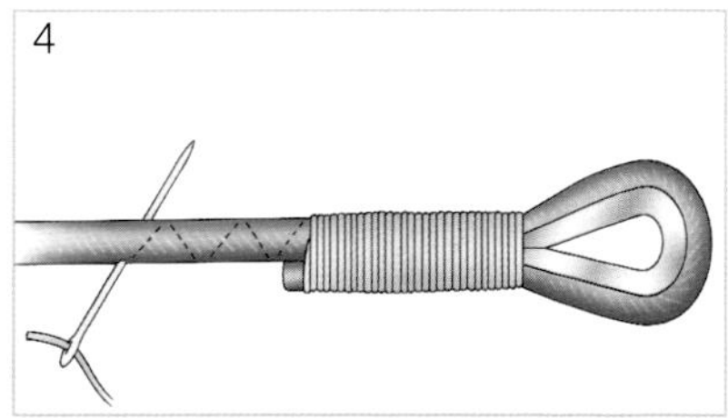

Seizing Bend

When boating, as when climbing, it is sometimes necessary to get a heavy rope across a divide, for example, to a boat in distress that needs a tow. The weight of the rope makes it impossible to throw, so a lighter heaving line must be attatched. The recipient can catch this and pull the heavier rope after it. A heaving line must stay firmly attached to the cable that it is pulling across a chasm and the knot shown here, while a little more complicated than others, is extremely secure. If ever needed, it will certainly justify the effort spent in tying it. The illustrations show everything very loose, but in practice they are close together and tighter.

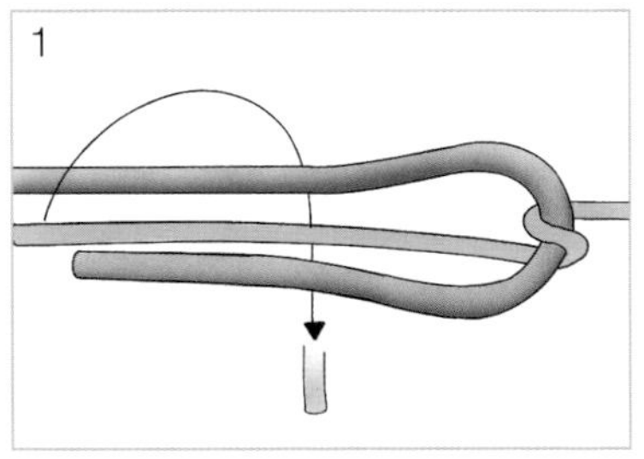

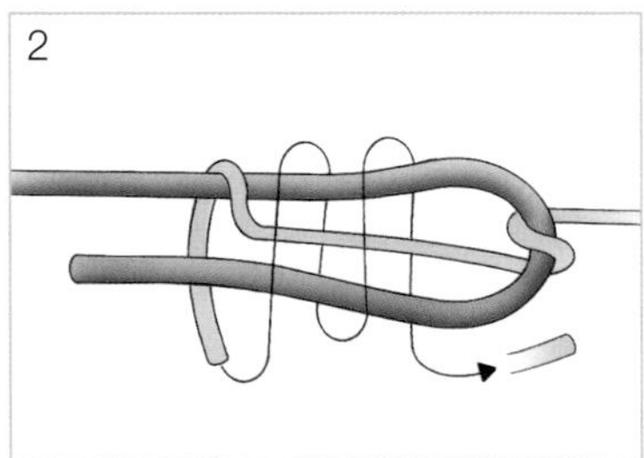

1 Form a bight at the end of the thicker rope or cable. Take a turn with the heaving line about the end of the bight and lead the tail down between the legs of the bight.

2 & 3 Make five or six tight turns with the heaving line around both parts of the bight, working back toward the eye, ensuring that the second turn traps the starting turn.

4 While supporting the turns, pull on the turn around the bight to bring some heaving line in through the eye of the bight. Take this slack and bring it over the end of the cable and up between both parts of the bight. This will act like the frapping on a seizing to lock everything in place. For added security, fasten the end of the light line to itself with a bowline.

The illustrations show everything very loose, but in practice they are close together and tighter.

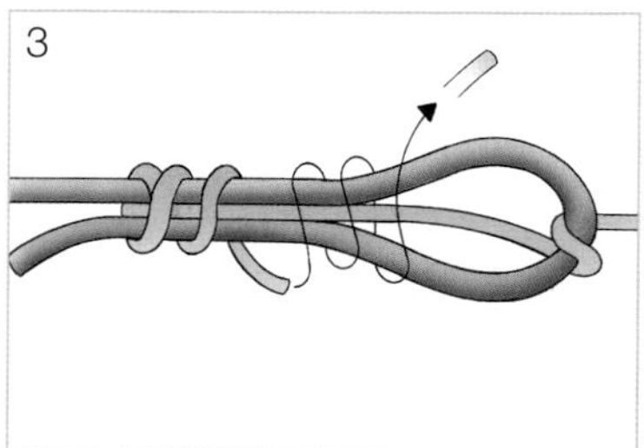

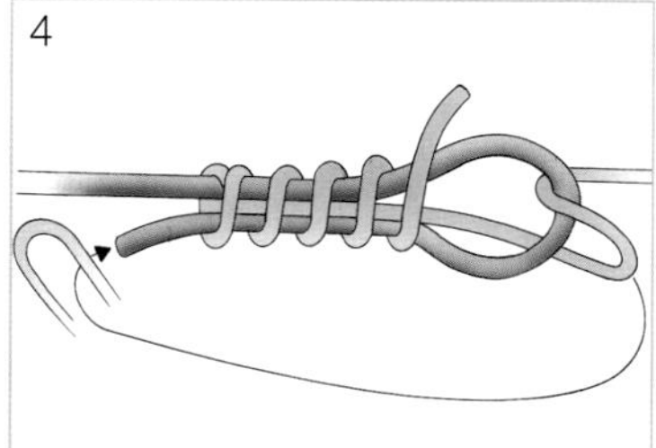

Ground Line Hitch

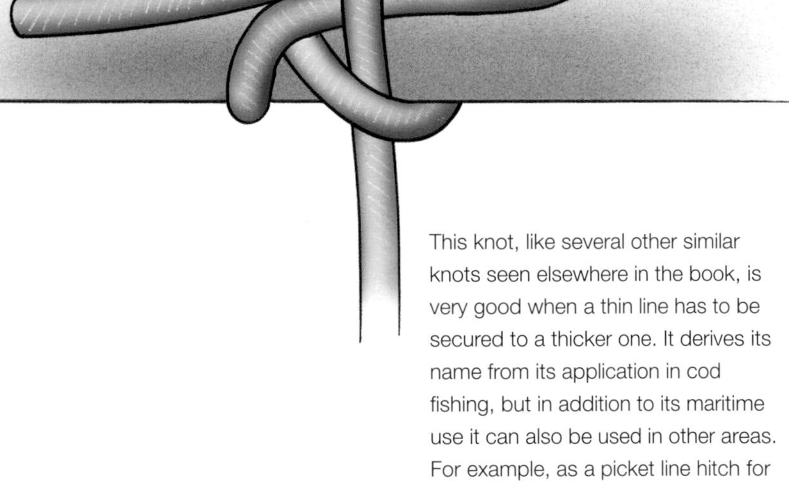

This knot, like several other similar knots seen elsewhere in the book, is very good when a thin line has to be secured to a thicker one. It derives its name from its application in cod fishing, but in addition to its maritime use it can also be used in other areas. For example, as a picket line hitch for securing horses.

If a bight is passed when tucking the end, the knot may be rapidly released, but this is not a good idea when used as a picket line knot, as it becomes less secure.

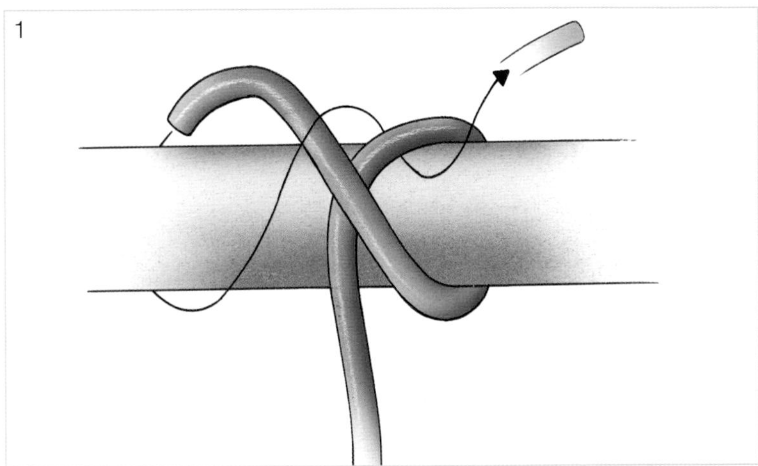
1

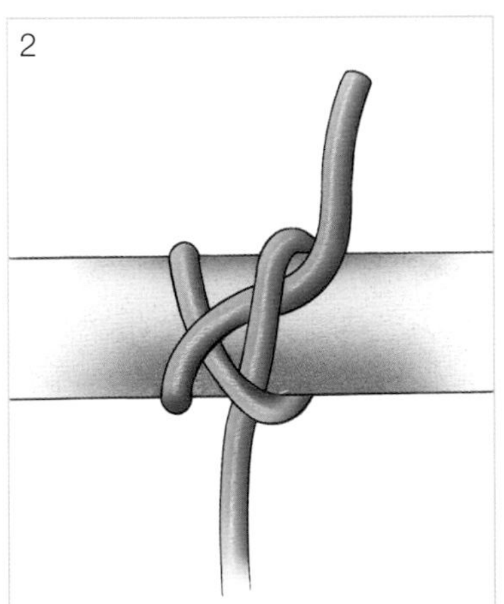
2

1 Commence as for a clove hitch by taking a turn around the main line or post. Cross in front of the first turn and form a second turn, bringing the end over to lock the second turn.

2 Tuck the end (or a bight as previously discussed) under the first turn. Pull taut to finish.

Carrick Bend

This old sailing knot was traditionally used to join two thick cables and this is still a good use for it. The method shown is the simplest to use when the rope is thick and heavy, as there is a minimum of interweaving to carry out. However, the design is also used decoratively in various guises.

1 With one end, form a loop, with the standing part resting over the working end.

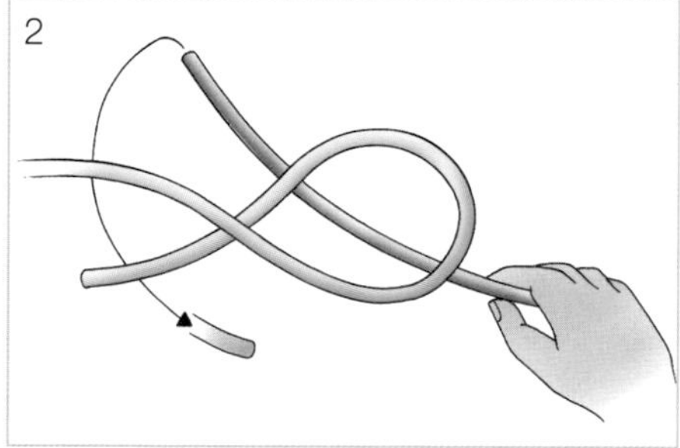

2 Drag the other cable under this loop and rest it on a block as thick as the rope.

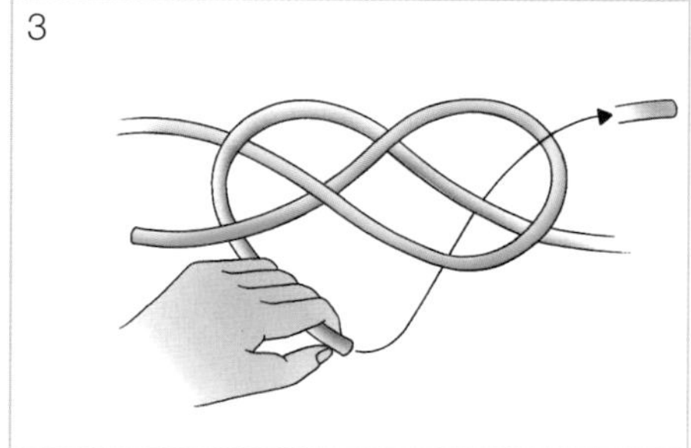

3 Bring the working part around over the other standing part and maneuver it under the first working end. Now for the only weave: Bring the end around, over the first rope, under the second, where the block supports the rope, and out over the third part.

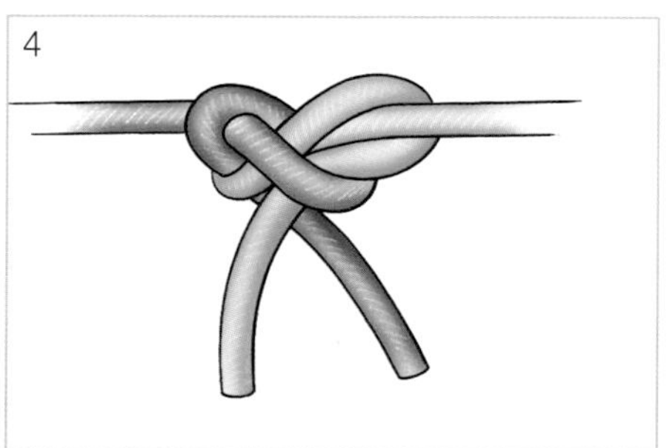

4 The working ends are now coming out on opposite sides, which is generally thought to give the strongest formation. A load should be applied carefully, as the knot will spill from the flat form to a more solid mass.

For decorative purposes, the knot may be adjusted so that the ends emerge on the same side.

Net Line Knot

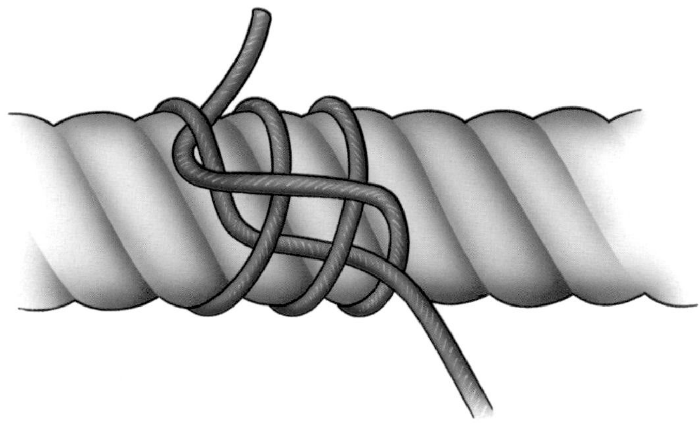

The headrope of a net will twist when wet and the net hanging under it may tangle. To combat this, you can tie two headropes of opposite twist together, as this will prevent this problem if they are firmly secured. This applies only to laid rope and if a suitable braided rope has been used as the headrope you need not anticipate inconvenience. To make it easier to demonstrate, only one rope has been shown in the illustrations, so remember that when laying your two ropes together that the twists should be in opposite directions, and that the ropes should lay tight alongside one another.

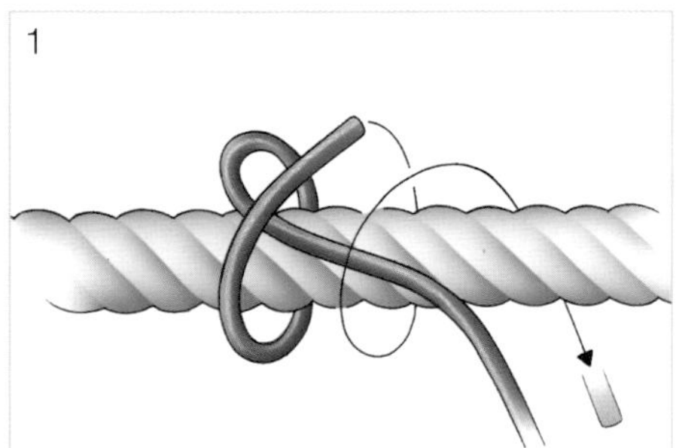

1 Bring the line diagonally across the thicker rope and take two turns over the line, trapping it as in the start of the rolling hitch.

2 & 3 Take the end up and across the two turns, tucking it under the furthest turn.

As seen in the illustration on the opposite page, the final tuck may be from either side of the furthest turn. Use whichever is most convenient or tidier.

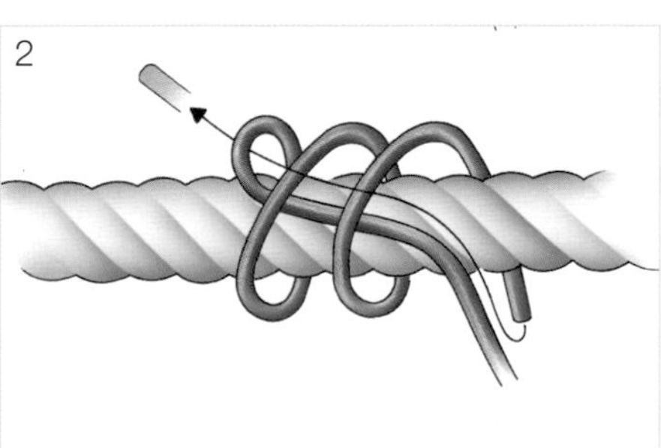

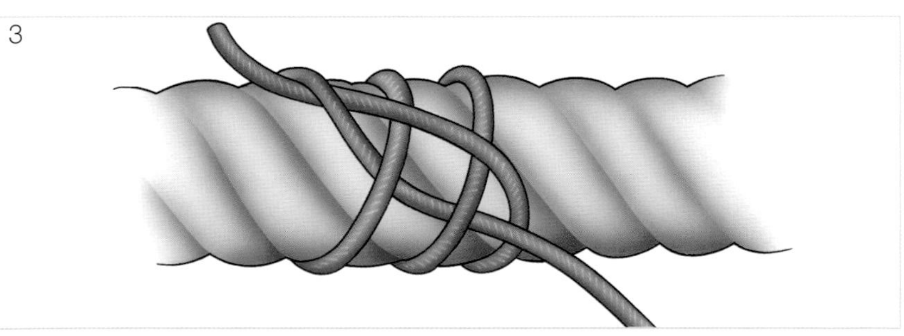

Turk's Head Knot Three Lead Four Bight

Used these days purely for ornamental purposes, this old seafarers' knot, and the next, can be formed flat around a ringbolt on the deck to make a thump mat to protect the planking, or can be made around a handle for identification and to give a grip.

The number of bights in the title refers to the number of lobes around the edge of the knot, while the leads are the interwoven strands needed to complete one circuit of the knot. It does not have anything to do with how many times you double (or treble) the knot to produce the finished Turk's head.

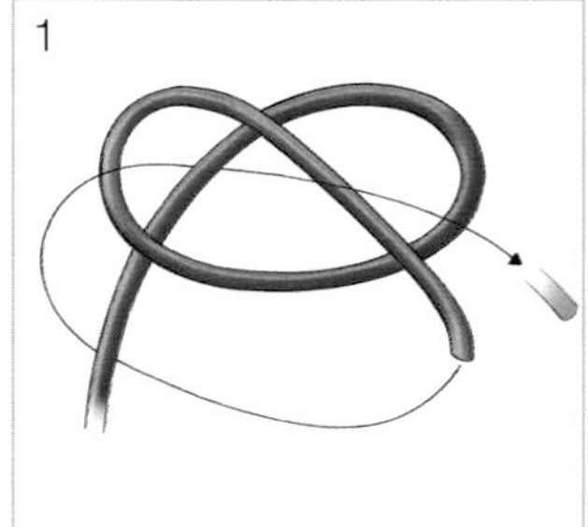

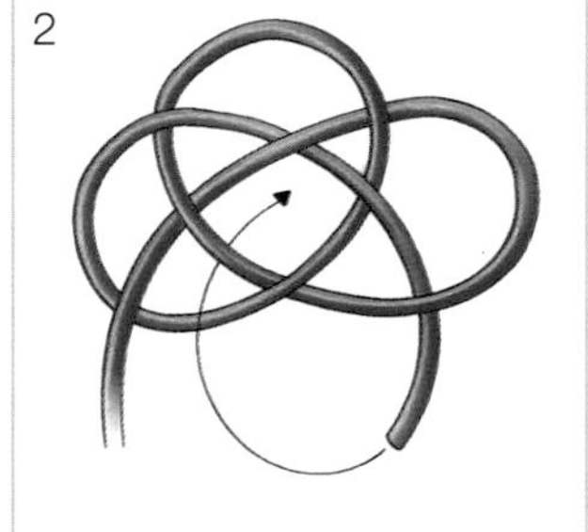

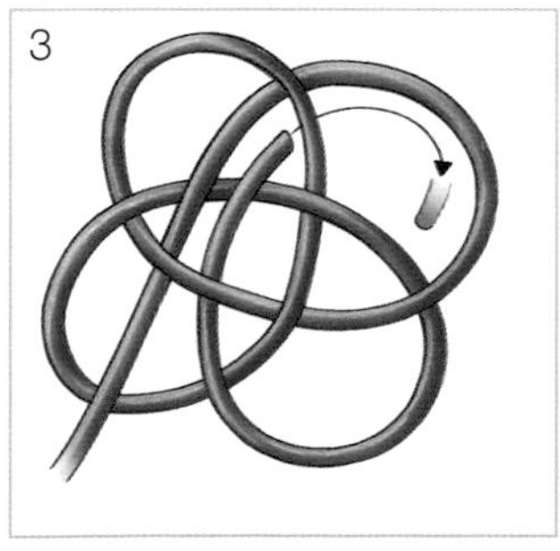

Learning a Turk's head is usually best done from the illustrations.

1 Form a loop and bring the end around over the loop.

2 Cross under the standing part and begin to weave. Over the first cord, under the next, over again, and then leave under the last cord. You will now have three interlooped lobes.

3 Bring the working end around and enter the knot alongside the standing part. This forms the fourth bight. Continue to follow the standing part and continue around the knot.

4 When you feel you have followed around enough, work the slack out and dress the knot into its proper shape. The ends are cut off underneath a loop and either sewn or carefully melted to keep it all from unraveling. If done in large cord, the strands of the mats should be sewn together for safety.

Turk's Head Knot Three Lead Five Bight

This knot makes a flatter mat than the previous one and is thus better suited as a coaster for drinks, though it may be used in many places.

Working out how much cord is required is almost impossible, as so much depends on what cord you use, how tight the knot will be pulled, and what its final job will be. Trial and error is the most effective way to learn how to tie this knot (it's unlikely that you will get it perfect the first time around). If you work any slack back toward the standing part, you will not waste much cord.

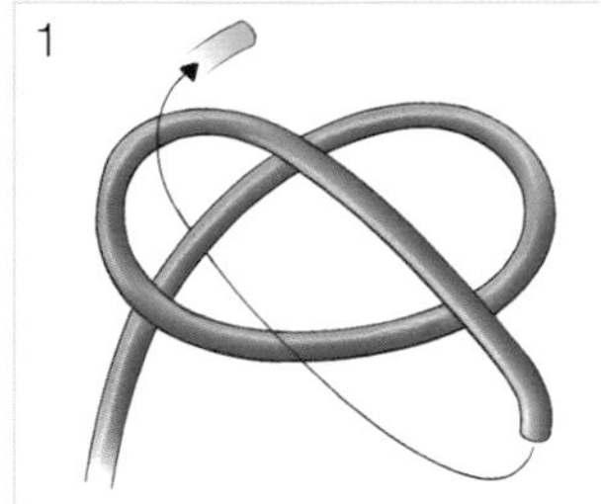

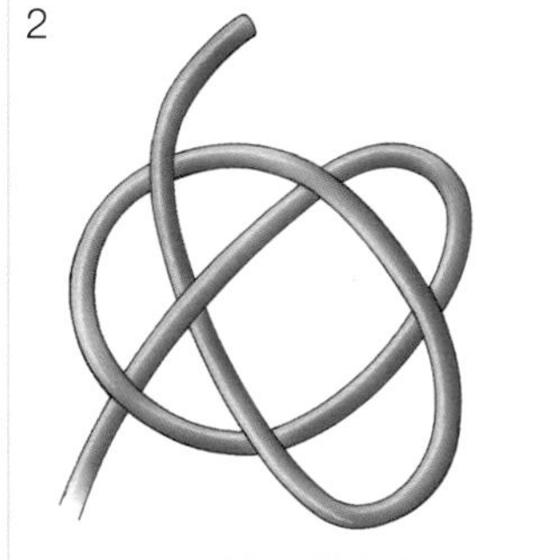

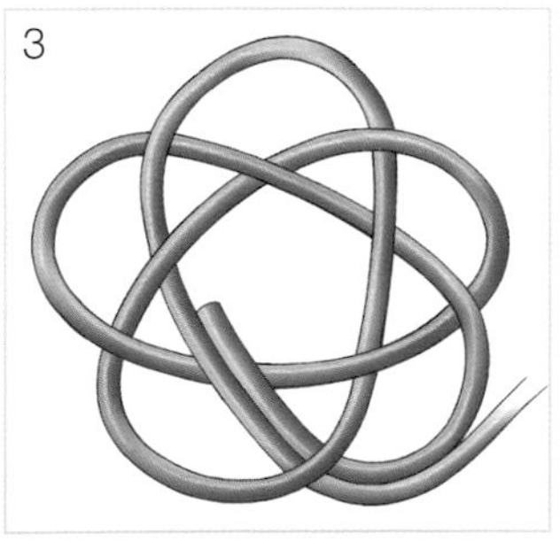

1 Form a loop as before and bring the working part across the loop.

2 Start weaving at once. Bring the end over the first cord, under the next, and leave over the last cord. Turn again and enter the knot under the next bight, going under, over, under, and leave over the last cord. You should now have four bights.

3 The fifth bight is formed by bringing the working end up alongside the standing part where it enters the knot, and you then follow around. The bights were formed in the order 3, 1, 4, 2, and 5 if you are following the third illustration.

4 When the following round is complete, you must work out the slack and dress the knot into the form you desire. The ends are treated in the same manner as the previous Turk's head.

Fishing Knots

Many of the knots in this section are similar in form and construction to those used in larger cord elsewhere and the most important thing to learn here is how to handle small lines. This comes with practice, but the basic grounding you will have already acquired if you have been tying the larger knots earlier in the book will make it much easier.

You may find that some of the specialized fishing knots will also work in larger cord, enabling you to perform a task that would otherwise be a problem. I recently had to rethread a particularly awkward blind and used the Albright knot to join some lines.

Contents of Fishing Knots

Knute Hitch 216
Double Turle Knot 217
Arbor Knot 218
Half Blood Knot or Clinch Knot 220
Blood Knot 222
Trilene Knot 224
Grinner or Uni Knot 225
Double Grinner Knot 226
Domhof Knot 228
Cat's Paw 230
Albright Knot 232
Dry Fly Knot 234
Perfection Loop 236
Vice Versa 238
Nail Knot 240
Blood Loop Dropper Knot 242
Jansik Special 243
Netting 244
Square Knot Netting 247
Spade End Knot 249
Palomar Knot 250

Knute Hitch

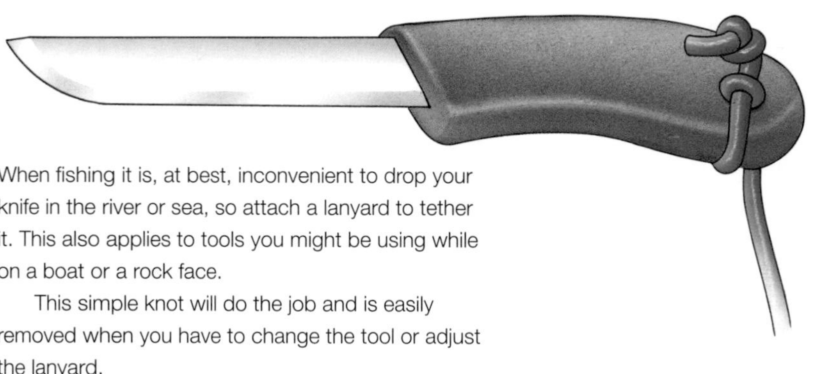

When fishing it is, at best, inconvenient to drop your knife in the river or sea, so attach a lanyard to tether it. This also applies to tools you might be using while on a boat or a rock face.

This simple knot will do the job and is easily removed when you have to change the tool or adjust the lanyard.

1 First tie a small stopper knot at the end of the lanyard line. Pass a bight through the lanyard hole, which should be just large enough for two thicknesses of the line. Bring the end up and pass it through the bight. Pull the standing end to tighten.

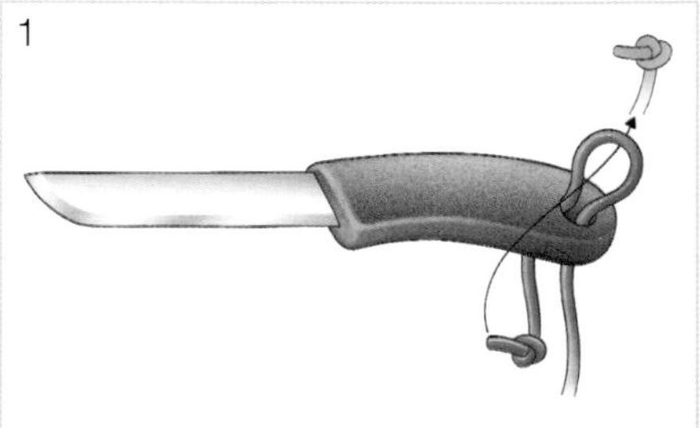

Double Turle Knot

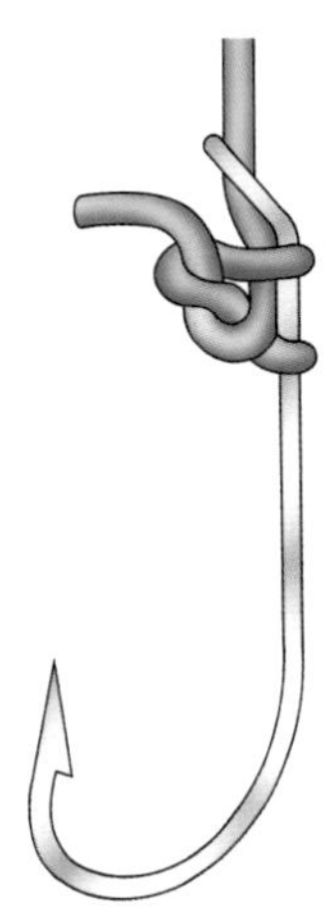

This knot is used to join a line to an angled eye or offset eye hook, and has been well known for over 160 years.

1 Feed the line through the eye. Form two loops, perhaps around a finger, and tie a thumb knot around them.

2 Remove the finger and pass the body of the hook through the two loops. Lubricate with saliva and pull tight. Trim the end.

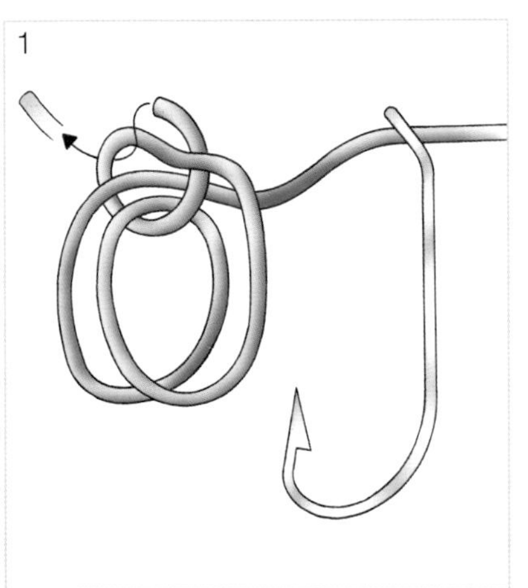

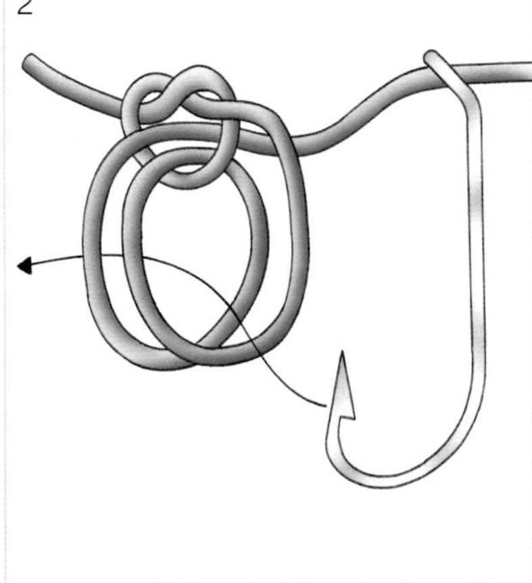

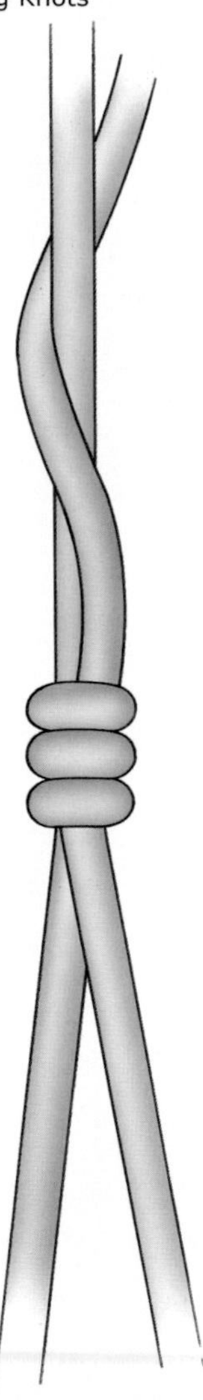

Arbor Knot

A fishing line is fastened to the reel with this knot. The axle or center of the reel is the arbor. This blood knot will slide down the standing part to lock against the axle and secure the line to the reel.

1 Pass the line around the axle, bring it forward, and make an open loop, which is then held next to the standing part.

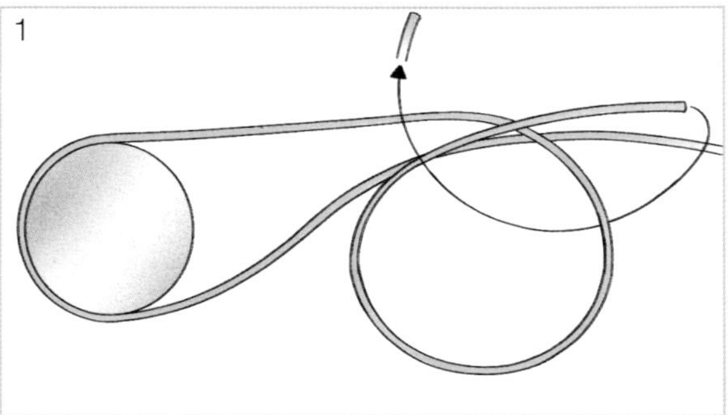

2 & 3 Take several turns around the loop and the standing part, and finish off as a blood knot. Pull taut. This blood knot will slide down the standing part to lock against the axle and secure the line to the reel.

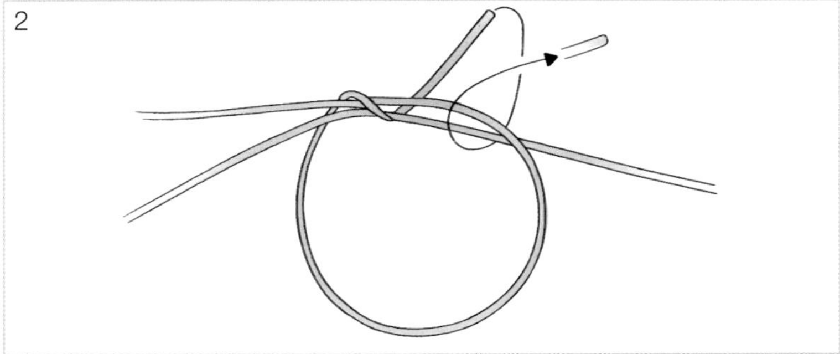

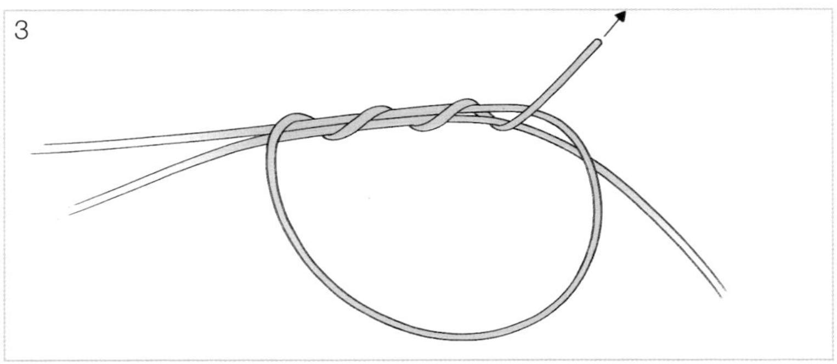

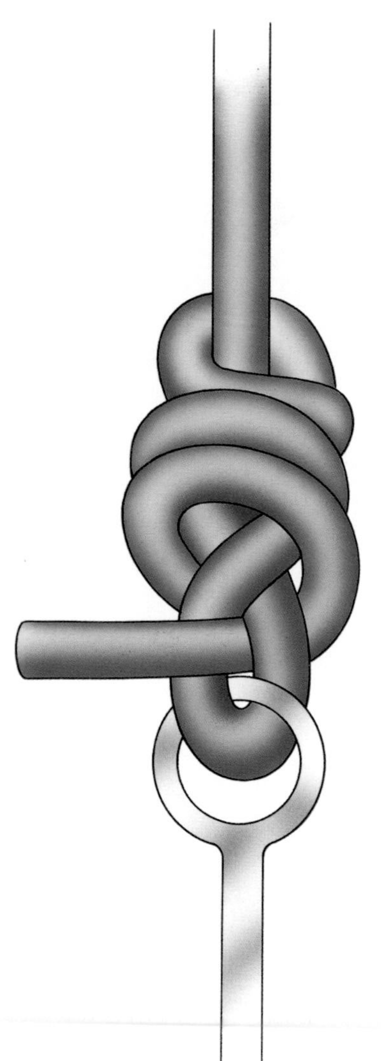

Half Blood Knot or Clinch Knot

This is one of the simplest knots you can use to join a line to an eyed hook or swivel, but like most fishing knots it does require practice and a certain amount of dexterity, as fishing line is far finer than the cords that have been used in other chapters of this book.

Most nylon lines pull up easier if lubricated. The lubricant of choice is usually saliva, as a separate carrying container is not required, but if you are going to put fishing equipment in or near your mouth, be very aware of the hook and be careful that your equipment is clean and has not come in contact with polluted water.

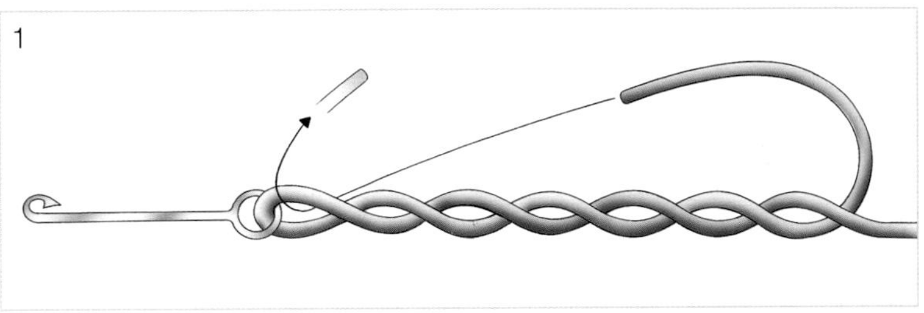

1 Pass the end of the line through the eye and double it back on itself. Roll the hook or swivel between finger and thumb, thus imparting a twist to the line.

2 Lead the end of the line down, over the twists, and through the gap where the line emerges from the eye. Lubricate and gradually pull taut. Trim the end short.

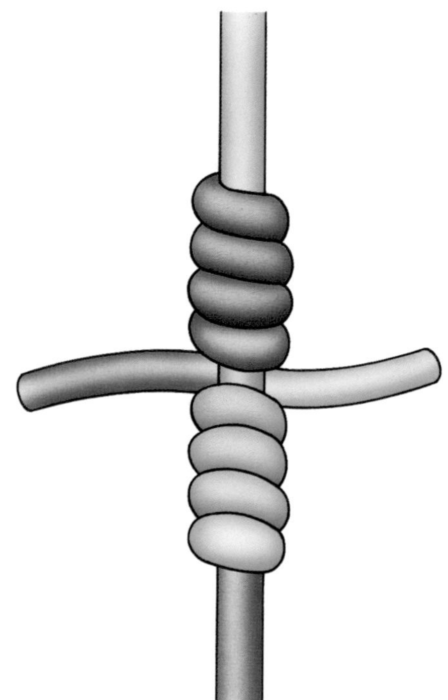

Blood Knot

This is one of many knots in the blood knot family, but is probably the best known. Used to join two lines, it may be used with success in regular-sized cord as well as in fishing lines. It may come in very handy should your line break.

1 Overlap the two ends of the line from opposite directions. Take several turns around one line, holding the core line straight.

2 Bring the end back and up between the standing part and the first turn.

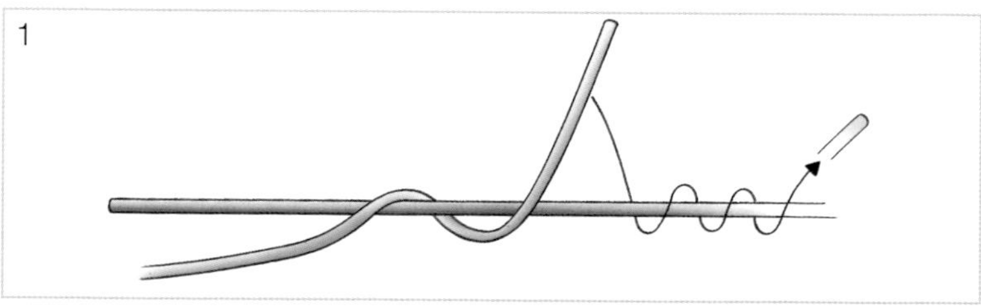

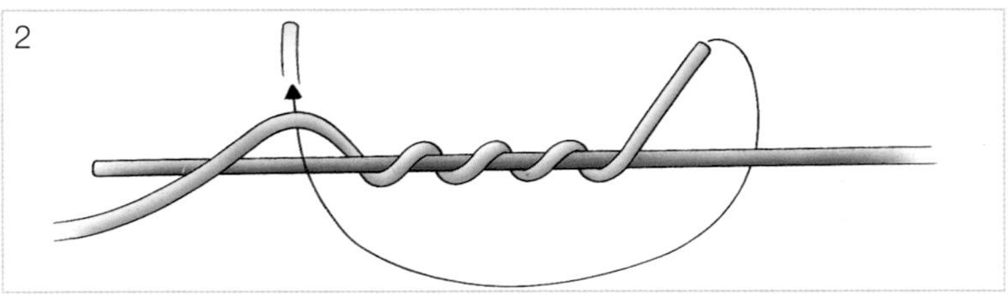

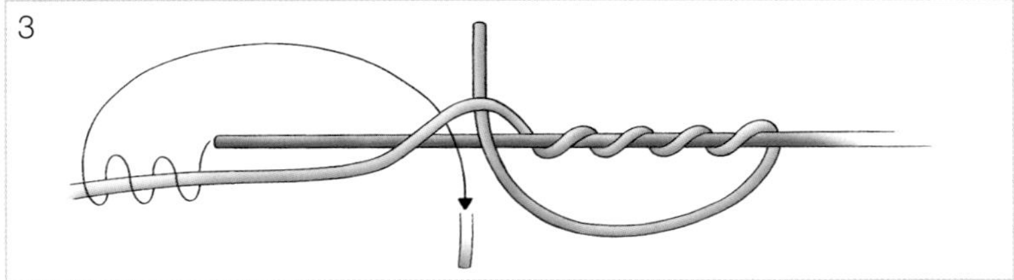

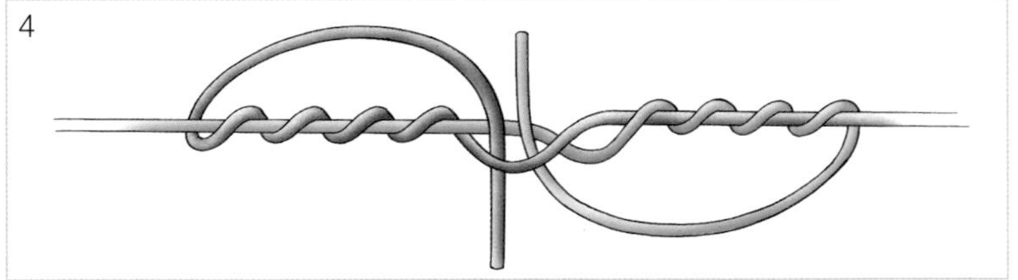

3 Turn the whole thing around and with the other line take the same number of turns, in the same direction around the first line, and bring the end back in the same fashion.

4 The two ends will be leaving the center of the knot on opposite sides. Lubricate and gently pull taut. Trim the ends.

Trilene Knot

This knot may be thought of as a blood knot with a round turn. In the same way a bowline with a round turn eases the load when a jerk is applied, this knot will also be stronger than a simple blood knot. This is of obvious use to a fisherman.

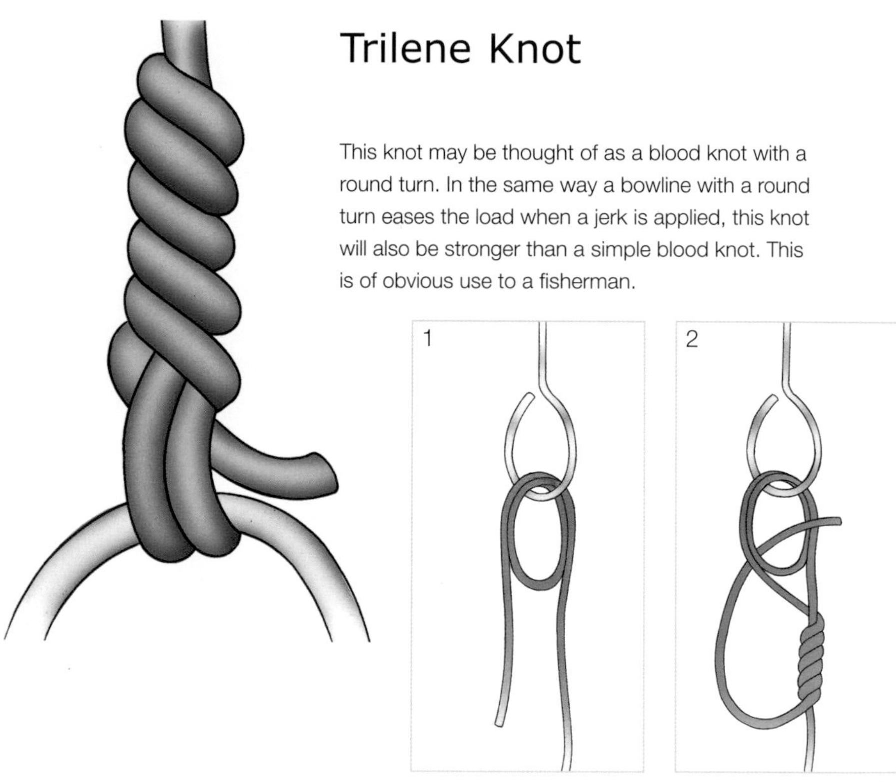

1 Take the end of the line through the eye and then pass it through again.

2 Form about half a dozen turns along the line, working away from the eye. Bring the end back and feed it through the round turns. Lubricate and pull taut. Trim the end.

Grinner or Uni Knot

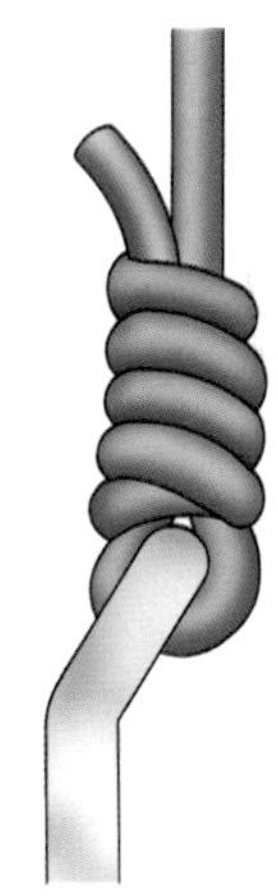

This knot is almost a reversed version of the double fisherman's knot and is used to join a line to an eye.

1 & 2 Pass the line through the eye and bring it back alongside the standing part so the eye will be at the end of a bight. Take the line back to the eye and put four or five turns around both arms of the bight and lead the end out from the loop. Lubricate and pull tight. Trim the end.

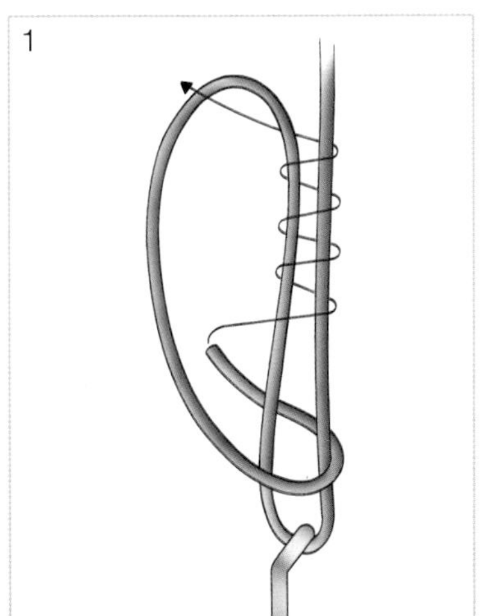

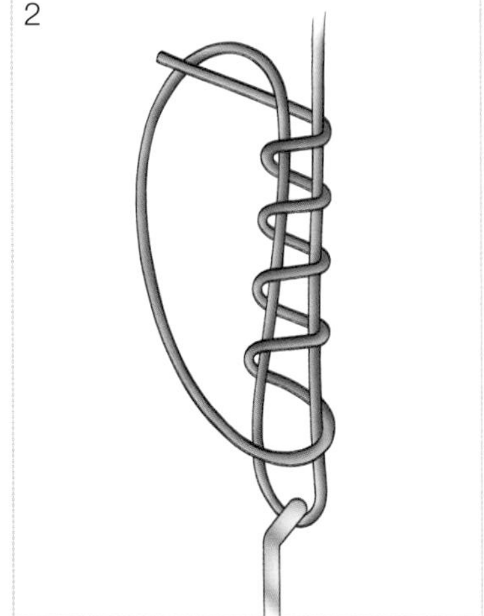

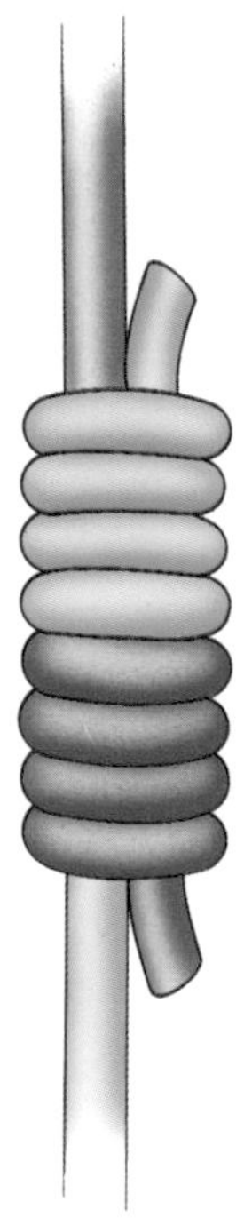

Double Grinner Knot

This uses the same principle as the grinner to join two lines. It is the fisherman's equivalent of the climber's grapevine, but more turns are usually taken, as the material is much more fine and slippery.

1 Bring the ends together from different sides. With one end form a grinner knot around the other line.

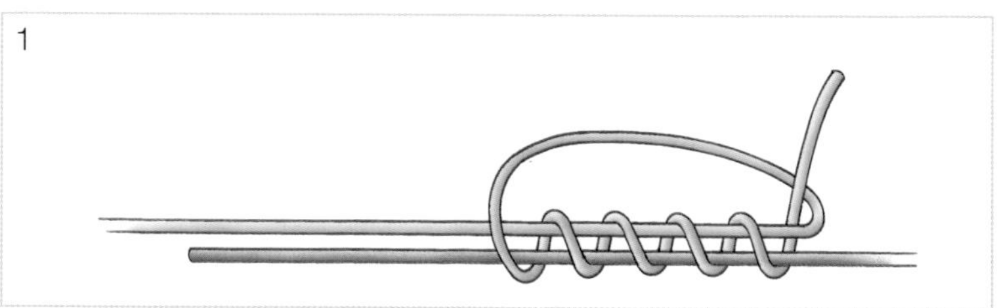

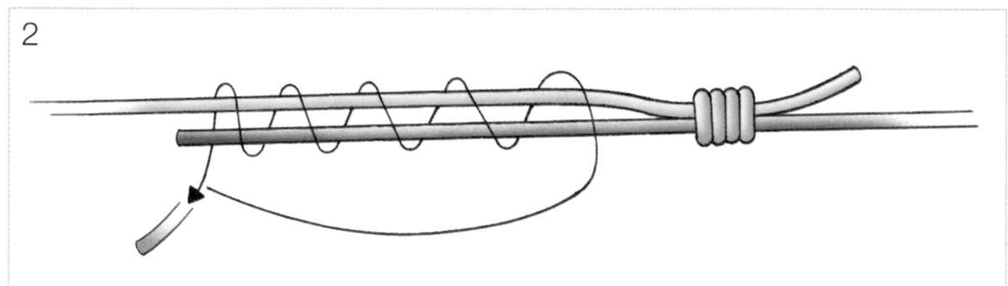

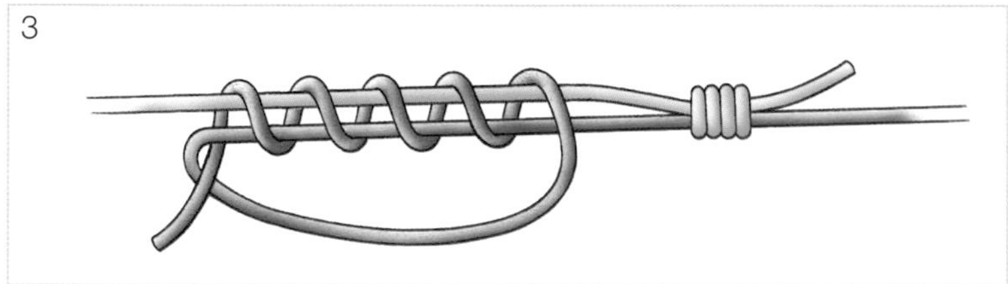

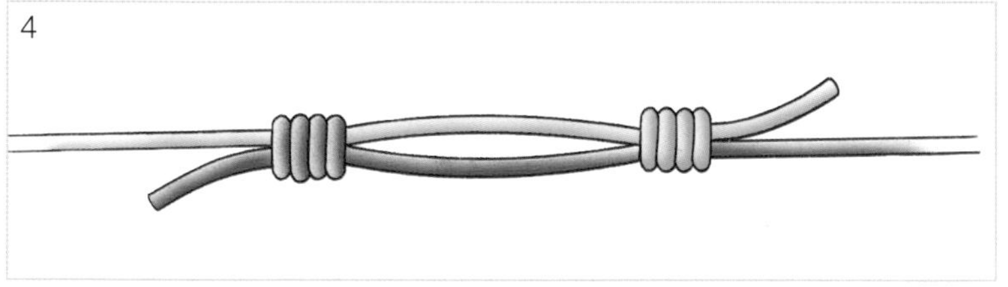

2 & 3 Turn around and form a grinner with the second line around the first.

4 Lubricate and work each knot firm, then pull the two standing parts to slide the grinners together. Pull tight and trim the ends.

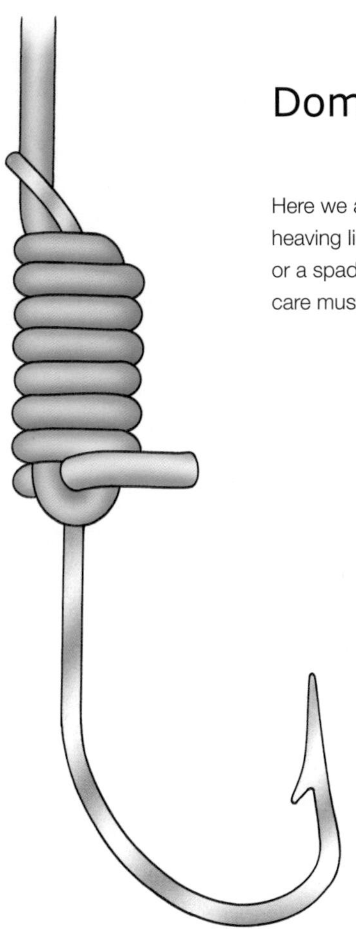

Domhof Knot

Here we are using the idea of the hangman's or heaving line knot to fasten the line to an eyed hook or a spade end hook. In the latter case, a little more care must be taken.

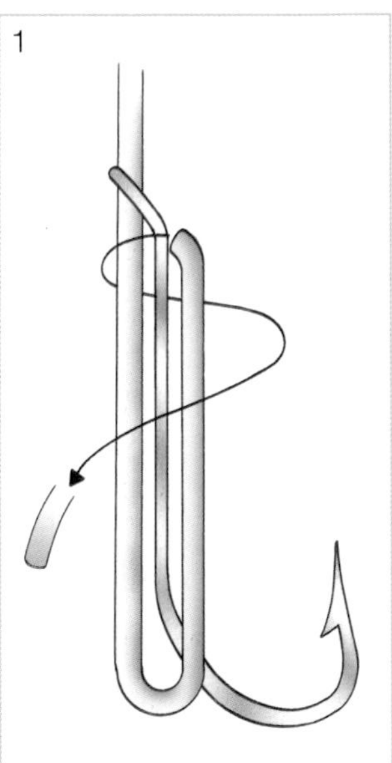

1 Pass the line through the eye, take it down the hook to the end, and then double it back.

2 Start to wrap around the two strands of line and the shaft of the hook until you reach the end.

3 Feed the end through the bight at the end of the hook. Lubricate and pull tight, sliding the knot toward the eye. Trim the end.

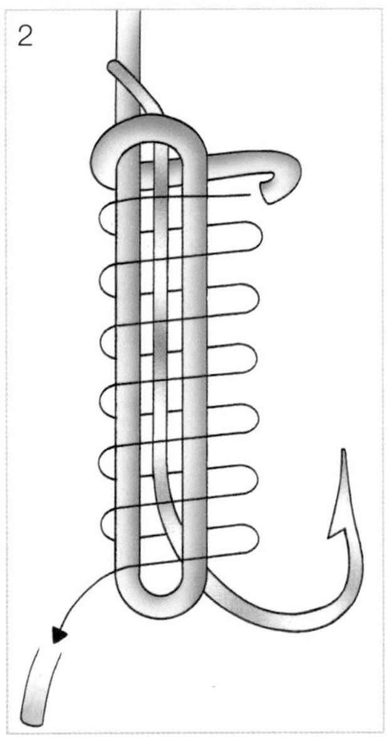

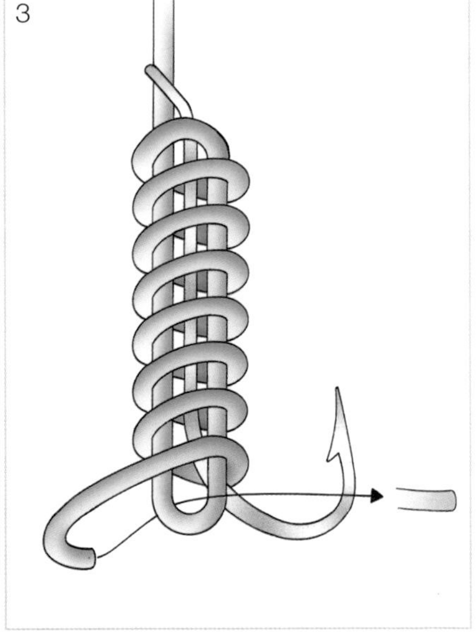

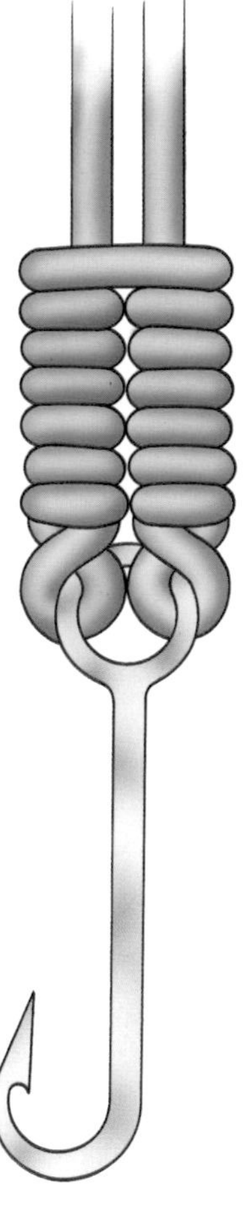

Cat's Paw

This is another application of the cat's paw used earlier in the book to suspend a slung load, but formed in a slightly different manner to hold a hook on a double line. It is also known as the offshore knot.

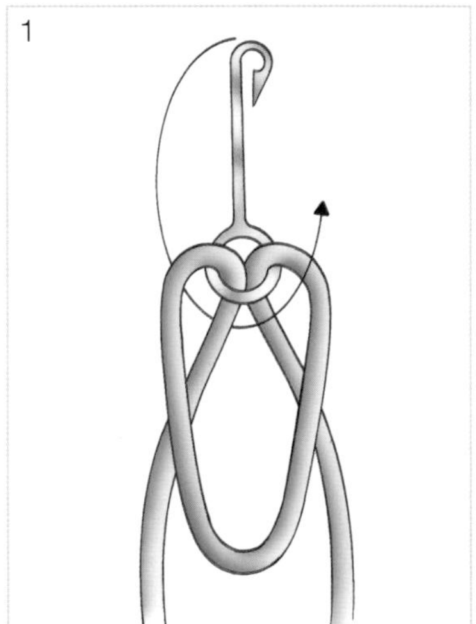

1 Pass a bight of the line through the eye of the hook or swivel and let the loop drop down in front. Let the hook fall back and come up through the loop. This will impart a twist to both sides of the cat's paw.

2 Repeat this seven or eight times.

3 Lubricate and pull the ends of the line while pushing the turns. Pull tight and trim the end.

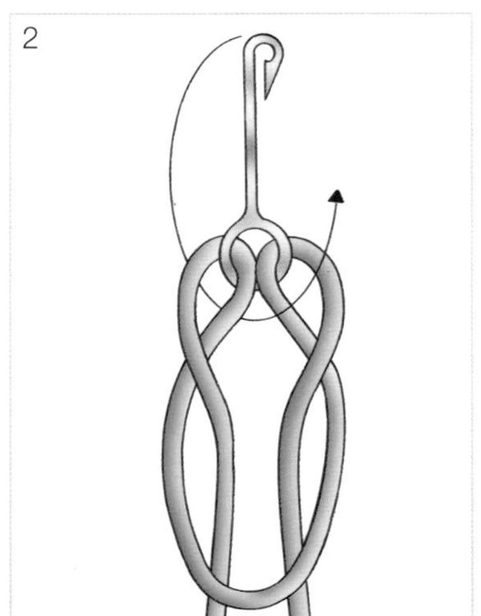

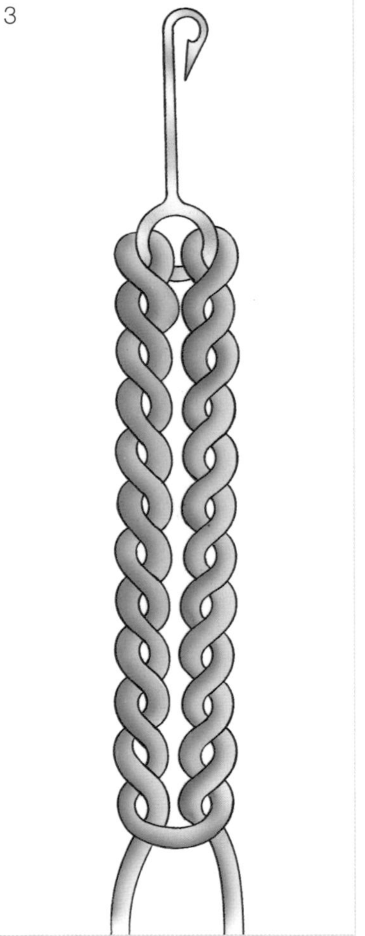

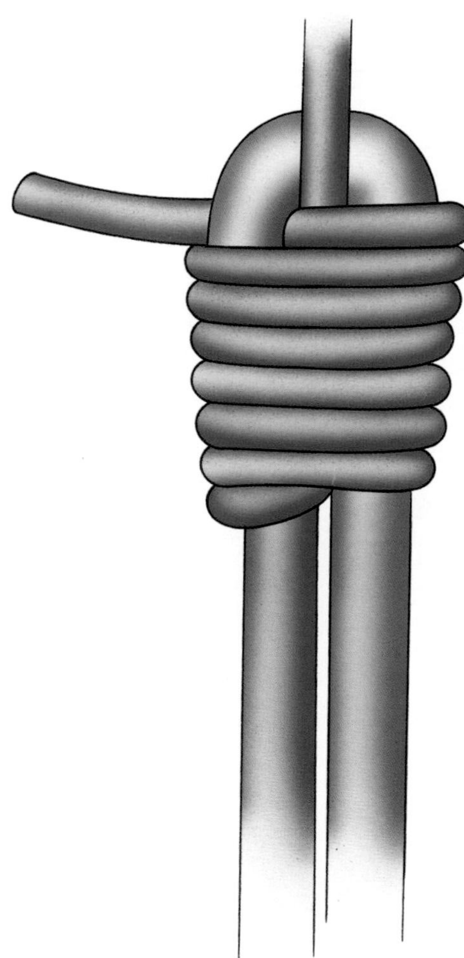

Albright Knot

This is very close to a seizing bend, but one that can be applied to small lines. It is used to join monofilament to wire or other monofilament of widely different sizes.

1 Double the thicker line to give an overlap of about three inches. Bring the thin line in at the bend of the doubled line and take it up between the two thick lines.

2 Start to wind the thin line over itself and the doubled thick line, working back toward the bend in the thick line, making sure that the turns are even and do not overlap.

3 Feed the end of the thin line through the loop at the end of the thick line, holding everything firm. Lubricate and work the knot along so that the end of the line is trapped at the bend of the thick line. Pull tight and trim the ends.

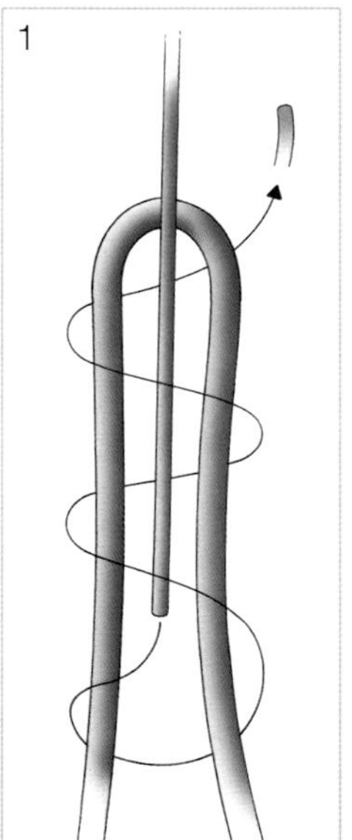

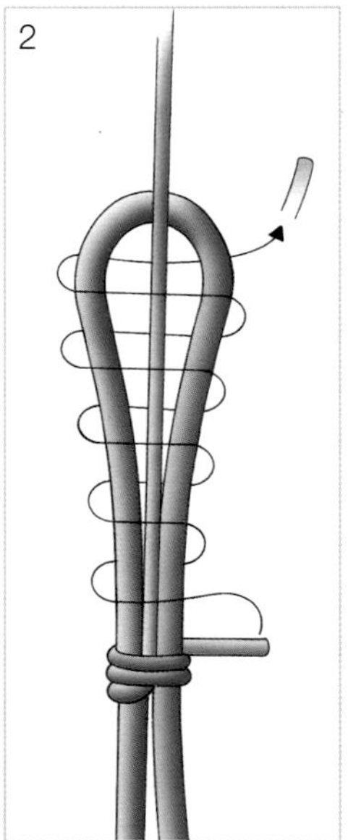

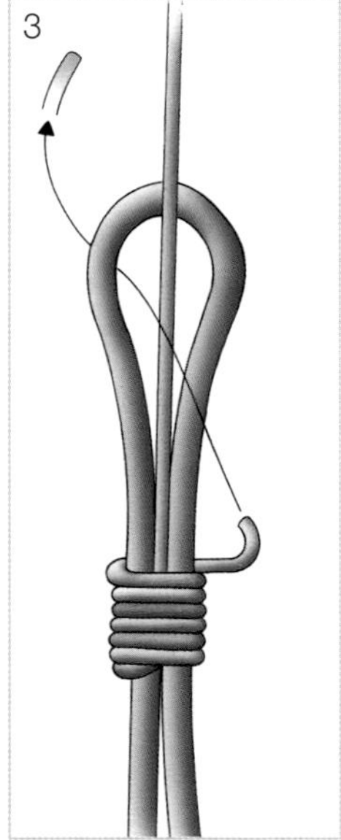

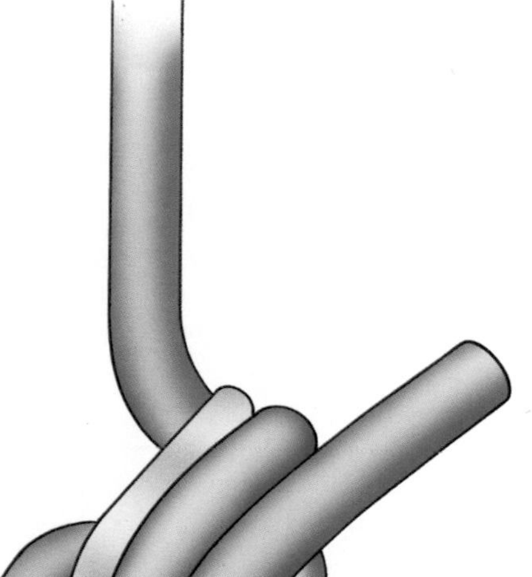

Dry Fly Knot

Of the many knots available to attach a fly, dry or wet, to a line, this is one of the best. If you wish to specialize in fly fishing it is an excellent place to start, but you might wish to study a book dedicated to the subject as you progress.

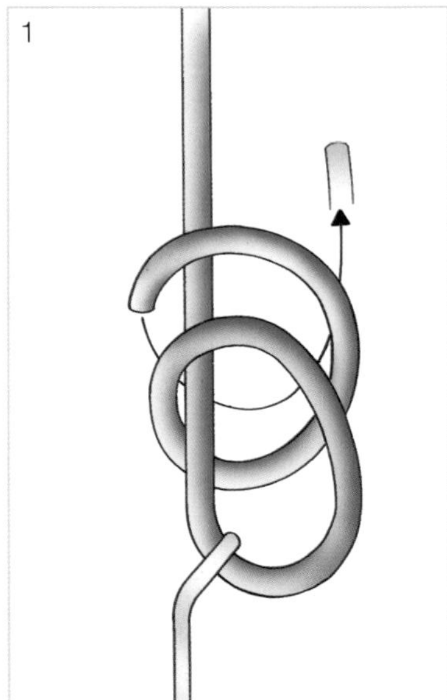

1 Pass the line through the eye and take two turns around the standing part to form two parallel loops.

2 Now take two turns through the loops and around the coils of the loops.

3 Slide the coils down onto the shank of the hook while simultaneously pulling on the standing part. You may need to lubricate at this point. When the knot is grasping the hook, tighten and trim the end.

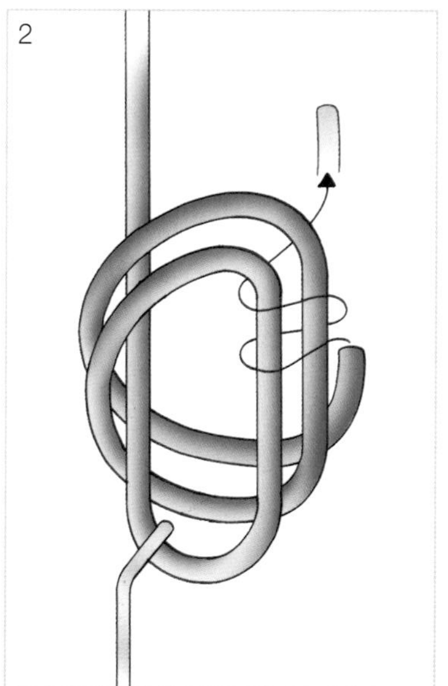

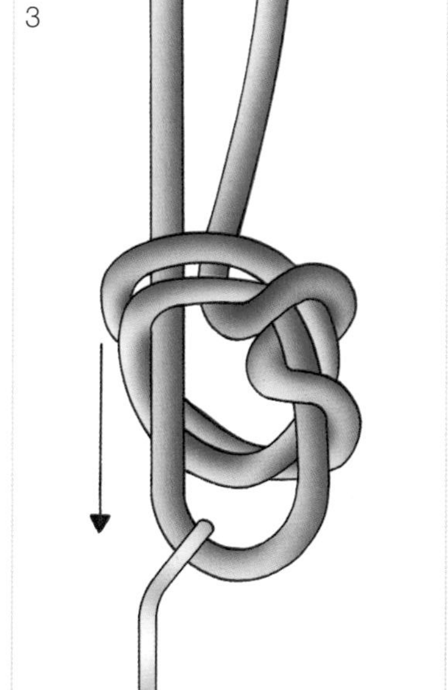

Perfection Loop

Here we have a knot that goes back to at least the 1600s and which works as well in modern materials as it did with the gut and horsehair lines of Isaak Walton. Indeed, though it is best known by fishermen, it will even remain secure in bungee cord (but don't trim the tail short if you're using it for that purpose).

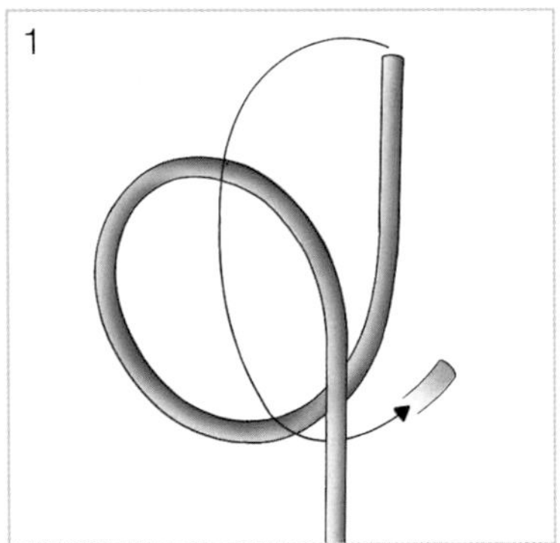

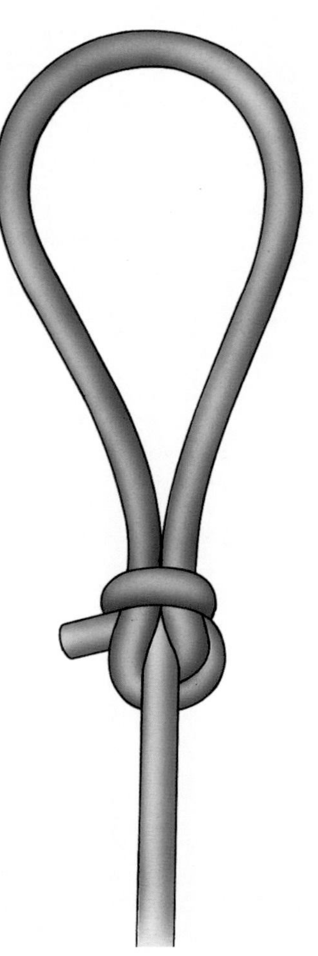

1 Form an underhand loop with the end coming out on the right.

2 Take a loose turn to form a second loop around the standing part, above and overlapping the first loop.

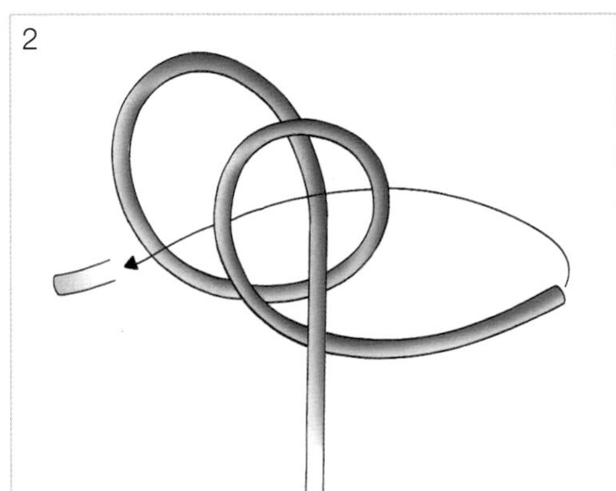

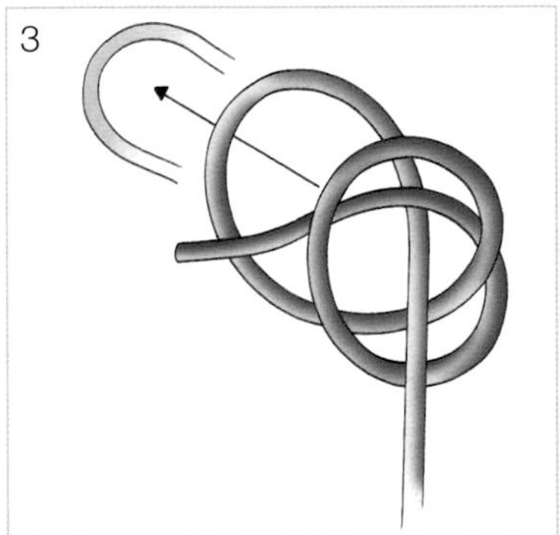

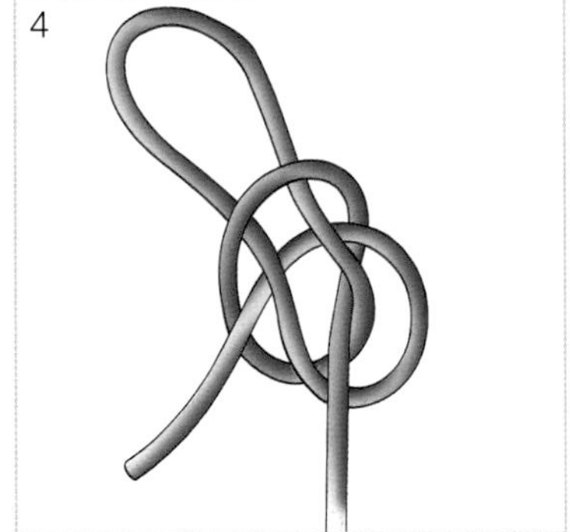

3 Lead the end between the two loops and pull the bight of the upper loop down through the first loop.

4 The end is now trapped and the knot can be worked tight.

Vice Versa

This knot is offered as a method of joining lines, as it holds well with slimy hide thongs, slippery sutures, wet yachting ropes, and even bungee cord. It was devised by the late Harry Asher, who made many invaluable contributions to the art and craft of knot tying. Try it and test it.

1 & 2 Bring the ends together. Take the end coming from the left around behind the other line and up in front of it but behind its own standing part. Lead the end coming from the right over the other line, down and up in front of its own standing part.

3 Cross this end behind the other end and lead it into the loop formed by the first line.

4 Take the first end and feed it through the loop formed by the second line. Gently tighten by pulling the ends and standing parts at the same time. When all is secure trim the ends, which lie neatly in line with the rest of the line.

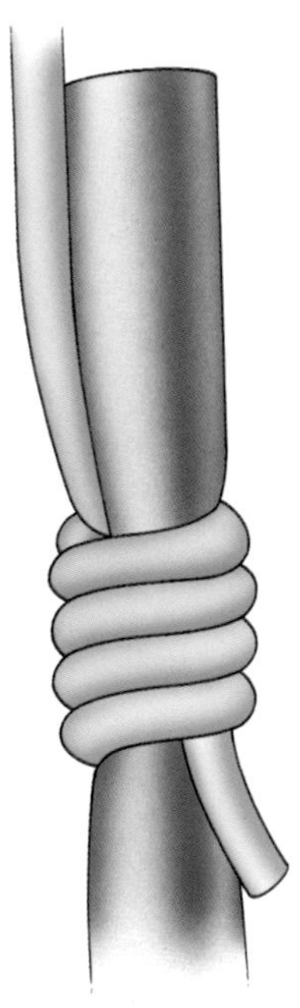

Nail Knot

Sometimes called the tube knot depending on the item used to assist in its construction, this is a means of joining a monofilament leader to a fly line. I prefer to use a small piece of fine brass tubing rather than a nail, but a section of a ballpoint pen ink tube, suitably free of ink, is just as good.

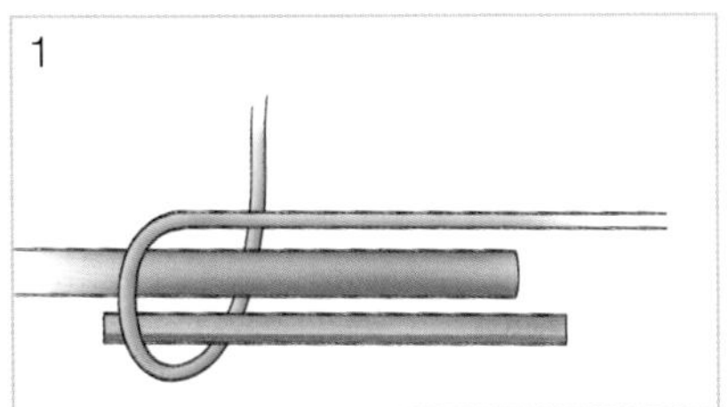

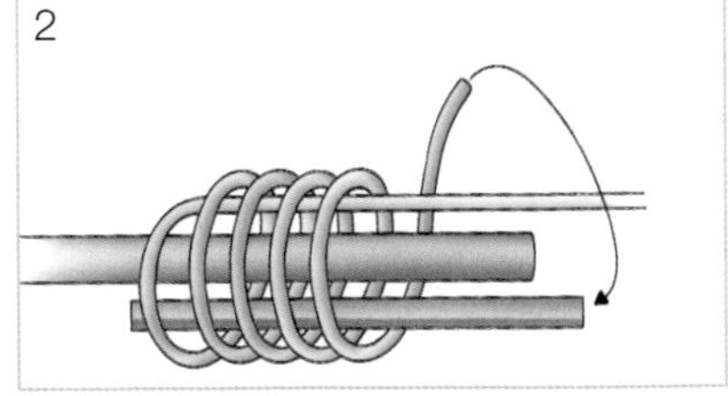

1 Place the tube against the end of the line and bring the monofilament up to it as shown in the illustration, with the standing part arranged along the top of the fly line. The tube should be placed beneath.

2 Start taking whipping turns around both the line and the tube, working toward the end of the line. As usual, these turns are kept close together without overlapping and are pulled fairly firm. Six or seven turns will probably be enough.

3 A little way from the end of the line, feed the monofilament through the tube.

4 Holding the whipping firmly, pull the tube free from the turns. This leaves a rather slack whipping, which must be tightened carefully before pulling completely taut and trimming.

If using a nail, the nail is removed and the end of the monofilament is fed down the space occupied by the nail. Using a tube makes life easier. Don't go too close to the end of the line when applying the turns, as there is a danger that they will all fall off and you will have to start again. In an emergency, should you not have a nail or tube, a doubled length of monofilament may be used instead. The loop where it is doubled can serve like the eye of a needle to pull the end through.

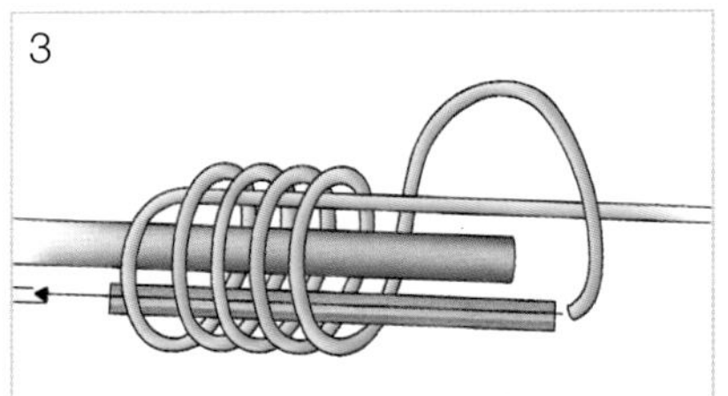

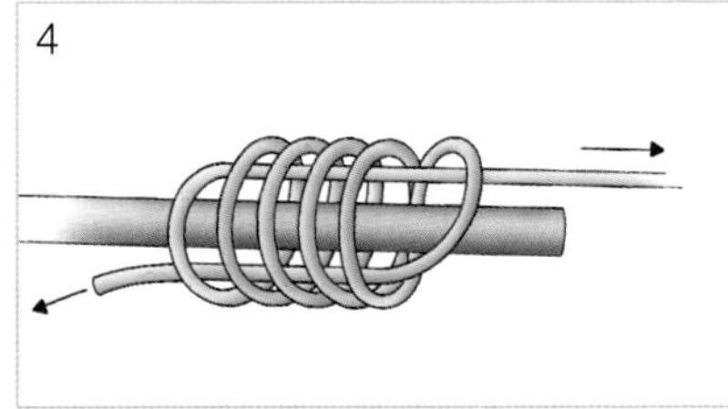

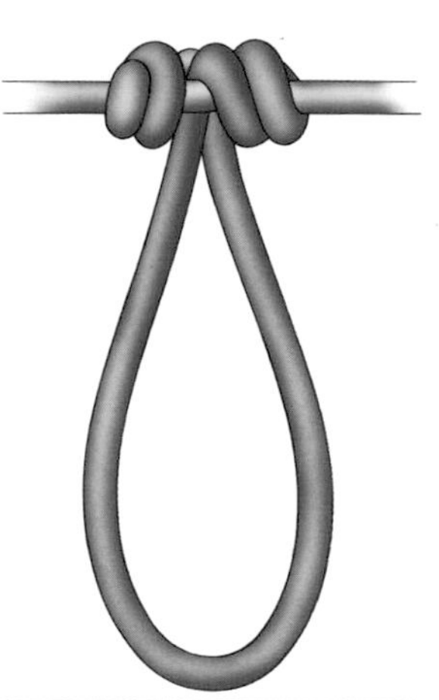

Blood Loop Dropper Knot

This loop, which should come out at right angles to the line, is excellent for attaching additional flies to the fly line, or weights and hooks for a paternoster system when fishing from beach or boat. An Alpine butterfly will do the same job.

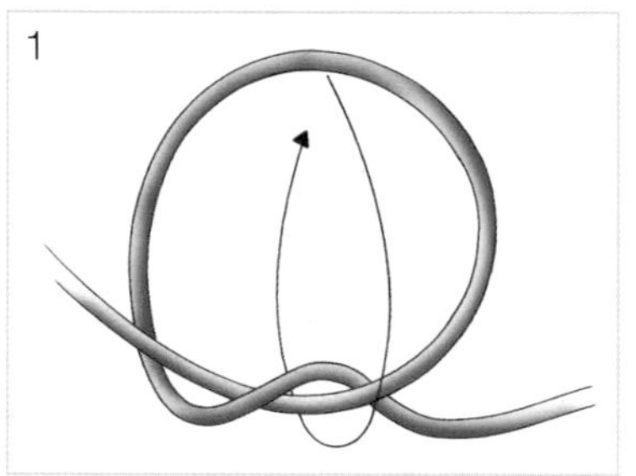

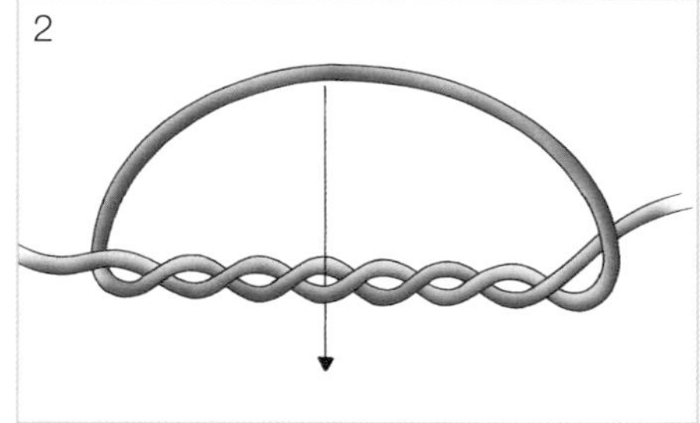

1 & 2 Form a thumb knot with a large loop and continue to add turns until there are at least eight. An even number is preferred.

3 Find the middle of the turns and separate them to produce an eye. Take a bight of the initial large loop through the eye and pull taut.

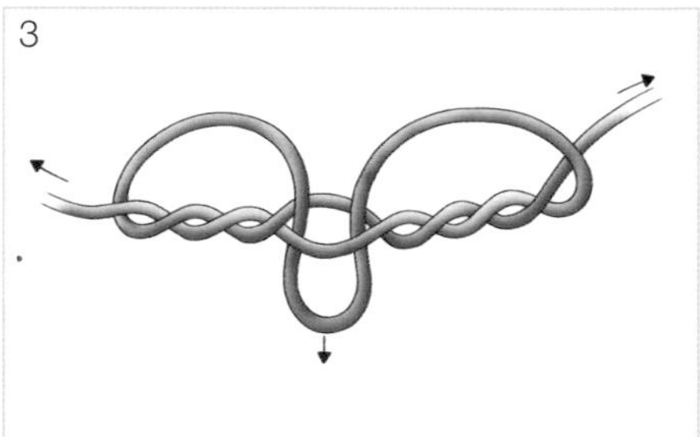

Jansik Special

This very efficient strong knot is good for attaching light monofilament to a hook or swivel.

1 & 2 Pass the end of the line twice through the eye of the hook, forming two loops.

3 Bring the end up to the eye as though you are intending to take a third turn, but instead change direction and take three turns around the three strands of line on the side of the loop approaching the eye. Work tight and trim the end.

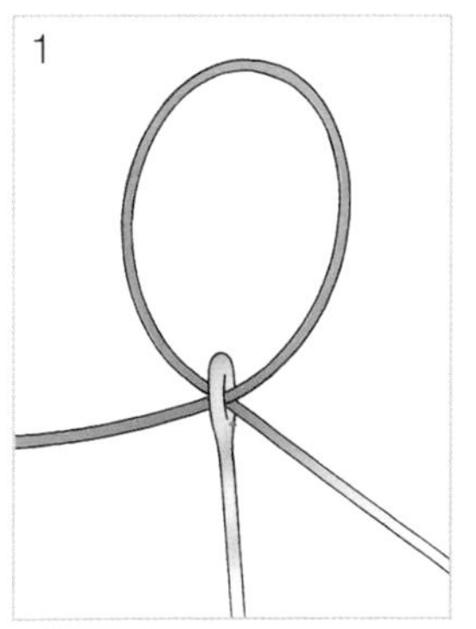

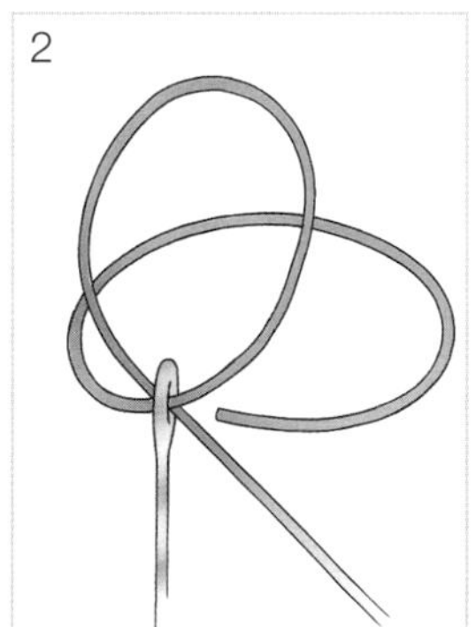

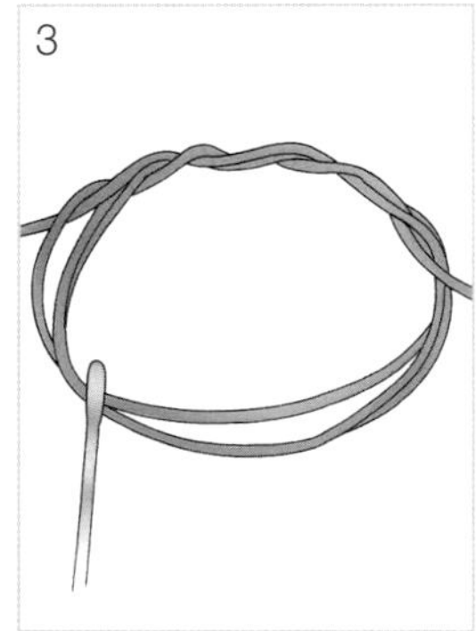

Netting

I enjoy eating fish, and nets, together with nightlines and traps (all in legal situations) have produced more food for me than the more "sporting" fishing techniques, so netting is included here, although it is such a useful skill to acquire that it would not be out of place in any of the other sections in this book. Hammocks, lightweight bags, and safety nets are but a few of the useful items that make life more bearable and can be made from knotted cord.

1 To save passing the ball of twine through the knot each time, you will need a netting needle. There are several different styles. The one illustrated is the most useful for our purposes.

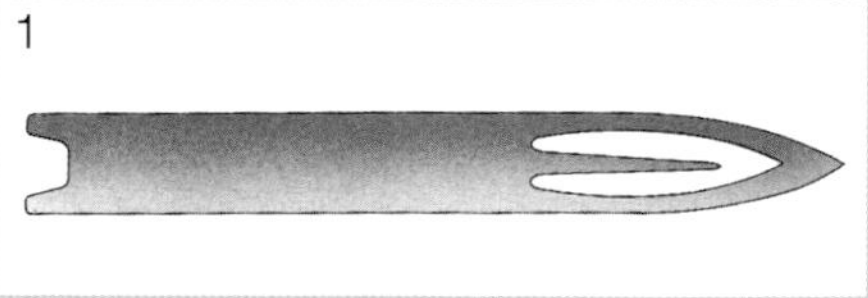

2 Loading the needle is accomplished by passing the cord around the prong and holding the end under the first turn while going down and up the other side, around the prong, and repeating until there is no more room on the needle.

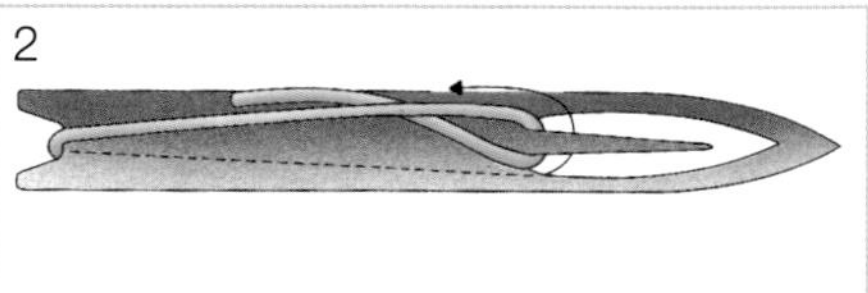

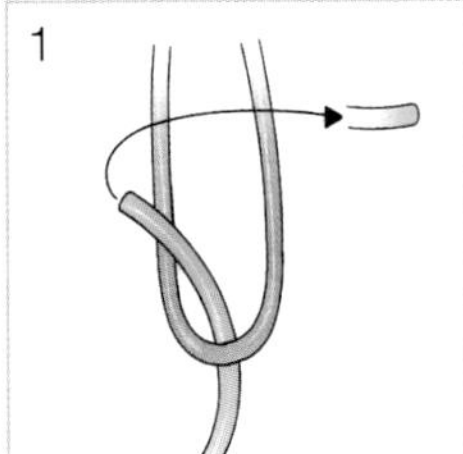

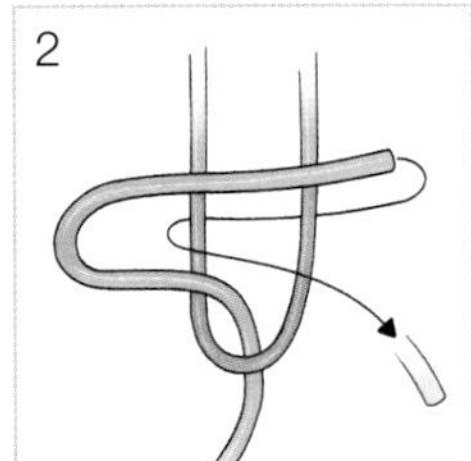

The first row of meshes is put on the headrope with clove hitches before the rest of the net can be built. This has not been shown, as this section is intended as a simple introduction to netting for those who may wish to learn it properly.

1 & 2 The common mesh knot is the sheet bend, and this you tie by bringing the needle up and through the first mesh from behind. Hold the twine at the base of the mesh with your thumb and bring the needle across to the left.

3, 4, & 5 Reverse direction, leaving a small bight, and go around the back of the mesh and out through the bight. Take the needle down to the right and pull tight.

This is the basic move in netting, although there are many refinements in setting up, repairing, and changing mesh size and shape.

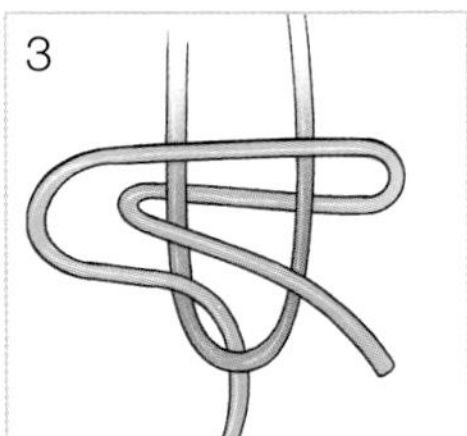

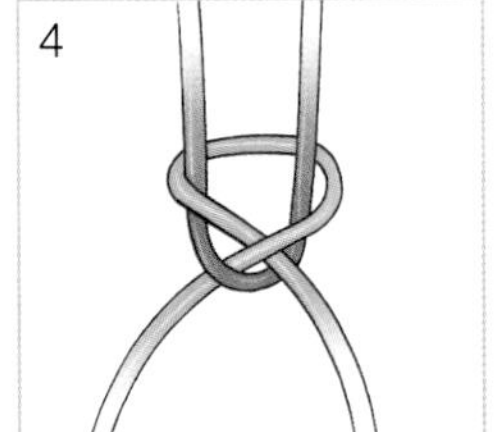

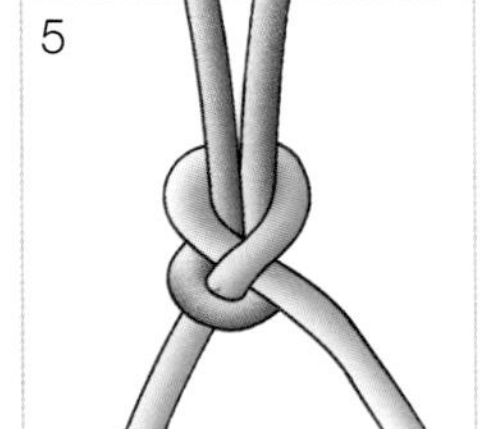

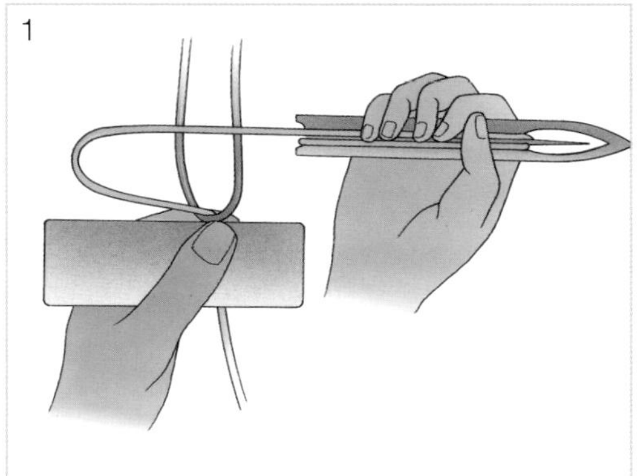

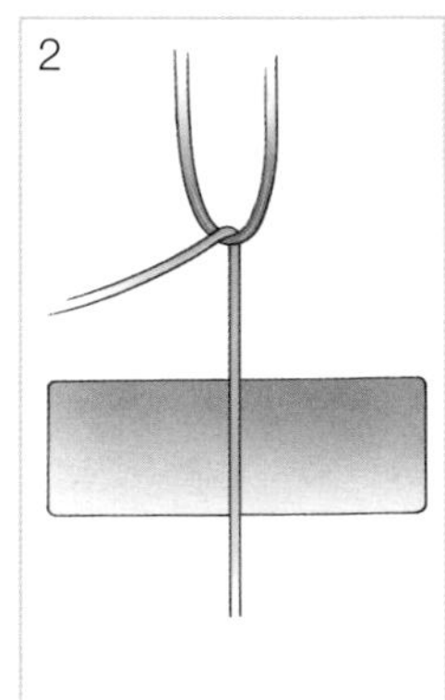

To keep the meshes all the same size, a mesh stick is used as shown. This can be seen in illustrations 1, 2, and 3. The needle goes around this each time between knots and so the size of the mesh is controlled by giving a loop that is exactly the same diameter as the stick each time.

When pulling tight, care must be taken to form a sheet bend and not to pull the knot off the mesh, which gives a slipped thumb knot that will not be of any use.

At the end of the row you can either work backward to the start or go to the other side of the net and carry on as before. This alternates the rows and prevents twisting of the finished net.

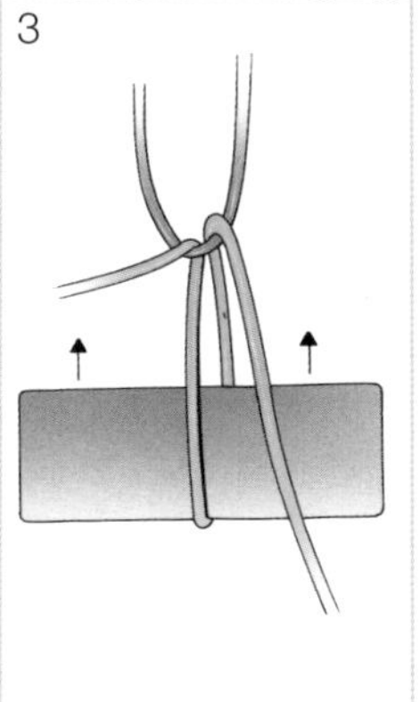

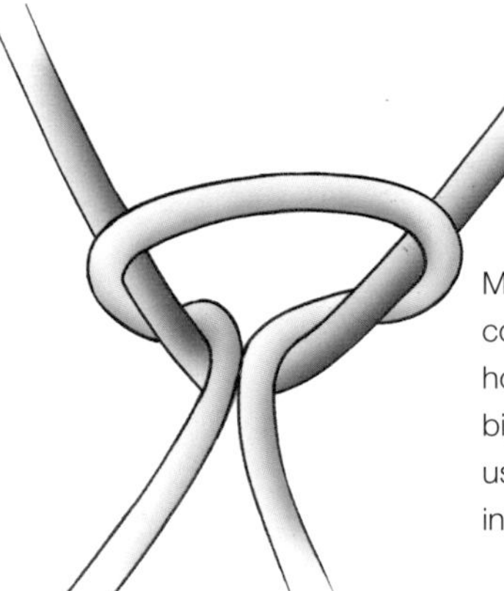

Square Knot Netting

Making large nets with thick cord can be very time-consuming if you are using a needle, as it will not hold enough rope. The ball of cord will also be too big to pass through the mesh. This method of netting uses a square knot and the ball of cord usually rests in a bucket.

1 Assume that the first row of meshes is in place and the end of your cord is anchored safely. Bring a large bight up from the bucket and pass it through the mesh and pull it down.

2 Pass the bucket through the bight from back to front and close the bight up a little.

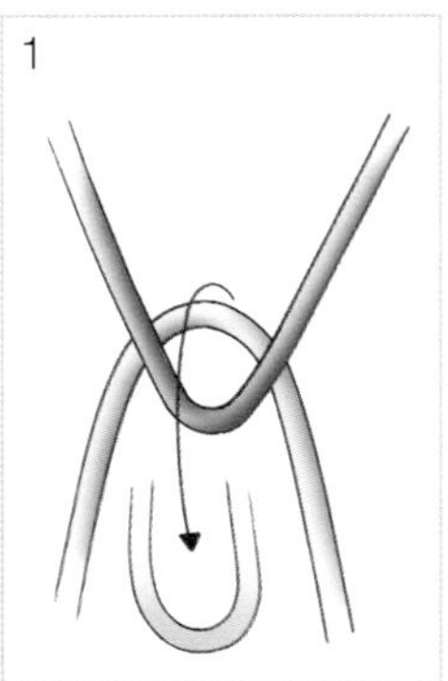

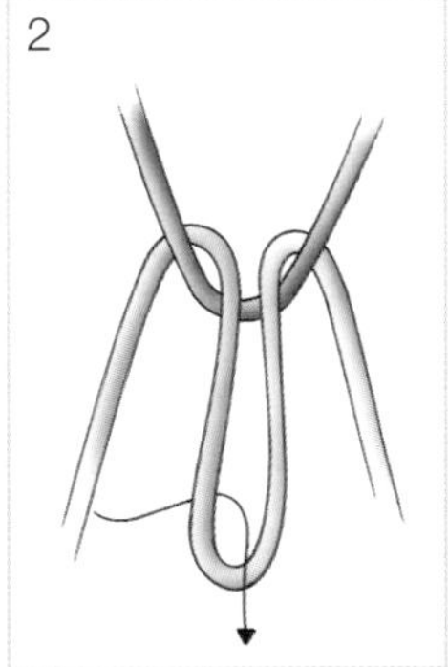

3 You now have a Munter hitch, and, if you remember, this will reverse itself when pulled in the proper direction.

4 Tweak the cord by pulling on the anchored side to reverse the hitch and pull down on the bight at the bottom of the hitch.

5 Pass the bucket again through the bight, from front to back. This leaves a lark's head or cow hitch. Lift the bottom of the cow hitch to form a reef knot and adjust the shape and size of the mesh. Pull tight and repeat on the next mesh.

A net can be built very quickly with this technique. All netting requires space and considerable practice, but the basic elements are simple and worth learning.

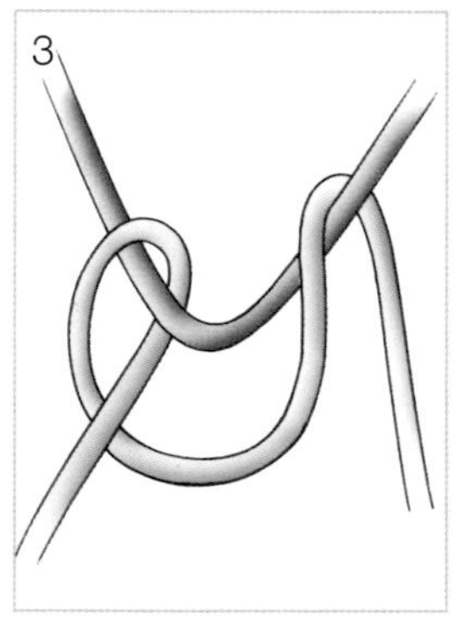

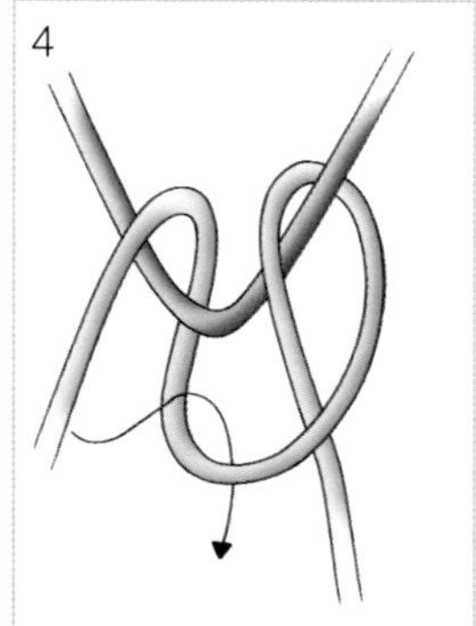

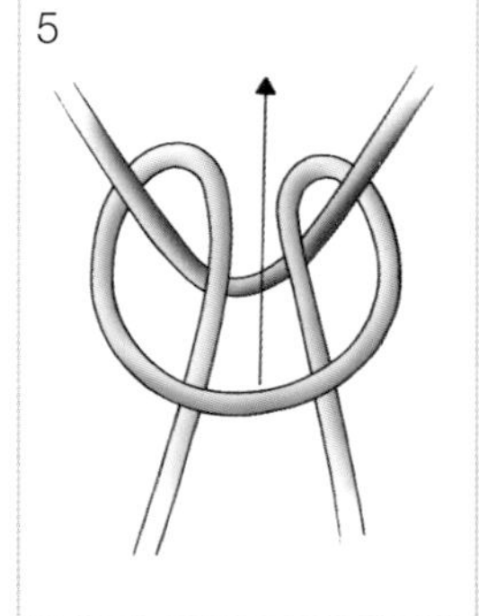

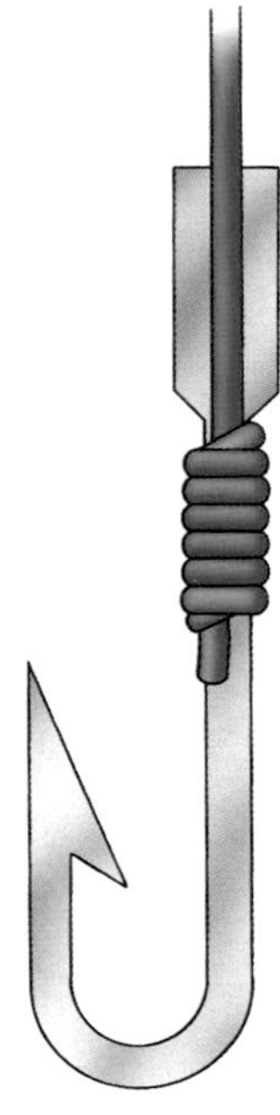

Spade End Knot

This knot has the same form as the nail knot but is tied differently.

1 Make a loop on the back of the hook, leaving an end, which you will need to be able to grip later.

2 Starting at the spade end, wind the loop around the shank of the hook, passing the curved portion of the hook and the loose end through the loop as necessary to prevent tangling.

3 When as much as possible has been wrapped, probably six or seven turns, carefully pull both the end and the standing part. The turns will tighten up and grip the shank firmly.

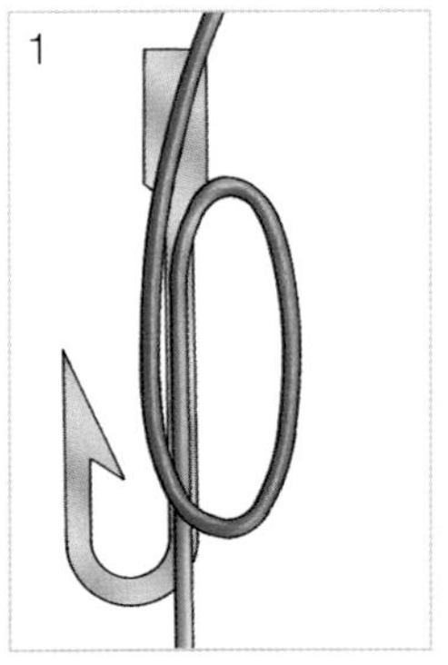

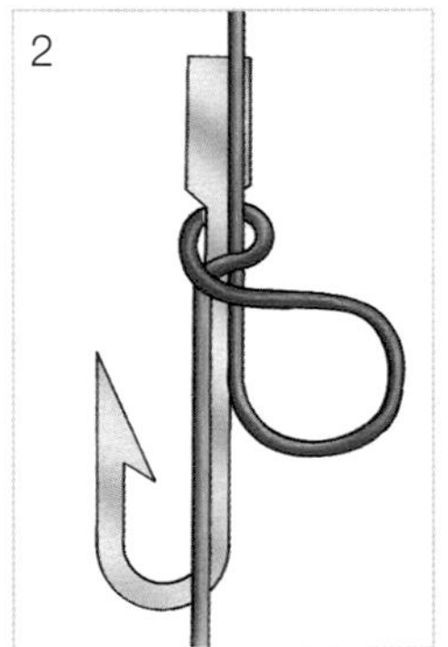

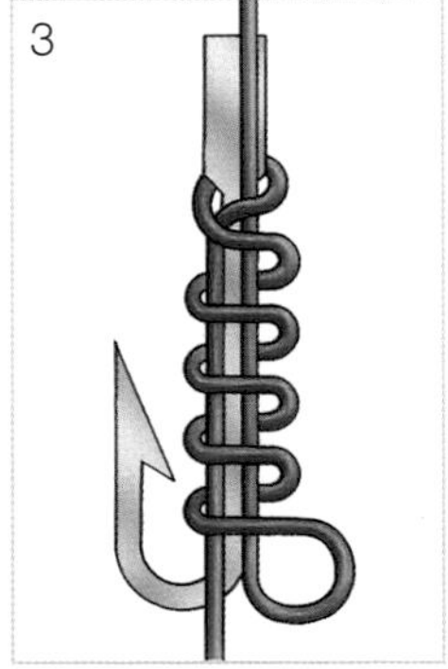

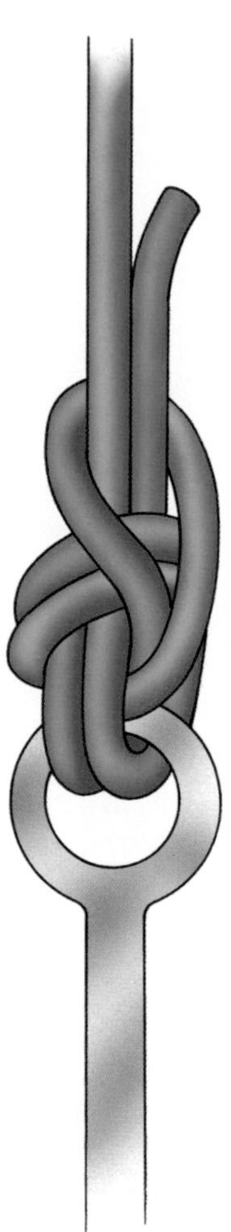

Palomar Knot

This popular knot is easy to tie and holds well for most purposes. It may be a little difficult to tie if your line is attached to a spool, and if that is the case then either give yourself a longer starting bight or choose a different knot.

1 Pass a longish bight through the eye of the hook and tie a thumb knot with the hook inside the loop.

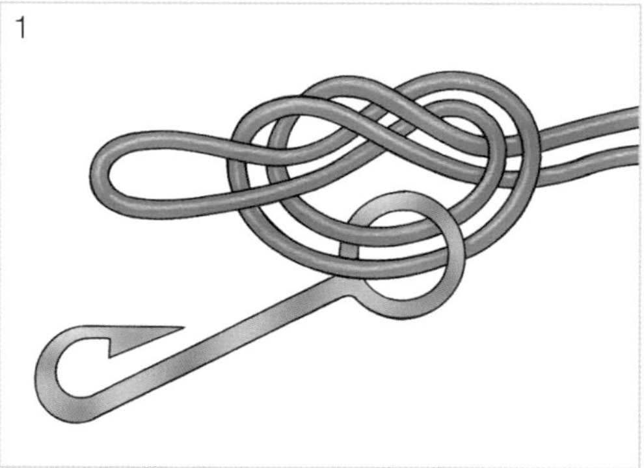

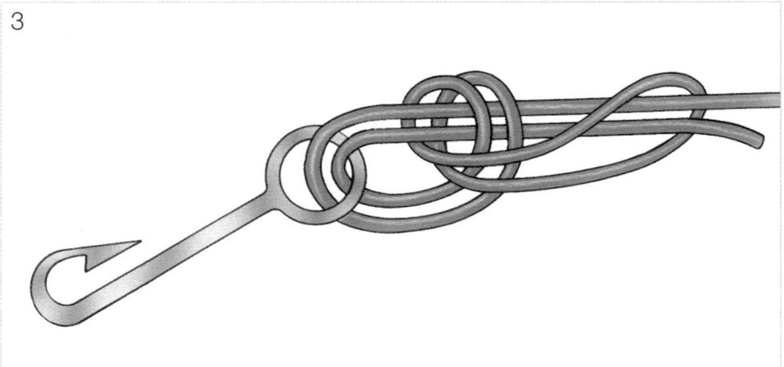

2 Bring the bight down, pass the hook through it, and then bring it back up behind the thumb knot.

3 Lubricate and slide the knot down to the hook and pull tight.

I have tried to avoid too much jargon throughout the book, but a few special words have inevitably crept in and I hope that this glossary will explain any terms about which you are unsure. Throughout the text I have used rope, cord, and line more or less interchangeably to indicate the material in which you are tying the knots.

Arbor The axle or center of a fishing reel.

Bend A knot that joins two ropes together.

Bight A tight loop formed by doubling back a length of cord.

Block A pulley.

Blood knot A family of knots formed with several wrapping turns.

Bollard A post at the side of a quay for holding the mooring line of vessels.

Braid Plaited or interwoven rope.

Carabiner A metal link used by climbers for various connection and attachment purposes. Often spelled karabiner and sometimes shortened to "crab."

Cast To make a bowline or cast a bowline.

Cast off To undo mooring ropes.

Crossing turn A loop of cord made when the cord crosses over itself. If the end is on top it is an overhand crossing turn, if the end is underneath it is an underhand crossing turn.

Eye A small loop either in cord or in the end of a needle or fishhook.

Fair up To adjust the position of the cords so that they lie in the correct places and will tighten up properly.

Fid A tapering wooden tool used to separate strands when splicing.

Frapping Extra turns put on a lashing or seizing to tighten them.

Gaffer tape Sometimes called gaffa tape, a fabric-backed, strongly adhesive tape used for locking the ends of webbing tape in knots. May also be used on the end of a rope instead of a temporary whipping.

Half hitch A crossing turn made around an object.

Heaving line A light line thrown from one site to another to enable a heavier line to be pulled across the intervening space.

Hitch	A knot used to fasten a rope to an anchor point.
Jury	Temporary or emergency replacement.
Kernmantel	Rope having a core surrounded by a braided sheath.
Laid rope	Rope made by twisting strands together.
Lead	The direction the end of a cord travels when forming a knot.
Loop	Formed when a bight is twisted to form a crossing.
Marlinespike	A pointed metal tool used to separate the strands of a rope when splicing. Needed when splicing wire rope, as a wooden tool wears away too quickly.
Noose	A loop, the forming knot of which can slide along the standing part.
Round turn	When a rope goes completely around a ring, pole, or rope.
Seize	To pull two ropes together by binding them with a thinner cord.
Spar	A wooden pole used on ships or in pioneering projects.
Spill	Accidental or deliberate distortion of a knot into a different form.
Standing end	The end of a rope not being used.
Standing part	The part of a rope between the working part and the standing end.
Strand	One of the thicker parts of a laid rope. Made up from yarns.
Swedish fid	A tool formed from a tapered metal channel with a wooden handle. Used for splicing and ornamental ropework but quite versatile.
Tackle	A pulley system.
Tape	A very strong woven webbing used by climbers.
Tuck	To pass the end of a rope under another.
Twine	A light cord, originally of two strands as in twins, but now a general term for soft, thin cord.
Whipping	A binding on a rope, made with a thin cord, to secure the strands and prevent unraveling. May be done around solid objects like fishhooks or knife handles.
Working part	That part of the rope involved in the tying of a knot.
Working end	The end of the rope being actively used to tie the knot.

There are hundreds of books on knots. Any of the titles shown will help you to find out more about this fascinating subject.

Asher, Harry. *The Alternative Knot Book,* A. & C. Black
Ashley, Clifford W. *The Ashley Book of Knots,* Doubleday
Budworth, G. *The Knot Book,* Elliot Right Way Books
Budworth, G. *Hamlyn Fishing Knots,* Hamlyn
Goodhind, W. *The Guide Association Knot Book,* The Guide Association
Graumont, R. & Hensel, J. *The Encyclopædia of Knots and Fancy Rope Work,* Cornell Maritime Press
Griend, P. van de, & Turner J. C. (eds) *The History and Science of Knots,* World Scientific Publishing Co.
March, B. *Modern Rope Techniques,* Cicerone Press
Padgett, A. & Smith, B. *On Rope,* National Speleological Society
Pawson, D. *The Handbook of Knots,* Dorling Kindersley
Pawson, D. *Pocket Guide to Knots and Splices,* Chartwell Books
Warner, C. *A Fresh Approach to Knotting and Ropework,* Published by the author
Vare, A. B. *The Hardy Book of Fisherman's Knots,* Camden Publishing

The International Guild of Knot Tyers

Founded in 1982, the guild has a worldwide membership of enthusiastic knot tiers. It is a registered educational charity working to preserve and promote the art, craft, and science of knots. Anyone may join. You don't have to be an expert tier, you just need to have an interest in knots. There are many local branches whose members would be pleased to welcome you.

For more information, contact the headquarters or try the web sites:

Nigel Harding
IGKT Honorary Secretary
16 Egles Grove
Uckfield
East Sussex
TN22 2BY
England

Secretary of the IGKT
Nigel Harding
Nigel@nigelharding.demon.co.uk

North American Branch
www.igktnab.org

Texas Branch
www.texasknot.tripod.com

Pacific Americas Branch
www.igktpab.org

Albright Knot 232
Alpine Butterfly 160
Anchor Bend 182
Arbor Knot 218
Asher's Bottle Sling 118
Ashley's Stopper Knot 58

Bachman Knot 167
Back Splice 134
Blood Knot 222
Blood Loop Dropper Knot 242
Boa 78
Boom Hitch 196
Bowline (1) 60
Bowline (2) 62
Bowline on the Bight 190
Bowline with Yosemite Tie Off 157
Buntline Hitch 195

Camel Hitch 113
Carrick Bend 206
Cat's Paw 230
Cat's Paw 88
Clara 73
Clove Hitch (1) on a Bar or Ring 64
Clove Hitch (2) over a Pin or Bollard 66
Constrictor Knot 76
Crown Knot 132

Diagonal Lashing 142
Domhof Knot 228
Double Fisherman's Knot or Grapevine 48
Double Grinner Knot 226
Double Overhand or Blood Knot 37
Double Sheet Bend 56
Double Simple Simon 95
Double Turle Knot 217
Dry Fly Knot 234

Extended French Prusik 172
Eye Splice 136

Figure Eight 51
Figure Eight Loop 52
Figure Eight Loop: Threaded 53
Figure Eight with Three Loops 150
Figure Eight with Two Loops 148
Fireman's Chair Knot 92
Fisherman's, Englishman's, or True Lover's Knot 46
French Bowline 158
French Prusik 171
Grinner or Uni Knot 225
Ground Line Hitch 204

Half Blood Knot or Clinch Knot 220
Handcuff Knot 90
Hangman's Knot 82
Hangman's Knot: A Fishing Application 84
Highwayman's Hitch 74
Honda or Bowstring Knot 69
Hunter's or Rigger's Bend 44

Icicle Hitch 114
Interlocked Bowlines 185

Jansik Special 243
Jug or Bottle Sling 116
Jury Masthead Knot 120

Killick Hitch 68
Klemheist or Headon Knot 169
Knute Hitch 216
Kreuzklem or Heddon Knot 168

Lapp Knot 119
Lark's Head or Cow Hitch 126
Lighterman's Hitch 198

Mariner's Knot 170
Marlinespike Hitch 80
Midshipman's Hitch 128
Miller's Bag Knot 129
Monkey's Fist 86
Mooring Hitch 197
Munter or Italian Hitch 152

Nail Knot 240
Net Line Knot 208
Netting 244

One-Handed Bowline 174
One-Way Sheet Bend 57
Overhand Knot with Draw Loop 39
Overhand Loop or Thumb Knot in the Bight 38

Palomar Knot 250
Pedigree Cow Hitch 127
Perfection Loop 236
Pile Hitch 111
Pipe Hitch 112
Prusik Handcuffs 166
Prusik Knot (1) 164
Prusik Knot (2) 165

Reef Bow 42
Rolling Hitch 70
Rope Ladder 124
Round Turn & Two Half Hitches 59
Round Turn Bowline 156

Seizing Bend 202
Shear Lashing 144
Sheepshank 106
Sheet Bend 54
Short Splice 138
Simple Simon Over 94
Simple Simon Under 95
Single Cat's Paw 89
Single Strand Diamond or Lanyard 96
Sliding Figure Eight Bend 186
Slipped Figure Eight 100
Slipped Zigzag Hitch 102
Spade End Knot 249
Spanish Bowline 162
Speir Knot 104
Square Knot (Reef Knot) 40
Square Knot Netting 247
Square Knot with Fisherman's Knot 151
Square Lashing 140
Stitch and Whip Eye 200
Strangle Knot 109

Tarbuck Knot 178
Tent Pole Hitch 122
Thumb or Overhand Knot 36
Timber Hitch 67
Tomfool Knot 91
Transom Knot 110
Treble Fisherman's Knot 49
Trilene Knot 224
Triple Bowline 194
Tundj 72
Turk's Head Knot —Three Lead, Five Bight 212
Turk's Head Knot —Three Lead, Four Bight 210

Vice Versa 238

Waggoner's or Trucker's Dolly Knot 130
Water Bowline 184
Water Knot 154

Zeppelin or Rosendahl Bend 188